Armed
and
Dangerous

JIM KELLY

With Vic Carucci

Armed
and
Dangerous

DOUBLEDAY

New York London Toronto Sydney Auckland

PUBLISHED BY DOUBLEDAY
a division of Bantam Doubleday Dell Publishing Group, Inc.
666 Fifth Avenue, New York, NY 10103

DOUBLEDAY and the portrayal of an anchor with a dolphin are
trademarks of Doubleday, a division of Bantam Doubleday Dell
Publishing Group, Inc.

Library of Congress Cataloging-in-Publication Data

Kelly, Jim, 1960–
Armed and dangerous / Jim Kelly with Vic Carucci.—1st ed.
   p.   cm.
1. Kelly, Jim, 1960—   . 2. Football players—United States—Biography.   3. Quarterback (Football).   4. Buffalo Bills (Football team)—History.   I. Carucci, Vic.   II.
Title.
GV939.K37A3   1992
796.332′092—dc20
[B]   92-13807
          CIP

ISBN 0-385-42451-5

JIM KELLY

To Mom, Dad and my brothers—Pat, Ed, Ray, Dan and Kevin. Thanks for showing me the real meaning of love, loyalty and family. I couldn't have done it without you.

VIC CARUCCI

To Rhonda, Kristen and Lindsay. Thanks for putting up with me through another one.

ACKNOWLEDGMENTS

The authors gratefully acknowledge the following for their contributions to the production of this book: Ed Abramoski, Leroy Andre, Ron Baham, Scott Berchtold, Jim Bush, Bud Carpenter, John Carucci, Rhonda Carucci, Richard Goldstein, Tommy Good, Bryan Harris, Terry Henry, Kent Hull, Alice Kelly, Dan Kelly, Joe Kelly, Pat Kelly, Murray Light, Stan Lipsey, Sal Maiorana, Ted Marchibroda, John McClain, Bill Munson, Milt Northrop, Mike O'Shea, Scott Pitoniak, Carol Recicar, Frank Reich, Leo Roth, Mark Rush, Lisa Scherer, Howard Schnellenberger, Fred Smerlas, Howard Smith, Dan Trevino, Roger Trevino, Frank Vuono and Will Wolford.

We wish to give special thanks to David Gernert, for his belief in this project; Joel E. Fishman, for his patience, brilliant editing and helpful advice throughout; Wendy Goldman, for her great support work, and the Basil Kane Literary Agency.

Contents

Introduction

Risky Business

I CAN'T BE a hundred percent certain, but I think I was sitting in front of my locker, alone, trying to sort a few things out. Nothing complicated. Just little things, like my name, where I was and what I was supposed to do next.

The first two were pretty easy. I remembered I was Jim Kelly and I was at the Metrodome in Minneapolis.

But the third one was giving me trouble.

I had showered. I had received head-to-toe treatment from the trainers, Ed Abramoski and Bud Carpenter. I had even put on my street clothes without any help.

Now if I could only figure out what I was supposed to do next . . .

Finally, Scott Berchtold, the Buffalo Bills' director of media relations, broke through the fog in my head with the answer: It was time to go to the interview area and talk about our 37–24 loss to the Washington Redskins.

Unfortunately, I did recall what I was doing at the Metrodome on the night of January 26, 1992—I had just finished playing in Super Bowl XXVI. I also remembered the disappointing outcome of the game, which had been over for almost an hour at that point.

As the two of us began the long walk to the interview area, Scott looked at me kind of funny. I guess I was saying some pretty strange things. He also walked close enough for me to grab on to him if I had to; a couple of times, my feet just started dragging and I stumbled.

Mild concussions have a way of doing that to a person.

Somehow, I managed to make it up to the podium without falling. I asked the small army of reporters to bear with me. I told them that I couldn't guarantee everything I said would make sense, that I couldn't remember a whole lot of details from the game. And maybe it was better that way.

"The part I can remember," I said to the media, "I didn't like."

One segment that was still fuzzy at the time was the play that left me feeling like my head and my body weren't connected anymore. I had been scrambling for a nine-yard gain in the fourth quarter. As I began my hook slide, cornerback Martin Mayhew hunched down and drove his helmet into the right side of my chest. The force caused me to fall on my left shoulder, snapping my head so hard that my helmet bounced off the artificial turf.

Say good night, Jim.

I wish I could tell you that was my first visit to la-la land. Not by a long shot. Before the Super Bowl, the last time I had been there was just a few months earlier, in a game against Indianapolis. And it's a scary feeling. At first, you have no idea where you are or what you're doing. For instance, after I got dinged in the Super Bowl, the trainers were trying to get me off the field and I wouldn't go. They kept tugging on my arms and I kept pulling away, yelling and cussing at all of them. I was so out of it, I didn't even know why I was putting up such a fight. They were doing the right thing, because the officials had called an injury time-out. Once that happened, it was mandatory that I miss at least one play, or we'd be penalized. They finally got that point across to me, and I left.

Because of my woozy state, and the Redskins' 37–10 lead, the trainers and our doctor thought it would be best for me just to stay on the sidelines and let Frank Reich finish the game. I refused. Maybe I didn't have all my wits about me, but I was still aware of the importance of that game. As bad as things were, I intended to keep searching for the miracle we needed to avoid losing our second Super Bowl in a row. It wouldn't have been our first amazing comeback. As an offense, we know we're never out of any game until that final gun.

Besides, how could things have gotten any worse? I had already been sacked five times. I had been knocked down after releasing 10 passes. I had been hurried into 13 bad throws. I had made three scrambles for 16 yards. And I had two balls batted back in my face.

I caught the second one for an eight-yard loss.

There are a lot of things I like about being rated among the top quarterbacks in the National Football League, but there is one hell of a downside: You're always the first person the other team tries to eliminate from the game.

You're the one at the control panel for the offense, trying to press all the right buttons to blow the defense to kingdom come. So they figure if they can kill you first, the rest of the offense will die soon thereafter.

The Redskins, with their very large and very physical defense, did their best to get me out of Super Bowl XXVI. And when I came back after the concussion to throw two touchdown passes they tried some more. Whether it's the Super Bowl or an exhibition game, it's a risk you take each time you set foot on the field; there might as well be a bull's-eye painted on your jersey.

You go out there knowing everything you have to do to help the team win—the right plays to use, the right reads to make, the right audibles to call. You go out there expecting to throw all kinds of perfect passes, just as you did through the entire week of practice. And you go out there hoping you can make all these wonderful things happen before the defense succeeds in its all-out effort to pound you into a memory.

No matter how good your offensive line is—and the last few years I've had one of the best in the NFL in Will Wolford, Jim

Ritcher, Kent Hull, John Davis and House Ballard—you are going to get hit. That's a fact of quarterbacking life. You're going to get hit before, while and after you throw the ball.

Blitzing linebackers and defensive backs will come flying out of nowhere and try to open a new hole in your body. A 300-pound defensive end or tackle will beat his man at some point and be on top of you before you even have a chance to set your feet. Or maybe you'll just hold the ball too damn long, searching for an open receiver, and that'll give one or more pass rushers all the time necessary to bring you down. Hard.

Not all sacks and hits you take are the offensive line's fault. In my case, quite a few result from my constant desire to make the big play. I always want to wait until the last possible second so I can do something to bring a roar from our 80,000 teammates at Rich Stadium.

There are some days when you walk away without so much as a scratch—days when you have not only a great team and individual performance to be proud of but also the ability to celebrate without wincing or limping.

Then there are other days when you feel like the victim of a terrible accident—days when you get beat up, down and sideways. Everything hurts, from the top of your skull to the soles of your feet. Of course, if you win, the pain seems to fade a lot faster. If you lose, there isn't enough ice in the world to give you relief. That's just part of being a professional football player.

I'm sure every quarterback would agree that the worst kind of hit is one where the defender follows through on you. If it's just plain and simple contact, it usually doesn't hurt all that much. But when somebody hits you and grabs you and body-slams you, that's when it can cause some damage. Big-time.

In most cases, I never see the guy coming. But when I do, and depending on the kind of hit I receive and the angle the guy takes, I try to be smart in breaking my fall. You know that if you land the wrong way—like square on your shoulder or elbow or knee—you stand a good chance of having something rip or tear or break inside your body. The right way for me to land is rear end first, because that's where most of my padding is.

I hardly ever know who has sacked me until I see the play in the film room the next day. I just never take the time to look at the guy's number. (Or should I say license plate?) That's because my eyes are always focused downfield. I'm always thinking about the next play to call in our no-huddle offense.

Strange as it might sound, there are times when a big hit can be exactly what I need. It acts like a wake-up call. I can remember quite a few games where I've taken a big hit, staggered off the field, then come back to play a lot better than before. A big hit just seems to get me excited. (Maybe, in the Super Bowl, somebody should have clocked me *before* the game.)

Now, don't misunderstand. I'm not saying I enjoy having people beat the daylights out of me. I don't. I'm not saying I wouldn't prefer having the Great Wall of China in front of me at all times. I would.

But it seems like when I get hit hard, when someone truly hurts me, I'm able to come back strong. I guess I just want to prove to the defense that it takes more than one shot to get me out of there.

When it comes to scrambling, no one will ever confuse me with Randall Cunningham. I'll pick up as many yards as I can, then do the old hook slide. But I'll also do whatever it takes to reach that first-down marker, or get into the end zone, even if it means going helmet to helmet with somebody.

And getting knocked goofy.

When I finished my news conference after Super Bowl XXVI, I stepped slowly off the podium. The fog in my head was as thick as ever.

Once again, I asked the question: "What am I supposed to do next?" Once again, Scott Berchtold was there with the answer: "Time to get on the bus and get out of here."

That sounded good to me. So I walked with him to the chartered buses that were parked outside the Metrodome. Scott insisted on carrying my large duffel bag; I guess he figured I was having a hard enough time keeping my balance with my hands free. As he put the bag inside the compartment under the bus, I said, "Make sure you remind me that's under there, because I know I'm never going to remember once we get off."

Scott gave me that funny look again and said, "Don't worry, Jim, I won't let you forget it."

There weren't many of us on board. Besides Scott and me, there were just a few other players. Marv Levy, our head coach, and Bill Polian, our general manager, climbed on just before the bus pulled away.

We were on the road for about ten minutes when I suddenly turned around to Scott, who was sitting right behind me, and asked, "Why am I on this bus?"

"Jim, you're on this bus because we're all going back to our hotel in St. Paul," he said. "You remember the hotel, don't you?"

"Yeah, but I already checked out of there two days ago. I definitely remember that."

"Oh, OK. Well, where are you supposed to be?"

"With my family. We were all getting together after the game. I'm supposed to be with my family."

"OK. Where?"

"At a hotel."

"Which one?"

"I have no idea."

Scott then said he'd help me find them once we got back to the team hotel, the Radisson St. Paul. So we grabbed my duffel bag from the bottom of the bus, went inside through the back door and headed up to Scott's room.

I sat there for a few minutes, trying to recall exactly where I was supposed to meet my father, five brothers, four sisters-in-law, and a whole bunch of friends from Buffalo and my hometown of East Brady, Pennsylvania. Everybody would be there except Mom. Because of her emphysema, she had stayed in East Brady with one of her friends.

All along, we knew the gathering that night in Minnesota was going to be either a wild victory party—or something along the lines of an Irish wake.

Then, suddenly, it came to me.

"They're at the Holiday Inn," I said.

"Good," Scott replied. "Now, there are about seven Holiday Inns in the Minneapolis–St. Paul area. Which one is theirs?"

"The one to the left."

"To the left of what?"

"You know, on a map. When you're looking at a map, it's on the left side, the west."

"That really narrows it down."

So Scott pulled out a phone book and started looking up the

numbers of all the Holiday Inns in and around the Twin Cities. Then he began calling to see which one had someone from my family registered. Finally, on the last try, he found it: the Holiday Inn Minneapolis West, which was about a half hour away by car. Scott spoke with my brother Dan, who oversees my business affairs, and told him everything that happened. Then he arranged to have a bellman from the Radisson drive me over.

When I arrived, Dan was waiting outside.

"How come no one was at the 'Dome after the game to take me here?" I asked.

"What are you talking about, Jim?" he said. "There was a limo waiting for you."

"What limo?"

"Man, do you ever have a concussion."

Dan then refreshed my memory: Once I finished with the postgame news conference, I was supposed to do a one-on-one interview on the field for *The George Michael Sports Machine* TV program. After that, a limousine, hired by the show, would take me to the Holiday Inn. It had all been set up long before the opening kickoff, and I was even reminded of it afterward.

Thanks to that little fourth-quarter collision between my helmet and the Metrodome carpet, I had forgotten about the entire plan.

"Sorry, bro'," I said to Danny.

He led me to the ballroom so I could join the "Irish wake" that was already several hours old. When I got to the door, the crowd of nearly a hundred and fifty family and friends stood and gave me a long, loud ovation. I was coherent enough to appreciate the response. And I was really touched.

I only wish I could have been walking in there with a Super Bowl championship to share with them.

But this wasn't the end. If there's one thing I learned during my thirty-two years on this planet, it's that with support from the people you love, anything's possible.

Armed
and
Dangerous

1

The East Brady Bunch

I NEVER THOUGHT it could happen. Never in a million years.

I watched guys like Terry Bradshaw, Joe Namath, Roger Staubach. I watched them throw touchdown passes and win Super Bowls. I watched them making all those big plays in all those big games, and I dreamed. Maybe . . . just maybe . . . one of these days . . . that's going to be me out there.

But whenever I would take a reality break I had to ask myself the same question: How was it going to happen? I mean, here I was, a kid from a town of barely a thousand people. You just don't go from East Brady, Pennsylvania, to the top of the world. Even if I showed that I had the right stuff, nobody in that little Irish Catholic community really believed that anyone on the outside would ever notice, would ever provide some freckle-faced dreamer with the chance to make the climb.

It was hard enough to find East Brady—which is located

along the Allegheny River about sixty-five miles northeast of Pittsburgh—let alone to find me. We're talking about a town with no traffic lights, just stop signs. We're talking about a town whose nearest department store is twenty-five miles away. We're talking about a town whose nearest McDonald's is a thirty-mile hike.

The coal mines have long since shut down. The Rex-Hide rubber plant, which used to be the town's lifeblood, is history. Not to mention all kinds of smaller businesses that have also bitten the dust through the years.

Basically, what you have in East Brady are bars (where Iron City beer flows faster than the Allegheny), churches and a lot of great people. Basically, what you do in East Brady—although I'm proud to claim it as my hometown—is try to make a better life for yourself.

I never stopped chasing my dream.

During idle moments when I was in the fifth grade, I liked to draw pictures of clowns and other cartoon characters that I saw in different books. And under each one, I'd practice my signature. I'd move the pen very deliberately across the paper as I made a big loop at the top of the J, an equally large K, and a giant loop at the bottom of the Y that ran through the bottom of the K. Then I'd give the pictures to a girl in class whom I was trying very hard to impress.

"Someday that autograph's going to be worth a lot of money," I told her. "Know why?"

"Why?" she said, pretending to sound interested.

"Because someday I'm going to be a pro quarterback—just like Terry Bradshaw."

She just rolled her eyes, as if to say, "Keep dreaming, Jim."

That's exactly what I did.

One thing I learned early in life is that owning a dream doesn't cost a cent. And that was particularly important in the Kelly household, because we couldn't afford much else. Our family wasn't dirt-poor, but we did scratch and claw for everything we had. My father, Joe, did the best he could. He put in long hours as a machinist at Daman Industries, which repaired parts for steel mills, and he performed carpentry work on the side. My mother, Alice, was a master at stretching every dollar Dad brought home as far as it would go. And then some.

But the task they faced each day was overwhelming. There were six mouths to feed, six bodies to clothe—and all of them belonged to boys.

When it came to athletics, though, Dad made each of us feel rich with his tremendous support, encouragement and instruction. And the amazing thing was, the man had never played a down of football himself, or a second of any other organized sport for that matter. His parents passed away when he was two, and he was raised by nuns at an orphanage just outside Pittsburgh, which didn't have an athletic program to speak of. He spent most of the next fourteen years there working—on a farm, at a shoemaker's shop. You name the chore, Dad did it.

Talk about growing up fast!

At seventeen, he left the orphanage to join the Navy. At twenty-one, he met my mother at a dance. A year later, Joe Kelly and Alice McGinn were married. They talked a lot about having a big family—the family my father never knew growing up. And between 1951 and 1961 they made five trips to St. Francis Hospital in Pittsburgh. On the first four, Mom delivered Pat, Ed, Ray and yours truly. She and my father then decided to give it one more try for a girl. Instead, they wound up with twin boys, Danny and Kevin.

I came along on February 14, 1960, weighing in at seven pounds three ounces. "The best Valentine I ever received," my mother would say years later. "Not even Hallmark has one as good."

Excuse me while I blush.

During his time in the Navy, Dad did some boxing and developed a casual interest in team sports. He liked watching games on television, but he knew it wouldn't be long before his oldest son started asking how those games were played. Dad didn't want to embarrass himself by just throwing up his arms and saying, "I don't know, Pat. You'd better ask somebody else about the difference between a strong safety and a free safety . . . or an infielder and an outfielder . . . or a guard and a center." So he went to the library and checked out every instructional book he could find on football, baseball and basketball.

Then Dad took the time to share his knowledge with each and every one of us.

• • • •

We all learned to be tough from the time we started talking. That was the only way you could survive in our house. When two of us would get into a fight (which seemed to happen every other day), Dad would break it up, take us into the garage and make us put on boxing gloves and football helmets. Then he'd step aside and let us pound the crap out of each other. Once Dad was satisfied that all the anger and hostility was out of our systems, he would always make us shake hands.

Call it Main Event Therapy.

When I was six, though, I came very close to going down for the count—permanently. We were living in West Deer, Pennsylvania, and I was chasing the twins around the house one summer afternoon. Dan and Kevin opened the sliding-glass door leading to our patio and Kevin quickly slammed it behind them. Sure enough, I came motoring along, thinking the door was still open. The next thing I knew, CRASH! As I exploded through the glass, a jagged piece cut the right side of my throat, just nicking my jugular. Mom grabbed a towel and jammed it into the cut. Then I was rushed to the hospital, where it took about forty stitches—twenty inside, twenty outside—to stop the gusher on my neck. The doctor said it was a close call, because being as little as I was, I couldn't withstand too heavy a blood loss. He told my mother that if she hadn't reacted as quickly as she did with that towel to slow down the bleeding, I'd have been history.

I guess you could say it was my first experience with LOTI: luck of the Irish.

A couple of years later, we moved to East Brady. Our house, located on Purdum Street at the top of a hill (which kept us dry whenever the Allegheny's banks would overflow), looked nice and pleasant enough on the outside. My parents, who are very proud people, did everything they could to keep the property in the best shape possible.

Inside? With six boys bouncing off the walls and ceilings, suffice it to say that the house and most of the furniture took one hell of a beating. So did Mom's sanity. We managed to bring her to tears two or three times per week. It's a wonder she didn't have a nervous breakdown. She always tells people now,

"I wouldn't trade my boys for the world—but there were days I would have gladly given them away."

For putting up with the six of us, that woman has definitely earned her way into sainthood.

One of our favorite indoor sports was basketball. We'd cut off the tops and bottoms of Clorox bottles, staple them to the walls and presto! we had our own basketball court right in the living room. We started out using one of those foam-rubber Nerf balls, but it would always get lost. So most of the time the ball was a couple pair of rolled-up tube socks. Since you couldn't really dribble, you'd take a lot of outside shots. Or you'd just bull your way to the basket, knocking down everyone and everything in your path.

We also played our share of indoor football. Because of the limited space in the living room, we had to modify the game a little bit. The three oldest brothers would get on their knees and form a defensive line, and the three younger guys would take turns as running backs trying to dive over the pile. We all wore helmets, and there was some serious body-slamming that resulted in bumps, bruises, bloody noses, broken bones and concussions.

And you wondered how all those fights could get started?

The dinner table also provided its share of challenges. Although Mom knew about a million different ways to prepare ground beef, most of the time there was just enough food to go around. So we all followed one simple rule: The faster you ate, the more you got. If there was ever steak on our plates, it would have to be the biggest of celebrations. Some dinners consisted of baked beans, period. There were other times when the only thing we ate all day was a peanut butter and jelly sandwich. But our parents always saw to it that we went to bed with something in our bellies.

The sleeping arrangements were a bit cramped, to say the least. I can remember, at one point, four of us—Ray, Danny, Kevin and me—in the same room on two bunk beds. Being the senior members of the East Brady Bunch, Pat and Ed had a room all to themselves. But, again, the six of us had to be thankful that we always had a roof over our heads (even if there were times when our combined rambunctiousness threatened to blow it off) and clothes on our backs (even if mine were handed down through three older brothers).

Christmas was the best time of the year for our family, but it wasn't because of all the great presents we found under the tree. Some parents shower their kids with gifts; ours showered us with a true sense of what the holiday is supposed to be all about. They always found a way to make it special, to create a joyous atmosphere around the house, to promote the feeling of togetherness that we have to this day. And they did it by providing a loving example, among themselves, that we all followed. You can't put a price on that.

Which isn't to say we were always understanding of our family's economic state. I doubt many kids in that situation would be. Sometimes, the best Mom and Dad could do at Christmas was a shirt and a pair of pants for each of us. And, sometimes, after hearing about the bicycles and minibikes that other kids got, we felt we had to make up stories about the tremendous haul we had also made. The year a strike shut down the plant where Dad worked, we were lucky to get anything.

But there was one Christmas I'll never forget. I was thirteen, and all I wanted was a sleeping bag. I must have bugged my folks about it every single day for a year. When I found it under the tree, I was the happiest kid in the world. In fact, I slept in it that night on the living room floor.

To help Mom and Dad put food on the table, we all took different jobs. When Pat was fifteen, he had my mother change the date on his birth certificate from 1951 to 1950 so he could receive a working permit; you had to be at least sixteen to get one. Pat then went to work as a stock boy in a department store. But he didn't have any means of transportation, so after school, he hitch-hiked six miles to the store. Fortunately, someone was always able to give him a ride most of the way home.

The rest of us did odd jobs around the neighborhood. We shoveled sidewalks, cut grass, delivered newspapers. Being a kid, however, I didn't have the world's greatest grasp on what it meant to share. I'd say to myself, "Wait a minute! I'm the one out here busting my ass. Why can't I keep some of this money for myself?" So there were times in the winter when I'd shovel, say, four sidewalks, but tell Mom and Dad that I had cleaned three—and they'd get paid for three.

I realize now that taking advantage of the two people who had worked so hard and sacrificed so much for all of us was a terrible thing to do. At nine years old, that was one of about a million lessons I had yet to learn.

The kids in our neighborhood were extremely competitive. I'm sad to say I don't see much of that attitude anymore, in East Brady or too many other places around the country. Kids today seem to have more important things to do with their spare time than play sandlot games. But we had such a close-knit group— about twenty of us, including my brothers and a whole bunch of friends, the closest of whom were Jimmy Hiles, Kevin Morrow, Paul DeBacco, Dan Bigley and Tim Simpson. We'd always play our hearts out, always try to outperform each other.

I can't recall a single day when we weren't competing in one type of athletic activity or another. For instance, to trace the origin of the arm strength I have today, I'd have to go back to when I got together with a bunch of friends to see who could throw rocks the farthest across the Allegheny River. No kidding. We'd pick out different-sized rocks along the bank, and whoever had the best throw got to pick out the next size. Nine times out of ten, I'd make the choice. I'd look for the heaviest ones I could find, naturally, and I know that that went a long way toward helping to develop the muscles in my right arm.

Our house didn't have a basketball net outside, but there were plenty of others in the neighborhood that did, and they were the sites of some pretty intense three-on-three and four-on-four action. We also played a lot of backyard whiffleball. Usually there were enough guys around to form three teams in both sports, so we'd stage our own basketball and whiffleball tournaments. We even pitched in a quarter apiece to buy little prizes for first, second and third place.

Serious stuff.

In the winter, we'd put on our good dress shoes, with the real slick soles, then go down to the river—after it froze, of course— and play hockey.

In the summer, our favorite river sport was diving from the big steel bridge that connected East Brady with its sister town, Bradys Bend. I'll admit, this wasn't one of the brightest things we did. It's a wonder none of us wound up severely crippled or dead. But, as always, those competitive juices were flowing. We'd have contests to see who could land with the least amount of splash and who could jump from the greatest height. Everybody would start out at the bottom of one of the X-shaped girders. After that, you'd climb to the middle of the X. After that, you'd climb all the way to the top. Only, most of the guys were too afraid to go all the way, and with good reason. The jump wasn't nearly as dangerous as the climb. We're talking about a seventy-five-foot drop into twenty feet of water.

We're also talking about a ten- to fifteen-foot cluster of rocks extending into the water under the end of the bridge where you began your climb by shinning up an I beam. We're also talking about trying to keep your balance while walking along a foot-and-a-half-wide beam for about forty feet to the point where you'd be jumping into the deepest water. Of course, my brothers and I were usually the ones doing so from the top.

Three rules: First, you never looked down; second, you always yelled at the top of your lungs when you jumped to keep your ears from popping; third, and the most important rule of all, when Dad was working the seven-to-three P.M. shift, you never jumped around three o'clock because that was when he would be driving across the bridge on his way home from work. If he ever caught us, our asses were grass . . . and he was the mower.

According to my father, my first official taste of football came when I was three, maybe four years old and he took me to a high school game. While we were there, I happened to pick up a football. Dad told me, "Throw it here!" He said I threw so hard that it stung his hands. Right then and there, he knew I had some potential. At the time, though, I was probably more interested in having another hot dog.

My first taste of organized football came when I was eight years old, in the North Butler County Midget Football League. My first position was tight end. And my first reaction to the game was boredom. That's because I rarely got to touch the ball; all I did was block. Friends of mine who weren't on the team seemed to be having a lot more fun riding their minibikes. So I decided to quit and hang out with them. That is, until my older brothers found out and threatened to kick my ass if I didn't change my mind.

Two days later, I was back on the squad.

The following year, the coach moved me to quarterback. My attitude toward football improved right away. I loved the idea of being in control of the offense. We threw the ball a lot and scored a whole bunch of points. Most of the time there wasn't much defense. It was just a matter of us outscoring the other team. And this was *with* a huddle.

Over the next two years, I really began sprouting and, all of a sudden, I found myself standing a good five inches taller than most of my teammates. As a result, it became harder and harder for me to stay under the weight limit of 132 pounds. A scale was even brought onto the field before each game, and both head coaches supervised the weigh-in process. If you were overweight, you couldn't play. It was that simple.

Through my third and final season, I was on a diet consisting of fish and boiled chicken. I also followed a stringent exercise routine. After practice, I'd run ten laps around Graham Field, which my dad helped build for use by every team in East Brady from midget league to high school. In addition, I'd run along the railroad tracks, which were near the field, and up and down a hill that was also near the field. Most of the time, Art Delano, our offensive line coach, would run with me for moral support. And when it was really hot out, like 85 degrees, we'd go inside our own personal sauna—Art's Volkswagen Beetle with all the windows rolled up. We'd just sit there and sweat it out for a good ten or fifteen minutes.

Yet even with all that work and suffering at the dinner table, I'd still barely make weight. To be on the safe side, I made sure I wasn't carrying any excess baggage when I stepped on the scale. I'd wear tennis shoes instead of cleats. I'd put on the lightest shoulder pads I could find. I'd even strip down my thigh pads so that all I wore was the plastic.

But nothing was going to help me the morning of the league championship game at Slippery Rock, which we entered with a perfect record of 7–0. The night before, at a Fellowship of Christian Athletes (FCA) outing, I blew my diet, stuffing myself with two or three hot dogs and a couple of cupcakes. When I stepped on the scale, the arrow stopped at 133. Exactly one pound beyond the max.

Unaware of my hot-dog-and-cupcake binge, which I kept to

myself, my father and my coach were stunned. They insisted that something was screwy with the scale, that the opposing coach had rigged it to give a false reading. So we jumped in the car and Dad rushed me to a butcher shop to see what that scale would indicate. When it, too, showed I was a pound over, we headed back to the field. I watched from the sidelines, still wearing my pads and uniform. All dressed up and nowhere to play.

I cried.

We lost, 12–0.

As usual, however, Dad took me aside afterward and found the right words to make me feel better—well, a little better. He taught us all that with winning comes losing, that you had to accept the fact that, sooner or later, you'll go up against somebody better than you.

Even if it's a cupcake!

Although Dad worked with all my brothers and pushed them to be the best in any sport they played, he saw ability in me that he thought was unique. Books may have showed him how the games were supposed to be played. But after a while, the man developed his own instincts when it came to recognizing talent.

As he would say years later, "I knew Jim had the potential to be a heck of an athlete. He had the size and the big hands. The way he threw that football when he was little showed me something. And when he started rolling out and throwing, it was so natural. It really showed me that he had something the other kids just didn't have."

The first intensive football coaching Dad gave me was before I took part in my first Punt, Pass & Kick competition. I swear, he had me in the backyard every day. Not only after school but also during my forty-five-minute lunch breaks, which, because school was within walking distance from home, I could spend at the house. At this time, Dad was working the three-to-eleven shift, so he would head out after my lunch break was finished. First he would wait at the door for me with football in hand. I mean, every day, rain or shine. As soon as the winter snow melted, we were out there.

He'd take our clothesline and stretch it on the ground from one end of the yard to the other, marking off the inches and feet. Then I'd punt, pass and kick off a tee, trying to get the ball to land right on the line or as close to it as possible. After each attempt, Dad would mark the distance between the rope and the spot where the ball hit the ground, and deduct accordingly for my final score, just like they did in P, P & K.

I had to do a certain number of repetitions in each drill before I could eat lunch. And more often than not, lunch was forgotten. Sure, there were times when I'd get sick of it, when I'd refuse to come home or hide just before I got there, hoping my father would get tired and leave. Then again, if I missed the noon session, that only meant we'd work longer and harder after school. There were other times when I complained through every drill and probably used a profanity or two—making sure, of course, I said them low enough so that my father couldn't hear.

"What was that, Jimmy?" he'd ask.

"Nothing, Dad," I'd say. "Nothing."

"I thought so."

Everything my father did was with an eye toward the future. He loved East Brady; he never wanted to live anywhere else. But he was realistic enough to admit that it wouldn't offer much in the way of career opportunities for his sons. He knew we'd have to go elsewhere if we were going to have any chance at success as adults. Dad saw sports as our ticket out.

"Someday you're going to thank me for this," he always told me. "If you want something bad enough, you have to work for it. If you work hard for it, chances are you'll receive it. All you have to do is put your mind to it and be patient, and everything will work out."

In 1970, when I was ten, I made it all the way to the Punt, Pass & Kick national semifinals. Representing my boyhood heroes, the Pittsburgh Steelers, I made my first airplane trip across the country to San Diego. Unfortunately, I slipped while kicking in the preliminaries and wound up losing to the eventual national champion for my age group by a measly 15 feet.

The following year, I won my second straight area P, P & K title at Three Rivers Stadium. Beforehand, at a special function for the contestants, I got to meet the No. 1 Steeler of them all, Terry Bradshaw. (We both had a lot more hair back then.)

"I'm going to take your job away, Mr. Bradshaw," I told him.

But that didn't stop him from giving me his autograph. Or showing me how he held a football—by pressing his index finger on the back tip of the ball and his ring finger on the first lace. That, he explained, maximized his ability to guide his throws exactly where he wanted them to go. Naturally, from that moment on, I used the Bradshaw Grip. I was convinced I was onto something special, that I was the only kid in the world who knew the secret to being a successful NFL passer. (That is, until I got older and developed the Kelly Grip. I put my index finger just below the back tip of the ball and my ring finger on the second lace, because, in my opinion, that provides even better control. But I'm not going to argue too much with a guy who has four Super Bowl rings on those fingers.)

Bradshaw's quick lesson notwithstanding, the bulk of my early instruction came from my father. Dad had a great coaching technique. Although he knew how to zero in on the things you did wrong, he always made it a point to recognize the things you did right. That does wonders for a kid's confidence. I can still hear him yelling, "That a boyyyeee!" or "That's my boyyyeee!"

He also was very knowledgeable when it came to baseball, and in fact coached my Little League and Pony League teams. He had a tremendous grasp of the strategy involved in baseball, and he made it his business to know everything about every player on the team so he could identify the exact part of your game that needed work. Playing for my father put a little extra pressure on me to be at my best. And I liked that.

It wasn't until junior high school that our backyard clinics began to focus on the specifics of quarterbacking. By that time, my hands were large enough so I could wear Pat's ring from the University of Richmond. Now I could really grip a football. I practiced dropbacks and sprint-outs. I threw to different spots on the same clothesline we used for my P, P & K training. I even threw to my father, who ran some pretty decent patterns. Dad stressed accuracy, although he never had me try to put the ball through a hanging tire, because he didn't want me to aim. His goal was for me to be able to make all kinds of different passes without having to think about them.

It wasn't long before I started to do exactly that.

The first bit of proof that there really was a payoff from Dad's coaching came in 1974 when Pat was drafted by the Baltimore Colts, with whom he spent some time at linebacker. He also spent a little time with the Detroit Lions and two seasons with the Birmingham Vulcans of the World Football League, ending his pro career by my senior year of high school.

The only time I got to see Pat play in person as a pro was the summer of 1977, after my junior year. The whole family traveled to Canton, Ohio, where the Lions faced Denver in the annual Hall of Fame exhibition game. Sitting in the stands, I was in awe. I couldn't believe that that was really Pat out there on the field wearing an official NFL uniform. I made sure I told everyone around me, "That's *my* big brother out there." I just thought it was the greatest thing in the world. We were all going nuts, cheering his every move on special teams and at linebacker.

And the more I watched him, the more I thought, "Wow! Wouldn't that be awesome to be in the NFL and get to play in the Hall of Fame game? Maybe the next time we come to Canton, that'll be me out there."

My father already had that picture in his mind, which was why he refused to let up on me.

But Dad's instruction wasn't limited to sports. He also taught us compassion, to help out those who were less fortunate, always to get behind the underdog. Our next-door neighbor, David Groves, was a little slow, and unfortunately there were some kids who saw that as an invitation to pick on him. That is, whenever my brothers and I weren't around.

We just couldn't accept the idea of someone who was unable to defend himself being treated that way. And if anyone tried mistreating him in front of us, we usually mistreated them with our fists. To this day, Dave remains a close friend of our family.

The East Brady High School Bulldogs were the biggest thing going, not only in East Brady but also in the surrounding towns. And every Kelly boy was a proud contributor to the tradition. Pat started it all as a linebacker who kicked ass and took names. Ray did the same as a linebacker, and also played quarterback. Ed was a quarterback, Danny was a wide receiver, and Kevin played on the offensive line.

In football and basketball, the Bulldogs were always the team to beat. (I imagine that would have been the case in baseball and track as well, but due to a limited budget, we had no teams in those sports. In fact, due to declining enrollment, East Brady High no longer even exists.)

There were only twenty-three players on our team. So besides playing quarterback, I was also a punter, a place-kicker, a linebacker, a defensive end and, in my senior year, a safety. Back then, I liked defense the best. I preferred it so much more than offense because it gave me the chance to hit people.

One of the best shots I delivered was on Ray, when he was quarterbacking the varsity in a scrimmage against my junior high squad. I was playing defensive end, and on one play I broke through clean and just knocked Ray's jock off. He said he hadn't been hit that hard by any of his varsity teammates. Being closer in age to me than Pat or Ed, Ray was the brother I looked up to the most for guidance and approval.

After I became the starting quarterback on the varsity as a sophomore, we went on to a 7–2 record. I completed 50 percent of my passes for 1,108 yards and 14 touchdowns. The following season, we were undefeated, as I improved my completion percentage to 58 for 1,474 yards and 15 TDs. We were also undefeated in my senior year, as I hit 63 percent of my throws for 1,333 yards and 15 scores.

I didn't really get to play very much as a senior. We were usually ahead of everybody by something like 30–0 at halftime, so most of the starters watched the last two quarters from the sidelines. While sitting out the second half of one game that year, I turned to Jimmy Hiles, our halfback, and said, "Hilesy, do you think we're going to letter this year? We might not get enough playing time."

I was only half kidding.

By the end of my high school career, I had completed 57 percent of my passes for 3,915 yards and 44 touchdowns and helped the Bulldogs to a 26–2–1 record, half of one Little 12 Conference championship and all of another. (The conference was comprised of 12 small schools, most under 350 enrollment, in the middle and western portions of Pennsylvania.) I was an All-State selection, I received honorable mention honors for All-American and I became the first player in Little 12 history to be chosen for the Big 33 state all-star game.

Our biggest rivals were Union and Karns City, two towns just outside of East Brady. Not only did we have fierce competition on the field and the basketball court; we also vied for the best-looking cheerleaders. When the fights broke out, they usually weren't over something that occurred in the heat of the game, but over something really important—like who was dating which cheerleader.

Besides playing like champions, we also made an effort to look the part. Between games, we'd break out the Lemon Pledge and give our helmets a thorough polishing. I mean, those things sparkled when we took the field.

My brothers and I also had the cleanest and brightest uniforms on the team. No matter what shape they were in after a game, Mom would make them look better than new. Eventually, the mothers of the other players began calling her up and asking, "How do you do it, Alice? How do you get your sons' uniforms so clean? What's your secret?" Just like one of those television commercials for some "new and improved" detergent.

But it wasn't the detergent. It was all the scrubbing she did by hand to get out every last speck of dirt and the tiniest of grass stains. She didn't do it to impress anybody. She was just proud of her boys and in doing a job right. Some of the other kids on the team even gave me their uniforms for Mom to wash. She'd always oblige.

A big thrill for my younger brothers and me was when Ray would send us his used white football shoes from the University of Richmond. They were meant to be worn on artificial turf and we always played on grass. But it didn't matter. When we put those sporty white cleats on, with everyone else wearing black, we felt as cool as could be.

Our head coach, Terry Henry, was a jack-of-all-trades. He taped our ankles, tended to our injuries. He was a teacher, counselor and father all rolled into one. He also did a good job of keeping me out of trouble. One time, he took about six of us with him in a van to scout a game involving Montieau High School, one of our many rivals. A few of us started mouthing off to some kids from Montieau and nearly caused a riot. Terry got everybody back in the van and hauled out of there. But that wasn't the end of it. A whole bunch of Montieau kids jumped in their cars and chased after us.

All of a sudden, we decided we weren't going to run anymore. Terry slammed on the brakes, and we got out of the van to confront them, right in the middle of the road. They never expected that. They thought they were going to chase us all the way back to East Brady. But when they saw they had seven psychos on their hands, they quickly did a 180 and went home.

After my older brothers left home, Terry became someone I looked up to during my last couple years of high school. I owe that man a huge debt of gratitude. He helped me grow up fast, not only as a player but as a person. When you get into high school and have a lot of success as an athlete, you start thinking that your shit doesn't stink. I was cocky. I didn't like criticism. I always thought I was right.

And Terry was there to pull me out of that dream world and say, "Jim, your shit definitely has an odor."

I did have one humbling experience in my high school career that I'll never forget. We were playing Clarion-Limestone in my junior year. A win would give us the conference championship. We scored a touchdown in the second quarter, and I had a chance to kick what would prove to be the winning extra point. I booted it through—but my foot hit the ball just as the referee blew the whistle to start the play. So I had to do it over. Sure enough, the second one sailed wide left. The game ended in a 13–13 tie; we had to share the title with a 9–0–1 record.

It still eats at me.

When I was a senior, my twin brothers were sophomores. So for that season you had one Kelly throwing, another catching (Danny) and another blocking (Kevin; we nicknamed him "Battleship," after Bob "Battleship" Kelly of the Pittsburgh Penguins). At the end of that year, we were crowned Little 12 champions with a 10–0 record. After Danny and Kevin graduated from East Brady, a coach for one of the opposing schools came up to my father and said, "Thank God you've run out of sons to feed that program, Joe."

I was also the most valuable player on our basketball team, which reached the state quarterfinals in my junior year and the semifinals when I was a senior. Playing center/forward, I became the first man in school history to score 1,000 points and pull down 1,000 rebounds in a career. As a senior, I averaged 23 points and 20 rebounds per game, and had six games where I scored more than 30 points.

I wasn't the tallest guy on the team, but I could jump pretty high. And I was very, very physical. Usually, I cleared everybody out of the middle. Those who didn't get out of the way wound up tasting an elbow or two. At the end of each game, I was either sitting on the bench with five fouls or standing on the court with four. Charles Barkley would have been proud.

No matter how much noise there was in the gym, I always heard my father yelling at the officials. He and two of his buddies—Art Vasbinder and John Olcus—would constantly scream things like "Bad call! Bullshit!" You'd hear that as clear as a bell, as if there weren't anyone else around. I knew Dad was just looking out for his son, just making sure that I didn't get cheated. But there were a couple of times when, as I ran down the court, I looked up in the stands and shouted, "Dad, would you please be quiet?"

I actually like basketball better than football because when you practice basketball, you're in a game-type setting. You do your drills, then you get right into a five-on-five scrimmage, which is as close to an actual game as you can get. You're always competing in basketball, and I love being a competitor. But that's not the case with football. You can't duplicate game conditions in a football practice because you'd lose most of your players to injury before Sunday. Teammates just can't hit each other the way opponents can.

I knew my future was in football, however. As good as I might have been in high school hoops, it was obvious I didn't have the height to become anything more than a decent small-college player. Besides, my older brothers had all excelled in football; I had a tradition to uphold.

Basketball was just another sport to keep me in shape . . . and keep me out of trouble.

At the banquet following the Little 12 championship that we won in my junior year, the guest speaker was Rocky Bleier, my second-favorite Steeler after Terry Bradshaw. I'll never forget that night at the Holiday Inn in Butler, Pennsylvania. Rocky gave a fantastic speech about his experiences in Vietnam and the NFL, I won a bunch of trophies and the whole team got to relive our great season in the game films that were shown through dinner. But the best part came at the end of the night, when my father and I went up to introduce ourselves to Bleier.

"I'm going to play for the Steelers someday," I blurted out.

To my surprise, he seemed to take me seriously.

"You know, something, Jim?" Bleier said. "I was very impressed by what I saw of you in that film tonight. You're quite an athlete. And you're going to be somebody someday."

I left the place on a cloud. So did my father.

Dad also heard a couple of nice compliments from opposing coaches in the Little 12. One said that facing the Bulldogs with me at quarterback was like taking on Penn State. Another said I played like a professional.

By the time our class of 65 graduated, East Brady retired my No. 11 jersey, which still ranks among the greatest honors of my life. But not before I got to play in the Big 33 all-star game, one of the more prestigious sporting events in all of Pennsylvania. I'd love to say that I performed brilliantly at quarterback, that I threw for a whole bunch of yards and a whole bunch of touchdowns and led the West squad to a huge victory over the East.

The truth is, I didn't get to take a snap until the final minute and a half of the game. There were two quarterbacks ahead of me on the depth chart, Frank Rocco and Dan Daniels. They were from Class AAA schools in Pittsburgh—schools that were much larger and received a lot more publicity than East Brady High. People in Pittsburgh barely knew the Little 12 existed. Plus, Rocco's father, Frank Sr., was the West's head coach.

I understood the politics involved. I wasn't expecting to be treated the same as those glamour boys. I just wanted a fair chance to show what I could do as a passer.

It never came.

I did get to start at free safety, however. When the year began, Coach Henry had moved me there from linebacker to reduce the chances of my being injured and losing out on a college scholarship. I played pretty well, but it wasn't a good day for the West. We were favored to win by three touchdowns, yet wound up losing, 28–6. That was the only reason I got to play quarterback—we were so far out of it, the coaches weren't afraid to hand the mop to some country kid.

But after watching the two big-city quarterbacks practice and play, I felt a lot better about myself. I knew I was at least as good as they were.

It was just a matter of getting someone on the outside to notice.

2

From a Blizzard to a Hurricane

WHEN YOU GROW UP in western Pennsylvania, your college loyalties belong either to Penn State or the University of Pittsburgh. My heart was always set on playing football for the Nittany Lions, so that automatically meant I despised the Pitt Panthers. I attended the Penn State football camp after my sophomore and junior seasons in high school. I even liked those dull helmets and uniforms. I never thought about going anywhere else.

Much to my surprise, however, there were quite a few choices for me to consider through the fall and winter of 1977. Besides being recruited by schools close to home—Penn State, Pitt and West Virginia—I also heard from Tennessee, Notre Dame, Kentucky, Georgia, North Carolina State, Maryland, Arizona, Arizona State and Miami.

So much for the concerns over whether I'd be noticed outside of East Brady.

I was certain my prayers had been answered the day J. T. White, a Penn State assistant coach, came to my house and said, "We want you, Jim." All I could think about was playing in front of those 80,000 fans who jam Beaver Stadium on Saturday afternoons. All I wanted to do was help the Nittany Lions continue their reign as one of the best and classiest football programs in the nation.

White showed up at a lot of my basketball games, which, I assumed meant I was high on the Nittany Lions' recruiting list. I also assumed they were really impressed with my quarterbacking skills. Little did I know that they had already recruited two all-state quarterbacks from Pennsylvania—Frank Rocco, the starter for the Big 33 West squad in my senior year, and Terry Rakowsky, who started for the East in the same game. A number of college recruiters thought Rocco had the best arm in the country that year.

Once he got Rocco's and Rakowsky's letter-of-intent signatures, White revealed that the school was only interested in me as a linebacker. Period.

It wasn't exactly music to my ears.

After my senior year, I paid an unofficial visit to the campus and met Joe Paterno, a god to almost everyone who lived in and around my hometown. Relatives, friends and people I didn't even know just assumed I'd walk into his office holding a pen, ready to sign the first piece of paper he slipped under my nose. But all bets were off when Paterno repeated exactly what his assistant coach had told me. At the time, I stood 6-3 and weighed 195 pounds. In Paterno's eyes, my physique was better suited for tackling than throwing.

"With your frame and size, Jim," he said, "we could get you up to 230, 235 pounds in no time."

"You probably could. But you're not going to."

Sure, I took a lot of pride in being the best defensive player I could be in high school. As I said, I loved delivering punishment a hell of a lot more than taking it. I also couldn't help but feel somewhat honored that a college known for churning out some of the best linebackers ever to play the game, the place everyone called Linebacker U., wanted to give me a chance to follow in that great tradition.

But my brother Pat, who had played linebacker in the pros as well as high school and college, gave me the following advice: "You can play linebacker and get your teeth kicked in. Or you can play quarterback and make a ton of money."

Quarterback was the only position for me. And nothing was about to change that. Not even a full scholarship offer from Penn State.

I do give Paterno a lot of credit for being up-front with me *before* I signed on the dotted line. When talking to recruits, a lot of college coaches promise the moon, the stars and the sun . . . and the kids end up being left in one big fog. Joe came right out and told me, "Jim, I don't want you to come here expecting to be a quarterback and then having us tell you, after you sign, that we really wanted you as a linebacker."

After that, Jackie Sherrill, who was coaching Pitt at the time, talked about my playing quarterback for the Panthers. I just couldn't put aside my bad feelings for Pitt from my years as a Penn State fan to even make the short trip for a visit.

That left Tennessee, Kentucky, Notre Dame and Miami as serious contenders. If it were up to Pat McGinn, my mother's father, who emigrated to Pittsburgh from County Cork, Ireland, there wouldn't be any decision to make. All he ever wanted was for one of his grandsons to be a quarterback for the Fighting Irish of Notre Dame.

Sorry, Grandpa. This was one Irishman they were going to have to do without.

We were having a blizzard the day Lou Saban, entering his second season as Miami's head coach, and one of his assistant coaches, Ron Marciniak, flew up to East Brady to pay me a visit. The storm was so severe, in fact, their flight couldn't land in Pittsburgh, so they were detoured to Toronto. There they sat for six hours before the plane received clearance to return to Pittsburgh.

When they finally landed, the roads to East Brady were still snowbound. Marciniak had grown up near Pittsburgh, so he drove the rental car. While clinging to the wheel for dear life, he kept asking Saban if he wanted to turn back.

"Just keep it on the road," Saban said.

I guess he really wanted me.

Even after they reached East Brady, they still had to search for our house. But that was no simple chore either. As in every old mining town in Pennsylvania, the houses in East Brady all look alike. And snow made it impossible to read the numbers. So after the two of them found Purdum Street, they got out of the car and began knocking on the door of each house.

My mother had been out, and because of the storm, she was delayed getting home. Much to my amazement, Saban yanked off his tie, stuck a towel in the front of his belt and started to make dinner. He wasn't a bad cook. But it was the things Saban said that really made me drool, beginning with a reminder that, in Miami, there wouldn't be any bone-chilling scenes like the one outside our window. Instead, I'd be looking at a lot of sunshine, a lot of sparkling water and a lot of pretty women. (I loved the last part especially.)

Best of all, he promised I'd be quarterbacking a pro-style offense. He even pulled out a pencil and some paper and began to draw pass patterns, showing me how zone defenses rotated and things like that. It was so interesting, I kept moving up my chair to get a better look. I was really impressed with the guy, especially because of his experience as a pro coach with Denver and Buffalo.

Before Saban left, which was after midnight, he admitted the Hurricanes' football program was on shaky ground financially. Very shaky. It had had only one winning season in the previous nine and attendance at home games was down to something like 20,000 per game. People were saying that, if things didn't turn around soon, football might be dropped.

That made going there a pretty risky proposition, but once I visited the campus, on my first trip ever to Florida, I knew Miami was the perfect place for me. It was November and the weather was pleasant, as were Saban and his assistant coaches. The players showed me a pretty good time. I went to the beaches and saw all those beautiful coeds in bikinis. I went out to eat, then went to some discos, where I saw more beautiful ladies.

After that, my only question was: "Where do I sign?"

Actually, I didn't pick up the pen right then and there, but I did give Saban a verbal commitment. I went ahead with plans to visit Tennessee the following week, thinking it would be just a formality. As things turned out, however, the Miami commitment was put to a stern test. Everything about Tennessee appealed to me: the big-time college atmosphere, the campus, the people who went to school there (yes, they had their share of attractive women, too), the fans and the fact that I'd compete for the starting quarterback job as a freshman.

When I mentioned I was leaning toward Miami, the Tennessee coaches acted like I was crazy.

"Why would you ever want to go to Miami?" they asked. "Lou Saban's going to leave you stranded there. Don't you know about his reputation? He never stays in one place long enough to take his coat off. He'll be gone by your second year—if not sooner."

"No way," I said, figuring they were just saying those things in a desperate attempt to change my mind.

But I couldn't deny having some second thoughts. I was impressed by all that Tennessee had to offer. And if I hadn't given my word to Saban, I probably would have become a Volunteer.

Once I got to Miami in August 1978, I almost wished I had picked Tennessee after all. I discovered we were running a veer offense. *A veer!* I couldn't believe it. I mean, the guy had marched right into my living room and told me and my family he was going with a pro-style approach.

I just couldn't see a guy like myself, who had a pretty strong arm but wasn't exactly quick on his feet, operating an offense that is designed for a nimble quarterback and places greater emphasis on running than on throwing. A veer basically gives the quarterback the options of faking a handoff to a split back who dives into the line, handing off to that same split back, keeping the ball and running it himself, or pitching to the other split back who trails him stride for stride. It involves a lot of running and reading on the run, and I knew it wouldn't put my throwing skills to good use.

When I got to Miami, I found out the only skills being put to good use were those of senior running back Ottis (O.J.) Anderson, who would go on to star with the St. Louis Cardinals and New York Giants. The veer was O.J.'s offense. Surely, no kid from East Brady—or anywhere else for that matter—was going to come along and force a change.

Not that it made a tremendous difference in that first season anyway. I was redshirted, which meant I'd have an extra year of eligibility. The "official" reason for the red shirt was an ankle injury. In truth, I was being placed in storage because the coaches felt they were better off going with Ken McMillian, a sophomore, as the starting quarterback and using two other freshmen, Mike Rodrigue and Mark Richt, as backups.

In the meantime, I'd pick up some seasoning on the scout team in practice and by watching the mistakes the other quarterbacks made in games. It was quite a comedown, going from Mr. Everything at East Brady to Mr. Nobody at Miami. I couldn't even get my high school number, 11, because it had already been issued. I asked for 12, because it was Terry Bradshaw's number, and that had already been issued, too. So I had to settle for 7, because it was the only quarterback number available. That really underscored the fact I was just another player waiting for his opportunity.

Of course, at the time, Hurricane quarterbacks didn't do a whole lot with the ball except pitch it to O.J. I got my turn in practice, and Anderson would constantly complain because I could never get outside fast enough to get him the ball for the option. I just didn't have the speed to keep up with him.

"What's wrong with you, man?" he yelled one time.

"Hey, I ain't no option quarterback," I said.

"Well, if you want to be on this damn team, you'd better become one."

There was a lot for me to learn. For instance, during our very first practice, we ran all of our drills without pads. I called my brother Ray and said, "Gee, I thought college football was supposed to be tough. These practices are easier than high school."

Four days later, after my first workout in pads, I called Ray again.

"Man," I said, "I got killed about five times today."

It also was quite an adjustment for me to spend eight hours each week watching films of opposing defenses. And that was just with the quarterbacks. Counting what we saw as a team, it came to about thirteen or fourteen hours per week.

By the end of that first season, my eyes were about ready to fall out. But as time went on, I realized that the more time you spent studying defenses, the better your chances were for success on the field. The first major difference I discovered between high school and college was that in college there was greater emphasis on reading defenses, determining the possibilities, then choosing the correct receiver according to the situation. In high school I'd just drop back, look for the open man and fire.

It was a long season of watching, learning and fuming over the fact that I was just like any other spectator. And soon after it ended, I received a very shocking phone call from our backfield coach, Joe Brodsky.

"Jim, Coach Saban left for Army this morning," he said, sounding all panicky. "I just thought you ought to know."

"He did what? Enlisted in the Army? At his age?"

When Coach Brodsky repeated himself a bit more slowly, I felt both confused and angry.

I thought about transferring. I thought about it a great deal. And the first place I thought about going was Tennessee. Then I said to myself, "Why should I be mad? Saban favored a run-oriented offense, but no one complained about it because O.J. was such a great player. Now O.J. is gone and so is Saban. Who knows? Maybe the new coach will throw the ball on every down."

All kinds of people were offering advice, including my brother Pat, who thought I should stick it out until the dust cleared.

"Sometimes you have to play the waiting game, Jim," he said. "Sometimes it's better to do that than be hasty and make a change that could possibly cause you to go from a bad situation to a worse one. See who they hire next, see what kind of offense they're going to run. Then decide whether to transfer."

(As time passed, the bad feelings I had about Saban disappeared. In fact, we've become pretty good friends through the years. Now, whenever we see each other, we laugh about our one semi-season together at Miami.)

The next phone call I received from Coach Brodsky was to inform me that Howard Schnellenberger would be our new head coach.

His arrival was a miracle for me. He came from the Dolphins, where he had been offensive coordinator, and brought with him the pro-style passing attack he had used with such NFL greats as Bob Griese and Earl Morrall. He also brought a ton of coaching experience that included a stint at Alabama, where his students included Joe Namath and Ken Stabler.

With Coach Schnellenberger calling the shots, I was able to start fresh. Anderson's departure had given the coaching staff a reason to open things up on offense. That is, gradually. First, we went from a veer to a pro veer, a compromise that took advantage of the skills of the players Saban had recruited for the veer and some of the guys Coach Schnellenberger found to throw the ball.

Their coaching styles were as different as their football philosophies. Saban yelled a lot and tried to scare the players, while Coach Schnellenberger reminded me of my high school coach, Terry Henry—both were easy to talk to, they explained things clearly and they made a player want to do his best for them. Saban made you do things out of fear of being humiliated. And sometimes that worked, too.

Which isn't to say Coach Schnellenberger was some sort of pushover. In fact, he had quite an intimidating presence. He was a big, burly guy with a deep voice and the meanest-looking eyebrows you've ever seen. In many ways he was like a drill sergeant. We had an eleven o'clock curfew every night during the season that was strictly enforced. (OK, maybe I did sneak out a time or two. But those were rare exceptions. Honest.) You just didn't screw around with the man.

Besides the pass plays Coach Schnellenberger used when he was an assistant coach for the Dolphins and, before that, Baltimore (where he coached my brother Pat), he also brought along one of his former NFL players, Earl Morrall, to tutor his quarterbacks. It was the best thing that could have ever happened to my football career.

Coach Morrall taught me all the basics of throwing the ball, especially the deep pass. My arm was pretty strong, yet I wasn't getting all the distance I was capable of. Not until Coach Morrall showed me the wonders of "getting air under the ball." I had always tried zipping my passes, tried making them travel as straight as ropes. But Coach Morrall pointed out that, in time, I'd discover defensive backs would cover receivers a little tighter and completions would come a lot harder. So I started to put more loft on my passes.

"That way," he explained, "you can drop the ball into the

receiver's hands as he's running ahead of the defensive back. Plus, it gives the receiver a little more time to use his speed to get open deep."

Coach Morrall also taught me to hold the ball up by my ear, rather than down low by my belt, to improve the quickness of my release. Holding the ball low, you create the extra motion of having to lift, then throw. Holding it by your ear, all you have to do is pull back and let it fly.

Of course, there wasn't a whole lot of choice in that or other matters where Coach Morrall's instruction was concerned. He didn't care whether you started or played third string. You did things his way or you did them somewhere else.

He was as tough as they come. For example, after a two-and-a-half-hour practice, we ran gassers. A gasser consists of running back and forth across the width of the field four times; usually, we did three of them. They were hard enough to handle in the smothering heat and humidity of South Florida, but if we didn't finish each within 40 seconds (with a 30-second break in between), Coach Morrall would make us run four. And if we still didn't beat the clock, he'd have us do five. But never more than that, or we'd be dead.

Sometimes we'd finish the third or fourth in 41 seconds and that still wouldn't be good enough.

"Ah, come on, give us a break!" we would yell.

"On the line!" Coach Morrall would yell back.

End of conversation.

Things really started looking up in my second year. I got to switch jersey numbers from 7 to 12. And I moved all the way up the depth chart to second-string quarterback, behind Mike Rodrigue. We got along great, even though we both realized we were in competition for the top job. Mike had more speed than I did and was a much better practice player. I mean, the guy was All-World on the practice field. He threw the most perfect spirals I've ever seen in my life. They were the kind of passes any coach would love to see his quarterback throw.

On the other hand, I have never really been a great practice player. I worked hard in every drill; I just never looked particularly sharp. Maybe, deep down inside, I was feeling that no matter how well I performed, it wasn't going to count. Maybe, deep down, I needed to know we were playing for keeps.

That was when Mike had his toughest times—when we played for keeps. Through our first six games that season, he threw 14 interceptions and three touchdown passes, and our record stood at 3–3. Our seventh game was against Syracuse. Ironically, it was played at my future NFL address, Rich Stadium, because Syracuse was using nearby neutral sites for home games as it awaited the completion of the Carrier Dome. It was a cold afternoon in late October, and there were only 8,000 fans in the stands—and 72,000 empty seats. After we fell behind, 25–7, early in the third quarter, Coach Schnellenberger caught me completely by surprise when he pulled me aside and said, "Jim, I'm going to let you take over."

The first words out of my mouth were: "Oh, great!"

But inside I was thinking: *"Oh, shit!"*

Although I tried my best to hide it, I was as nervous as could be. The big opportunity to show my stuff for an extended period had finally arrived, and I was just so afraid of screwing it up. If I flopped, I might never get another chance to play the rest of my college career, let alone the rest of the season. I also knew it could be the biggest break of my college career.

We wound up losing, 25–15, but I came out OK. After throwing a 12-yard pass over the head of our split end, Pat Walker, who was wide open in the end zone late in the third quarter, I found him for a 39-yard touchdown in the fourth. I also hit fullback Gary Breckner for a two-point conversion. I finished the day with seven completions in 17 attempts for 130 yards.

I knew that I had what it took to be a big-time college quarterback. I knew I had the arm strength and the smarts. I just needed the opportunity to show what I could do—in actual game conditions, that is.

I thought I opened the coaches' eyes at least a little bit against Syracuse. I figured they might even consider giving me a chance to start and play a whole game down the road. But when Mike took all of the first-unit snaps in practice the following week, I assumed I was back to my same old spot on the bench.

I couldn't have been more wrong. The day of our next game, about four hours before kickoff, Coach Schnellenberger informed me that I was the new starter. Now, we're not talking about any old game. The team on the other side of the field on that November afternoon in 1979 would be none other than Penn State, which had a 5–2 record, was ranked 19th in the country and was favored to beat us by about 30 points. Penn State, the school I grew up loving. Penn State, the school that didn't want me as a quarterback.

The school I wanted to beat more than any other on our schedule.

We had just eaten the pregame meal at our hotel in State College, Pennsylvania. After meeting with the coach, I went back to my room and, well, returned the food back to the hotel —a pregame ritual that's going strong to this day.

Before then, we were mostly a running team, throwing as few as 11 passes in a game. But we weren't having a whole lot of success on the ground, so Coach Schnellenberger loosened things up a bit.

On the first play of the game, I combined with our fullback, Chris Hobbs, on a 57-yard pass-and-run play. I went six for six on our first two series as we built a 13–10 halftime lead on the way to a 26–10 victory. The whole day I felt like I was in a dream. Nothing went wrong. When the game ended, I still couldn't believe what had happened. It was one of the best feelings in my whole life. I was on an incredible high. And I couldn't wait to share it with the friends and family who were waiting for me (minus the twins, who were still at East Brady and involved in a conference championship game on the same day; Mom and Dad chose to come to my game because it was the only one on the schedule close to home and they couldn't afford to go all the way to Miami for a game).

I had wanted to go in there and show Paterno, his assistant coaches, 80,000 fans in Beaver Stadium and everyone else associated with Penn State that I had what it took to be a big-time college quarterback. I think my 18-of-30, 280-yard, three-touchdown performance did the trick.

"I've never seen a quarterback play as well and as poised in his debut as Kelly was today," Coach Schnellenberger told reporters.

Actually, it wasn't quite as simple as it looked. After I released that throw to Hobbs on the first play, defensive tackle Bruce Clark and defensive end Larry Kubin combined to dislocate my jaw. It wasn't until after the first series that the doctors finally got it pushed back to where it belonged. After that, my jaw kept locking up on me, which made calling plays tough because I couldn't open my mouth all the way.

But it didn't matter. No dislocated jaw, or any other injury, was going to keep me from finishing that game. If I could stand, I could play.

Afterward, Paterno shook my hand, but he didn't say much. I think he just wanted to get off the field. Fast.

Our next—and last—three opponents that year were Alabama, Notre Dame and Florida. It was a case of going from the frying pan into the flame thrower.

After we upset Penn State, somebody got the bright idea that Miami, with this "freshman sensation" at quarterback, would be attractive for national television. So the entire country would have an opportunity to watch us take on Alabama—which was only the No. 1-ranked team in the country at the time—at Tuscaloosa no less.

The attitude among fans and media seemed to be: "What else does the kid have in him?"

I'm sorry to say it wasn't much that day. I completed only two of 15 passes, I was intercepted three times and we lost, 30–0. To make matters worse, late in the first quarter I suffered a concussion when, while I was scrambling toward the sidelines, linebacker E. J. Junior (who would go on to become a first-round draft pick of the Cardinals) came up and knocked the living hell out of me and my head bounced off the Astroturf a couple of times. I didn't remember too much of what happened in the game after that, which was just as well.

My roommate, offensive lineman Clem Barbarino, who was also from western Pennsylvania, gave me all kinds of abuse for completing more passes to the Crimson Tide than to our receivers. He also started answering our phone, "Jim Kelly's ex-fan club."

The Notre Dame game was played in Tokyo, Japan. It was my first time overseas, and I couldn't have been more excited. I'll never forget how polite the Japanese were. They waited on us hand and foot. They treated us like kings.

Unfortunately, the Fighting Irish weren't quite as hospitable.

They pounded us, 40–15. I left the game early with cracked ribs.

The only other sour memory from the trip was when Japanese police wouldn't allow either team to leave the country, because a major-league crime had been committed at the hotel where we were both staying. Someone ripped off a $35,000 necklace, and all the players were immediately considered suspects. The authorities said they didn't want to know who did it; they just wanted the necklace returned. After a short while, it was back where it belonged and we were allowed to check out. To this day, I don't know who the culprit was . . . or whether he was from Miami or Notre Dame.

In only three games, I had suffered a dislocated jaw, a concussion and cracked ribs. To me, each week became a challenge to see if I could stand up to the pounding of big-time college defenders. And I wore every injury like a badge, just like when I was a kid. Growing up with three rough-and-tumble older brothers, I took my share of punishment. Whenever I thought I was man enough to take them on in a wrestling match—or was just acting like a typical wise-ass younger brother—I usually wound up in a lot of pain.

But you could never let them know they had gotten the better of you, because then they'd just beat on you some more. I might have been hurting like a sonofagun on the inside, but on the outside I was laughing in their faces. You always had to laugh. If you ever started crying, you were immediately branded a baby, a big puss. I wanted them to be proud of the fact that I could handle whatever they dished out.

It was the same after each of those three games. I wanted everyone, my brothers and everyone else in the world, to know I could take a licking and keep on ticking.

But in terms of my actual performance as a quarterback, I hardly felt like I was in one piece. I wasn't throwing the ball well. I wasn't making anything happen for our offense. And I started to lose a little bit of confidence in myself. I began wondering whether I had the right stuff.

Then along came just the boost I needed. We traveled to Miami for our season finale against Florida, one of our main rivals. To protect my ribs, I wore miles of tape around my chest and a flak jacket Coach Morrall borrowed from Delvin Williams, a running back for the Dolphins. It hurt just to take a breath, let alone a hit, yet I still managed to complete 10 of 17 passes for 165 yards and a touchdown in our 30–24 victory.

My brother Pat had gotten married the day before in Richmond. But he and his wife, Tricia, scheduled their honeymoon just so they could make the eighteen-hour drive down to Miami to watch me take on the Gators the following night.

"Jim gave me the wedding present I wanted—and more," Pat told a reporter afterward. After spending the next two nights in my dorm room, he and his wife left on their honeymoon cruise to the Bahamas from the Port of Miami.

The game worked out pretty well for me, too. After the Alabama and Notre Dame disasters, I needed a game where I ran the team with poise. That's what a quarterback's for.

Our 5–6 record wasn't so bad when you considered how young we were; we had only two seniors on the entire roster. But it was going to take many more wins to impress the school's administration, which was feeling heat from dissatisfied alumni.

The future of the football program continued to hang very much in the balance.

One of the greatest things to happen to me at Miami was the friendship I developed with our halfback, Mark Rush. We became roommates in that second season, and I still refer to him as my "sixth brother."

Mark caught my attention in one of our first practices as freshmen when I saw him run the 40-yard dash. He finished in under 4.5 seconds, and his great speed had everyone stopping and staring in amazement.

It wasn't long before Mark became my favorite receiver coming out of the backfield on third down. Besides what he could do with his feet, he had by far the best hands on the team. I loved to throw, he loved to catch. And whenever we needed a big play, all I had to do was look in Mark's direction.

Our third-down play was called a "56 Halfback Option." Every time the coaches sent it in from the sidelines Mark and I knew, one way or another, he was going to make the play work. We'd just look at each other in the huddle and there would be a mutual confidence that nothing was going to stop us from getting it done. There was a sixth sense between us where one guy always knew what the other was going to do. And that was especially important on the "56 Halfback Option," because depending on what kind of coverage the defense was showing, Mark could run one of three different pass routes—a six-yard hook in, a six-yard hook out or he could take it straight up the middle and split the safeties deep. More often than not, the last pattern resulted in a touchdown.

We called Mark Mr. High Stakes, because he had a vertical jump of around 37 inches and in short-yardage and goal-line situations, he'd always take the high road over the pile. It was almost like watching Superman leap tall buildings in a single bound. And I'd say, almost 100 percent of the time, Mark would get the first down or the six points.

We were sort of an odd couple. I was from the country and Mark was from Fort Lauderdale. He really knew his way around the beaches and night spots of South Florida. He was your typical tall, tanned, handsome surfer boy. At the time Mark was single, so he knew where to find all the good-looking girls. And it only made sense to me to hang around someone who knew where all the attractive young ladies were.

When we became roommates, our goal was to have the nicest, most modern bachelor pad possible. I had a king-sized water bed, which took up almost three quarters of the room. So Mark had to have a super single. We varnished all the cabinets, got everything in tip-top shape and kept it that way. Unlike the "Odd Couple" in the movie and television series, we were both pretty neat. And we both cooked. Fortunately, we often could enjoy the great home-cooking of Mark's mother, Joan, who was my mom away from home. Because the best thing I knew how to make was reservations.

We rarely failed to have a good time when we went out together. And if either of us had a problem, we didn't have to look too far for a helping hand or a sympathetic ear. We were pretty much inseparable. Anytime I would be somewhere and Mark wasn't close by, people would automatically ask, "Where's your shadow?" It would be vice versa with Mark.

When it came to physical conditioning, Mark was a workaholic. Many mornings, he'd get up around six and go for a three-mile run. He was always in shape, always working out.

Before college, I didn't worry a whole lot about the kind of shape I was in. But Mark's attitude was contagious and I became a pretty devoted weight lifter. It wasn't long before I was benching 300 pounds and squatting 450.

Part of my motivation, I have to admit, was to get one of the special T-shirts that our strength coach, Ray Ganong, gave out. They said "Bench Press Club 300" or "Squat Club 450." I'd always see those huge, thick-necked linemen and linebackers strutting around with them on, and I thought it would be neat for a quarterback—among the so-called weaklings of the game —to wear one.

I put my mind to it and got both shirts.

Another close friendship I formed in college was with Jeff Peck. He didn't play on the football team, but was in a couple of my classes. Jeff was among the elite students at the school. He also had a great personality and we just hit it off right away.

We became study partners, which definitely worked more to my benefit than to Jeff's. No matter what the subject was, if I had a hard time understanding something, I could count on Jeff to help me out. All those hours we spent in the library got me through a lot of exams and term papers.

During spring practice in 1980, I was suddenly promoted from Mr. Nobody to the primary leader of a team just beginning to find its identity. The air conditioner in the players' dormitory was blowing hot air for about three days. We were all dying, but nobody had the courage to complain.

Then one of our offensive linemen, Jim Pokorney, came up with a bright idea.

"Since you're the quarterback," he said, "why don't *you* go and tell Coach Schnellenberger about it?"

My first thought was to suggest he get off his fat ass and do it himself. But I knew he was right. We didn't have a true veteran at any position with a strong enough sense of security to act as our spokesman (or is it chief bitcher?). As the No. 1 quarterback, I'm the man everyone is supposed to have enough confidence in to follow into battle, so it was up to me to talk to the coach—like it or not. After a little bit of hemming and hawing, I finally got up the courage to walk across the campus to the football complex and go up the two flights of stairs to Coach Schnellenberger's office. I was nervous. Anytime you were headed for a face-to-face conversation with Coach Schnellenberger, your mouth would get a little dry. Just that deep voice of his was enough to frighten about 95 percent of the team.

But as I approached the football complex, I thought the worst he could do was say no and that would be the end of it. When I got to his office, I saw that his door was open and he was sitting behind his desk. He motioned me to come in. I cleared my throat, stated our case, thanked him for his time and walked out.

The next day, cold air was breezing through those air-conditioning vents. The thing I learned that day about Coach Schnellenberger was that his players came first. As long as you were reasonable with him, he'd see things your way.

By the fall, we were refreshed and ready to show how much we had improved over the previous year. We even had our sights set on a bowl invitation. I knew the school's administration was hungry for some positive results to show the alumni, whose patience was just about gone.

We came through with an 8–3 record and a bid to the Peach Bowl in Atlanta, ending a thirteen-year bowl drought for Miami. Two of the wins were upsets: We gave No. 3 Florida State its only loss of the season, 10–9, at the Orange Bowl and ended the year, just like the previous one, by traveling to Gainesville and beating No. 18 Florida, 31–7.

That was a particularly sweet win on two counts. First, the Gators were ranked and we weren't. Second, their fans had been a lot nastier than usual, pelting our bench throughout the game with oranges, tangerines, ice, rolls of toilet paper (at least they had the decency to make sure they weren't used), water, cups and anything else they could get their hands on.

Coach Schnellenberger was so furious that he shocked everyone in the stadium (as well as in the ABC-TV announcing booth) by calling for a 35-yard field-goal attempt after we recovered a fumble in the last second of the game. We made it.

"The field goal was my little way of telling the fans I was not happy with their conduct," he explained afterward. But the Florida players and coaches took it as a direct insult to them and vowed to get revenge when we met in the following season's opener. Al Michaels, who was a college play-by-play man before graduating to the *Monday Night Football* booth, closed the broadcast by asking, "Wouldn't that stick in Florida's craw somewhere down the line?"

We didn't have time to worry about that then. We had to prepare for our Peach Bowl game against Virginia Tech.

Not that I needed it, but my brother Pat gave me a little added incentive to be at my best. He said if we won, he was going to take me, Ray, Ed, Danny and Kevin on a skiing trip to a resort in northern Virginia. Pat had it all planned out: We'd have a victory party that night in Atlanta, then pile into our parents' van the next morning and head north.

We took command of the game right away. My 15-yard touchdown pass to Larry Brodsky and a 12-yard run by Chris Hobbs gave us a 14–0 lead less than two minutes into the second quarter. The Hokies cut it to 14–10 in the third, but our defense, anchored by nose tackle Jim Burt, stiffened and our place-kicker, Danny Miller, hit a pair of field goals to seal the 20–10 victory. That gave us a 9–3 overall record, the Hurricanes' best since 1966.

Burt, who'd go on to establish himself as one of the NFL's best nose tackles with the Giants, was a lot of fun. He liked pulling pranks on everybody, and he had to get in the last word on every conversation. We called him One-up because no matter what anybody said, Burt always had to go one better. On this day, however, the best he could manage with yours truly was a tie. Burt made nine tackles to take the defensive Most Valuable Player hardware. I completed 11 of 22 passes for 179 yards and the touchdown to walk away with the game's offensive Most Valuable Player trophy.

That night, the party was in my room at the Peach Tree Plaza Hotel. The entire team was there, along with my brothers. We had the bathtub filled to the top with beer, champagne and ice. Forgetting about the seven-hour drive ahead of us, I made the big mistake of trying to empty the tub all by myself.

I paid the price all the way to Virginia.

Longtime followers of University of Miami football began comparing me with George Mira, the Hurricanes' All-American quarterback in the early in 1960s. His nickname was the Matador because of his Spanish descent and because, according to legend, of his ability to sidestep defenders who blitzed like bulls. *Olé!*

It was nice to be mentioned in such outstanding company. But I wasn't entirely satisfied with my performance going into my junior season of eligibility. I had to work at being a lot quicker on my feet. I realized there was only so much improvement Mother Nature would permit in that area. But there were some finer points Coach Morrall stressed, such as the importance of keeping on my toes and not standing flat-footed in the pocket. That helped me see the field a lot better and get an even quicker release.

There was also plenty of room for us to grow as a team. We knew we had the makings of a national champion. With eight bowl teams on our 1981 schedule, we had an opportunity to make a strong impression on the rest of the country.

The only problem was, because of some minor NCAA recruiting violations, we wouldn't be allowed to play in a bowl game. And that, of course, would kill any chance of our winning the national title.

The Florida Gators were every bit as fired up for our home opener as they promised to be after the late field goal in our 24-point victory at their place in 1980. I left the game in the third quarter with a leg injury that I just couldn't walk off. And with six minutes left on the clock, we were down, 20–11. My backup, Mark Richt, was having his problems, but he finally settled down and came up with a big touchdown pass on third and 11 to make it 20–18 with 5:45 remaining. Our defense held, and with 41 seconds to go, Danny Miller kicked a 55-yard field goal to give us a 21–20 triumph.

We'd go 2–2 in our next four games, then catch fire and win all of our last six. Both losses were on the road, 14–7 at Texas and 14–10 at Mississippi State, and in each case the officials took a late touchdown away from us with a questionable penalty.

Our biggest victory that year came on October 31, 1981, when we knocked off No. 1-ranked Penn State, 17–14, at the Orange Bowl. It's still viewed as one of the bigger wins in school history. I connected with Larry Brodsky for an 80-yard touchdown pass and Miller hit three field goals before one of our few nationally televised games of the season. But the outcome wasn't secure until our defense came through with two big plays

—a fumble recovery by nose tackle Tony Chickillo with 2:29 left and an interception by free safety Fred Marion with 1:15 on the clock. Fred, who would become an awesome member of the New England Patriots' secondary and pick off more than a few of my passes through the years, was incredibly pumped up by the victory.

"All week, I kept hearing we didn't have a chance," he said. "Well, we did. And we did it before a national television audience. Now when people talk about the University of Miami, they will know it's a good football team."

Just in case there were any nonbelievers out there, we closed the season at home by crushing Notre Dame, 37–15. It marked the first time since 1960 and only the second time ever that we beat the Irish. At 9–2 and ranked ninth in the country, we should have been a cinch for a major bowl. But because of the recruiting violations, it wasn't going to happen that year. So we considered that our "bowl" appearance.

It was our game from early in the first quarter when Mike Rodrigue, who had moved from quarterback to wide receiver, ran four yards for our first touchdown from a trick formation that faked the pants off Notre Dame's defense. After we broke the huddle, I lined up as a flanker; Mike lined up under center, took the snap and ran untouched into the end zone. We generated 516 yards of total offense, averaging 6.3 every time we touched the ball. I hit 17 of 25 passes for 264 yards, giving me 4,643 career passing yards and breaking Mira's eighteen-year-old school record. My two touchdown passes gave me 29 for my career, which broke another school mark held by Mira.

George was very gracious about it, saying records were meant to be broken and "it couldn't happen to a nicer kid." I knew where he was coming from. One of my high school records, for career passing yards, fell while I was in college. I was happy for the kid, David Kerschbaumer, and I felt proud it was my record he had set out to break.

I also knew that the Hurricane records I set would probably be shattered soon after I graduated. In fact, during my junior year, Coach Schnellenberger assigned me to act as the official greeter for two stud quarterback recruits—Bernie Kosar and Vinny Testaverde. Given their credentials, I had no doubt they'd do a number on the record book, not to mention almost every opponent on Miami's schedule in the coming years.

They both signed and would be freshmen in 1982. Vinny kind of kept to himself, but I hit it off right away with Bernie, even if he did have the most awkward-looking throwing style I'd ever seen in my life. Bernie did everything against the book —slow dropback, sidearm delivery, high follow-through, little zip on the ball. I tried convincing him to go the more conventional route. Everybody tried.

But Bernie believed in doing it his way. And somehow he always managed to get off a perfect spiral. Somehow, even though it looked like he was doing it all wrong, it always turned out right.

In only two seasons, Bernie would establish 22 single-game, season and career records while leading the Hurricanes to a national championship in 1983. He also would be named the Most Valuable Player of the Orange Bowl after throwing for a record 300 yards as a freshman in a 31–30 upset over Nebraska. With those credentials, Bernie would set himself up to join the Cleveland Browns as the top overall pick of a 1985 supplemental draft.

Vinny? He would go on to finish as UM's all-time career leader in passing yardage on the way to leading the 'Canes to an 11–0 regular-season record and winning the 1986 Heisman Trophy. Then, he would join the Tampa Bay Buccaneers as the top overall choice of the 1987 draft.

The summer after my fourth year, I went to Virginia to stay with three of my brothers—Pat and Ray, both of whom had gone to the University of Richmond, and Ed, who was also living there. I took a roofing job to cover my expenses and have a little spare cash.

But after one week, I gave it up. I thought my time could be a lot better spent working on football and my overall physical conditioning. I figured if I was going to have any chance at a career as an NFL quarterback, I was going to have to get serious.

So I proposed a deal to my brothers.

"You take care of me during the summer while I work out—

keep me fed, pick up all my expenses—and I promise, when I make it big in the pros, I'll take care of all of you."

They looked at each other for a few seconds, then nodded and said, "It's a deal."

Determined to get their money's worth, they pushed me hard. They made certain I didn't skip a single workout or cut any of them short. And in their free time, they would lift, run and work on various aspects of my game with me. Especially Ray, who had just gotten out of college. He played linebacker at Richmond, but was a quarterback at East Brady and a real student of the game. In college, he made it a point to listen to the offensive coaches, as well as those on his own side of the ball, and picked up quite a few helpful pointers that he shared with me.

The thing Ray stressed the most was the importance of delivering the ball as high as possible to maximize the quickness of my release and the ability to get good loft on my throws. He constantly reminded me, as Coach Morrall did, to keep the ball up by my ear. He also stressed the importance of having good footwork because of the great speed of most of the pass rushers I'd face in the NFL.

He kept pounding those points into my head, over and over, and I kept working on them, over and over, until everything came naturally to me.

With workout partners, coaches and brothers all in one, how could I go wrong?

3

"Throw for the Dough"

BEFORE MY FINAL YEAR of college, Coach Schnellenberger gave me a compliment I'll never forget when he told reporters, "I don't think any one kid has meant so much to a program and its turnaround as Jim Kelly. Pitt was good before Dan Marino. So was Georgia before Herschel Walker. Jim's the most productive quarterback I've been around. And that includes Joe Namath and Ken Stabler. He's the grease that makes our offensive machine run, and our kids have a great deal of confidence in him. Every time he handles the ball, they know they have a chance to score."

Thanks, Coach. But nothing I accomplished as a player would have been possible without the instruction and guidance I received from you and Coach Morrall.

Nor would the fact I was being touted for the 1982 Heisman Trophy. I knew my chances weren't great. The previous ten Heismans had gone to running backs, and despite being a junior ballcarrier, Herschel Walker was the preseason favorite that year. A very heavy favorite. The other top candidates were also quarterbacks—Marino and John Elway of Stanford. I thought I compared favorably with those two.

But it was going to be tough for any of us to beat out Walker.

Still, Ron Steiner, our sports information director, campaigned like crazy for me. Every letter, postcard, brochure and press guide his office mailed to reporters throughout the country contained the words "Heisman candidate" next to my name. But I didn't want it to become too much of a circus. For instance, there would be no T-shirts or buttons, which a lot of schools make for their candidates. I thought they were silly. And I killed another idea about stamping oranges with the words "Jim Kelly and oranges—two of Florida's biggest producers" and sending a six-pack of them to every media member nationwide who received a Heisman ballot. That was taking things a bit too far.

Besides, what kind of impression would it have made if some of those oranges went bad before reaching their destination?

I did have an especially busy preseason of media interviews, though. Every Monday, I'd check with Steiner and he'd give me a weeklong calendar with the date, time and place of each session penciled in. I must have averaged two per day in the month leading up to our 1982 season opener at Florida.

Everybody was after a different hook. For instance:

• ABC-TV filmed me on jet skis off Miami Beach. They wanted something relating to the area where each candidate played. (I think they shot Marino in front of the picturesque setting of steel mills and smokestacks. Just kidding, Dan.)

• One newspaper took a photograph of me flashing the Heisman pose in my uniform while wearing a helmet without a facemask. The idea, of course, was to bring the statue to life through me. But all it really did was make me feel like George Jetson.

• A syndicated film crew from Philadelphia had me dressed in a three-piece suit, which was supposed to cover two themes: the fact that I was a business management major and that "Jim Kelly and the University of Miami mean business." I sure hoped so.

• • • •

The Heisman campaign—and the 1982 season—got off to a disastrous start when we traveled to Gainesville and lost to the Gators, 17–14. That snapped our four-game winning streak against them and gave us all plenty to think about through the remainder of what everybody in Miami assumed would be a great season for the 'Canes.

I knew we were in trouble when I didn't complete a pass to a wide receiver until 7:57 of the third quarter. Florida dropped more people into deep coverage than we were ready for, and I wound up throwing mostly short routes to our backs and tight ends.

Coach Schnellenberger didn't take the loss well at all. He carried it in his gut for four days. Then, during our next-to-last practice before taking on the University of Houston at the Orange Bowl, he exploded. He started yelling and screaming at all of us on offense for looking so bad against the Gators. We just looked on with our mouths open. I never saw anything like that from the man, which was probably what made it so effective.

We were definitely ready to face the Cougars two days later. And our 31–12 victory proved it. Offensively, we were back to our old selves, cranking out 351 yards against Houston's highly regarded defense. I completed 16 of 27 passes for 208 yards and a touchdown to Mark Rush. Mark also did his Mr. High Stakes routine for a pair of scores.

Our third game was against Virginia Tech at Blacksburg, Virginia. Once again, the offense was clicking. I was having my best game of the season, connecting on 17 of my first 24 attempts for 207 yards and a TD. Still, because of penalties and other mistakes, it was only good enough for 14 points through the first 47:30 of the game. That was frustrating.

But nothing was more frustrating, horrifying and, most of all, painful than what took place with 12:30 remaining in the fourth quarter.

We had a third-and-seven play from our own 14-yard line. I couldn't find anybody open, so I ran out of the pocket and began heading up the right sideline. With my "blazing" speed, I managed to avoid one tackler around the 19 and kept motoring. As I got to the 30, I thought to myself, "Maybe you really are fast enough to break it all the way." So I cut back to the

Relaxing in my first "hot tub" at six months old. (Author's collection)

My first taste of glory, representing the Pittsburgh Steelers as a national semifinalist in the Punt, Pass & Kick competition. (Leroy Andre)

With my boyhood hero, Terry
Bradshaw, when we both
had a lot more hair.
(Author's collection)

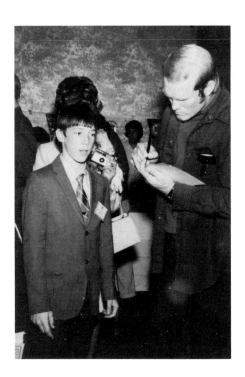

Showing my "blazing" speed on a scramble for the
East Brady High Bulldogs. (Leroy Andre)

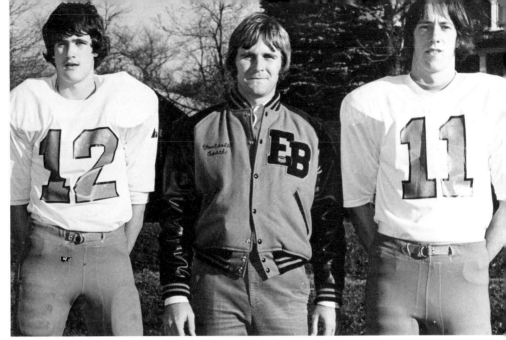

With my high school coach, Terry Henry, and close friend Jimmy Hiles. (Leroy Andre)

I always played basketball with the same intensity I showed on the football field. (Leroy Andre)

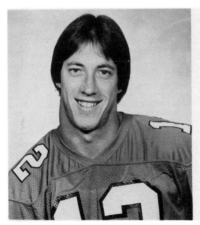

UNIVERSITY OF MIAMI

JIM KELLY
HEISMAN TROPHY CANDIDATE
SENIOR QUARTERBACK
6-3, 210
EAST BRADY, PA

Penn State wanted me as a linebacker, but I wound up throwing passes for the University of Miami. (University of Miami Sports Information Photo Files)

At the Miami Touchdown Club awards banquet with my closest friend in the world, Mark Rush. (University of Miami Sports Information Photo Files)

That's my college coach, Howard Schnellenberger, on the right, and the late George Allen—two men whom I'll always admire. (Author's collection)

Operating the run-and-shoot for the Houston Gamblers, I did a lot of throwing . . .

. . . and took a lot of hits, like this one from Keith Millard, then with the Jacksonville Bulls. (Houston *Chronicle*)

Mother's Day 1984, with St. Alice and my five brothers: Kevin, Ed, Pat, Ray, and Dan. (Author's collection)

A knee injury caused me to watch the last four games of the 1985 USFL season from the sidelines. (Houston *Chronicle*)

I was all smiles the day I finally signed with the Bills, August 18, 1986, as was the greatest man in the world, my father. (Robert L. Smith)

middle of the field. I didn't see a single Virginia Tech jersey in my path. While picking up another five yards, I figured I was gone.

Then, all of a sudden, WHAM! David Marvel, a six-foot, 219-pound defensive end, came flying in from my left. At least I think it was from my left. I never saw him. I mean, for all I know, he could have dropped out of the sky. His nickname *was* Captain Marvel, after all.

Anyway, he hit me like a ton of bricks and took me right off my feet. With no chance to brace myself, I landed squarely on my right shoulder. My passing shoulder.

And the instant it hit the ground, I heard a loud pop.

Incredible pain—pain like I never felt before in my life—shot straight down to the pit of my stomach. I tried lifting my arm, but it was no use. It wouldn't budge.

Dr. Joseph Kalbac, our team physician, didn't need long to come up with a diagnosis as he and our trainers hovered over me.

"Total separation of the AC joint," Dr. Kalbac said. "We'll have to operate when we get back home. I'm afraid you're done for the season, Jim."

At that very moment, I was in too much pain even to begin thinking about the consequences of the injury. But after I reached the locker room, it all started to sink in. And when it did, the first thought that ran through my mind was how hard I had worked—all the time and energy I had invested in becoming a top-notch, major-college quarterback.

Especially the time.

It wasn't something that happened in a year. It wasn't something that happened in two or three years. I had busted my ass for more than four seasons to get to that point, not to mention those countless lunch hours in the backyard with my father. I had done everything I was supposed to do to make myself the best player I could possibly be. I had taken the dream of throwing passes in the NFL and started transforming it into reality.

And now, all of a sudden, I felt it being ripped right out of my hands.

Why? Why was this happening to me?

We managed to hang on for a 14–8 victory, and it's a good

thing. Getting beat, on top of getting injured, would have been just too much to handle in one afternoon.

Afterward, I sat in a corner of the locker room with my right arm in a sling. Pat and Ray, who came over from nearby Richmond, sat with me, holding a huge ice pack against my shoulder. Finally, I stood and, while biting a hole through my lip, I walked slowly toward the door. Reporters started swarming around me, but I really wasn't in the mood to answer a whole bunch of questions just then. So I just quietly followed the path that my brothers and team officials made for me. Outside, Ray's girlfriend, with tears in her eyes, gave me a hug and a kiss. Coach Schnellenberger's wife, Beverlee, gave me a kiss, too. Then, much to my surprise, some guy came up and asked for my autograph. With my writing hand sticking out of a sling, that was a tall order.

But I took his pad and pen and did the best I could. I figured it might be the last autograph I signed for quite a while.

On Monday, September 20, 1982, I underwent surgery for the reattachment of the torn ligaments connecting my collarbone with the top of my shoulder blade. Dr. Kalbac inserted three metal rods, each about five inches long, into the shoulder to help hold everything together as it healed. In six weeks, they'd be removed and Mother Nature would be on her own. But until then, I'd have to walk around with the half-inch tips of each rod sticking right out of the skin around the front of my shoulder. Call it the Frankenstein look.

After I came out of recovery and returned to the hospital bed, where I would spend the next week, Dr. Kalbac came by to see how I was doing. He didn't pull any punches.

"I'm pleased with the way everything went," he said. "But I've got to be honest: This is a tough operation for a quarterback to go through. It's going to be very hard to get your throwing motion back. If you can do it, great. Not many people have."

Then the doctor paused.

"I sure hope you've been studying hard in your classes, Jim."

When I heard that, my heart sank right to my toes. What he was telling me was that my football-playing days were over, that it was time to start considering another line of work, that my NFL dream wasn't just dying; it was dead.

For about five minutes, I listened in silence and began to think about a future without football. Yes, I was paying attention in my classes. I already had enough credits for my degree in business management. I did have something to fall back on.

But the longer I lay there, the harder it was to accept that my football career was finished. I kept saying to myself, over and over, "I'm not going to let this happen to me. I'm not going to give up. I have never quit anything in my life and I'm not about to start. As long as I still have an arm, I have a chance."

And even if I wanted to, my family wouldn't let me quit.

"You're a Kelly," they reminded me. "You're tough, you're a survivor. We'll help get you through it."

There was some comic relief provided by Mark Rush. When he came to visit me at the hospital, he mentioned that, after just about every game since I became a starter, I had received the Chevrolet Player of the Game award, which was a certificate presented to the outstanding player of the winning and losing teams as selected by a media panel.

"So?" I said.

"So it pisses me off," Mark said with a sly grin. "You've won it all those times and because of that, I've never had a chance to even win it once. I'm sorry you're hurt, Jim. But damn it, I'm getting the Chevrolet Player of the Game award this week."

Actually, it was five weeks later, against Florida State, that Mark won the award, catching five passes for 124 yards in a losing effort.

I couldn't have been happier for him.

I was warned to do the best I could to avoid exposing the surgical area to bacteria, which meant activities such as swimming were out. I tried to resist the urge, and the heavy taping that kept my arm immobilized and a brace that went all the way around my back should have discouraged me further. But the Miami heat made me so delirious within my first couple of weeks out of the hospital that I forgot myself one day and took the plunge. Sure enough, my shoulder became infected; I had to spend another week in the hospital.

It was a hell of a price to pay for a few minutes of refreshment.

Finally, six weeks after they were inserted, the rods came out. Next to the actual separation of my shoulder, that ranks right up there among the all-time scary moments of my life. I'll never forget the sight of Dr. Kalbac walking toward me with a huge pair of pliers in his hand.

"Whoa! Whoa!" I said. "What do you think you're going to do with those?"

"I'm going to use them to pull out the rods."

"Like hell, you are."

"I promise, it won't hurt a bit."

"I think you'd better give me something to make sure it doesn't hurt, Doc."

"Trust me, Jim, it's not going to hurt."

I winced before he pulled out the first one, but I didn't feel a thing. I winced before he pulled out the second one, but that didn't hurt either. The third time I didn't wince at all, but his pliers slipped as he was pulling, the rod caught somewhere inside the bone and I screamed bloody murder.

Dr. Kalbac promptly injected me with a painkiller to finish the job.

Although there was a lot of concern over my future, I was having my share of problems dealing with the present—that is, watching from the sidelines as the Hurricanes struggled through a 7–4 season. That was really painful, because I knew we were better than 7–4. Way better. We were planning on such a successful season, and I knew I could have helped get us there. In a little more than two games, I had completed 51 of 81 passes (63 percent) for 585 yards and three touchdowns, and thrown only one interception. That was enough to give me school records for career passing yards (5,228), total yards (5,325), completions (376) and TD passes (31).

Of course, when you look at it, my playing time at Miami only covered a little more than two seasons. The 'Canes were 22–8 in games I started. Average attendance climbed from 20,000 in my first year to 40,000 in my fifth. Nine times we appeared on national television, and nine times I was named offensive MVP.

Still, I wasn't able to achieve all the goals I had hoped for. I had wanted to take us to a national championship. I had wanted to take us to a major bowl. The Heisman? It would have been interesting to see what my numbers were at the end of the '82 season, but it probably wouldn't have mattered. As everyone expected, Walker won the trophy in, well, a walk.

I guess you could say my college career began with disappointment—when I was redshirted as a freshman—and ended likewise. But the middle was pretty good.

If I didn't make it all the way back, if I couldn't recapture the throwing motion that was supposed to have vanished in surgery, it wasn't going to be for lack of effort. Or lack of help.

I had an incredible support base, beginning with Mike O'Shea, UM's football trainer, and his assistant, Frank Rice. They supervised my recovery from the time I left the hospital, even though I didn't have any eligibility left. My usefulness to the football program was, to all intents and purposes, gone. Yet they dedicated themselves to my return to the playing field.

And they weren't alone. My twin brothers, Danny and Kevin, actually moved to Miami that summer and took jobs as landscapers just so they could work out with me. And, of course, there was the unofficial member of the Kelly clan, Mark Rush.

I began my rehabilitation program in November, about two months after the injury. Each day started off with running until it hurt. Then I'd run some more.

Phase one in getting my shoulder to work the way it used to was regaining my arm's normal range of motion going up, down, sideways and across my body. I never imagined the simple act of raising an arm over my head would ever be so difficult. But until I worked out all the kinks and tightness that are a normal part of the healing process, I took nothing for granted when it came to moving my right arm.

After that, I spent three days a week on a Cybex machine, followed by weight lifting. The Cybex is a rehabilitation device for shoulder, hip, knee and ankle injuries. It's sort of rectangular—about eight feet wide, five feet deep and five feet high—with a chair on each side and a bench for the different workouts. It has hydraulics that allow you to work specific muscles against variable speeds of resistance. The faster the speed, the lighter the resistance; the slower the speed, the harder the resistance. As time went on, I steadily increased the resistance, pushing and pulling with my right arm bent at the elbow and fixed to my side (the trainers call that external and internal rotation) as well as with my arm stretched out (for extension and inflection). Sometimes I was sitting in the chairs and sometimes I was on my back on the bench. It all depended on what angle was needed for me to work specific muscles in my shoulder. And I worked every single one of them.

The main thing you have to remember about the Cybex is that it only puts out as much pressure as you put in. I definitely put in everything I had—to the point where I almost broke the machine. To me, it was a lot of pain and a lot of commitment. And there's no way of cheating because it gives a printout of everything you do, which lets the trainers know where your peak performance is and how you're progressing.

My right shoulder would be killing me during every session with that thing. Sometimes I would actually be crying afterward. I never got to the point where I wanted to quit, although each time I got near the Cybex, I'd moan and say, "Do I have to do *this* again?"

Mike and Frank would always be there, pushing me to the max. And when I was finished with the Cybex, they'd see to it that the rest of my five-hour day was spent in the weight room.

With the combined encouragement of the trainers, Mark and my brothers, I'd work so hard that I'd throw up. I'd work until there was nothing more my body could give. Whenever I felt like taking the easy way out, I'd think about my mom and dad. I'd think about all the sacrifices they made for us, and that I had to do everything possible to put myself in a position, financially, where I could take care of them.

I just kept busting my ass and telling myself, "Hey, you've come this far. Why give up now?"

Before he came to Miami, Mike was the trainer for the Colts. And to give me a little incentive, he told me a story about how he had worked with Colts quarterback Bert Jones after his shoulder separation just before the 1978 NFL season. Bert didn't have surgery, but he still had to undergo an intensive rehabilitation program. After about two and a half months of pushing him through all the same exercises I was doing, Mike had Bert playing again. As a matter of fact, his first game back was on Monday Night Football against Washington.

The Colts won. Bert gave Mike the game ball.

"Look, Jim, I've been through this before," Mike told me. "You're gonna make it. You're just too hard a worker not to."

For about the first two months of rehab, I never picked up a football. And when I did for the first time, the trainers were careful to limit my throwing to only 10 yards. After that, I'd be allowed to work my way up to 15, then 20 and so on. One of the earliest signs of encouragement I saw was when Mike or Frank started scolding me for throwing, say, 20 yards when I was only supposed to be throwing 10. But the more I had that football in my hand, the more chances I took, going a little further than I was supposed to . . . and a little further . . . and a little further still. After four months, I was finally given the OK to throw 20 yards.

But there was one chance I took that I'd have to put in the stupidity column, right next to going for a swim shortly after surgery. A bunch of us were on our way to see the Florida–Florida State game at the end of the season. I was riding in the back of a pickup truck and, with a few beers clouding my judgment, I sort of lost control of myself when I saw somebody drive by in a car wearing a hat that said "Miami Sucks." There were a bunch of lemons in the back of the truck. Without giving it a second thought, I grabbed one and fired it at the car. Suffice it to say that I put more oomph into that throw than the 10-, 15- or 20-yard passes with a football. All of a sudden, I doubled over, clutching my right arm. I did hit my target, but it definitely wasn't worth the pain. I had stretched some of the shoulder ligaments that hadn't quite healed yet, which made me see stars and set my recovery back a couple of weeks.

Through the entire program, I must have thrown 150 passes a day. When I wasn't passing, I was constantly squeezing a rubber ball to work the muscles in my wrist and forearm.

I began making steady progress. I knew that was so because there were more and more instances when I overdid it, when Mike and Frank had to yell at me to slow down.

Before the injury, most NFL scouts saw me as a first-round choice in the 1983 draft. Some even thought I'd go within the first three picks. Naturally, after the operation, the question everybody started asking was: "How much is Jim Kelly worth now?" Nobody really knew for certain, including yours truly.

The standard line most of the scouts gave me was: "When your shoulder's one hundred percent, we want to see you throw. Then we'll take it from there."

My shoulder wasn't going to be one hundred percent in time for the NFL's annual scouting combines in February, where coaches and personnel people from each team would get to see hundreds of draft-eligible players up close for several days in different locations throughout the country (they later merged and found a permanent home in Indianapolis). The players are weighed, measured, timed in the 40-yard dash and evaluated in several other agility and strength drills.

Although I wouldn't be able to do much with my arm—my throws were still limited to 20 yards at that point—NFL teams still wanted me to attend the combines so their physicians could examine the shoulder. They poked and probed and studied its every movement to determine the quality of Dr. Kalbac's work. That, in turn, would help tell them how big of a risk to take on me in the draft. Some were satisfied with what they saw, but others actually thought I would need more surgery before I could play. As far as I was concerned, Dr. Kalbac did a super job and I'm thankful for that.

I wanted to throw long so badly it was killing me. Especially when I saw some of the other quarterbacks launching bombs. One who really caught my eye was Tony Eason of Illinois. Not only did he look like he had a strong arm, he also delivered some pretty spirals. Others showing their stuff were Dan Marino and Todd Blackledge from Penn State, and they looked pretty impressive as well. (The only prominent no-show among the quarterbacks was John Elway, already thought of by everyone as the No. 1 overall choice.)

The more I watched them, the more frustrated and jealous I became because of my limitations. Part of me wanted to try to let loose with an 80-yarder, which had been my all-time best distance before the injury, and make everyone stand up and take notice. But part of me, the sensible part, knew that if I did try a pass like that, I'd risk throwing away the opportunity to play in the NFL, let alone become a high draft choice.

Besides, Coach Schnellenberger had a plan for me to stage my own combine at the University of Miami. All I had to do was tell him when I felt my shoulder was one hundred percent recovered, and he'd set a date and invite representatives of all twenty-eight NFL teams to come and watch me throw.

"But remember, Jim, come to me only when you feel you're a hundred percent," Coach Schnellenberger said. "I don't want you coming to me when you're ninety percent. I don't want you coming to me when you're ninety-five percent. When you feel that you can show everybody that you're absolutely, positively one hundred percent, that's when I want to hear from you. Understood?"

"Yes, sir."

I spent most of the next several weeks working with Mark Rush, who really pushed me to the limit. He wanted me to make it as badly as I did.

Around the end of March, after completing five months of rehabilitation, I informed Coach Schnellenberger I was ready. And on April 7, 1983, a few weeks before the NFL draft, I finally got to show my stuff at the Hurricanes' Greentree practice field. Some billed the session as the "Kelly Sweepstakes." Others called it the "Throw for the Dough." The fact was, my performance that day would go a long way toward determining whether I'd be a first-round draft pick. And the difference between the first and the second round alone was hundreds of thousands of dollars.

A total of twenty pro scouts and a few NFL head coaches—including my future offensive coordinator with the Bills, Ted Marchibroda, who was with Baltimore at the time—showed up, along with some people from the brand-new United States Football League (even though I already had been drafted by the USFL's Chicago Blitz). A whole bunch of media types were also on hand. Coach Schnellenberger had not allowed cameras anywhere near my rehab workouts. He had been insistent that no one should see me throw until we were all convinced I was at my best. Some photographers and TV camera crews had tried to sneak in, but they couldn't get past Coach Schnellenberger's security setup. At times, we would even move the sessions to a remote park or the back of Dr. Kalbac's house.

Much to my surprise, hundreds of spectators turned out to lend moral support that day at Greentree Field. I was really touched.

As I waited in the locker room beforehand, the thought of the pressure I was under left me feeling both nervous and excited. Then Coach Schnellenberger walked in and set me straight.

"You've been under enough pressure your whole time here," he said. "You've played before big crowds and nationally televised games. There's no reason to be nervous about this."

He was right. But I still made my routine visit to the toilet to toss my cookies.

After the coach left, the only other person in the locker room was Mark, who'd be among several pass catchers working with me that day. And just before I took the field, Mark and I sat down and said a little prayer asking God to look over me. The way I saw it, I had worked as hard as I possibly could. I had done everything I needed to do to get my shoulder back in top form. I was ready. If it was meant to be, it was meant to be. If it wasn't . . .

The spectators cheered the moment I set foot on the field. I went casual, wearing shorts, a sweatshirt and my lucky fishing hat that said "Charger Power." The hat was given to me by a San Diego Chargers scout at one of the combines. I had worn it a few weeks earlier on a deep-sea fishing trip when I hooked a fifty-four-pound dolphin fish, my first ocean catch ever. (Before any of you Flipper fans get upset with me, keep in mind that he's a mammal; what I caught was a fish.) I didn't know if the hat would now help me catch a first-round contract, but it sure wouldn't hurt.

I spent about ten minutes loosening up. Then, for the next forty-five minutes, I threw 125 passes. And I threw every kind of pass imaginable: out patterns, square-ins, comebacks, quick posts, short routes. I tried four bombs of around 70 yards and connected on all of them.

Dolphins head coach Don Shula stuck around long enough to watch me throw my first long pass—which the receiver caught without having to break his stride—then left.

"Where are you going?" someone asked. "You've only been here five minutes."

"I've seen enough," he said. "The kid can throw."

Bob Schnelker, offensive coordinator for the Green Bay Packers, agreed.

"We didn't think Kelly would be ready to throw until training camp this summer," Schnelker told a reporter. "But by throwing as well as he did today, it's obvious he has recovered."

"I think he looks as good as I've ever seen him," said Denver Broncos scout Lide Huggins.

Those comments were important. We had set out to make believers of the men who controlled the NFL draft, and that's exactly what we did. Of course, the ultimate sign of their belief wouldn't be known for certain until the actual draft.

But I did know one thing for certain that day: I couldn't have thrown the ball any better. Like other quarterbacks, I know when I'm throwing well. I know when I'm on. And I was on that day.

As I walked off the field, I looked up and thanked God for sticking with me through all the ups and downs of my rehabilitation. I also gave big thanks to Dr. Kalbac, Mike O'Shea, Frank Rice, Mark Rush and my two brothers, Dan and Kevin.

I'd never have gotten through it without them.

4

Running, Shooting and Making History

I DIDN'T SLEEP VERY WELL on the night of April 25, 1983. That was because April 26 was the day of the National Football League draft, and I was a nervous wreck wondering where—and when—I was going to go. There was a lot of talk, a lot of speculation.

But nothing concrete.

I knew where I *wanted* to go. My favorite teams since childhood were the Steelers and the Raiders. And I was hoping that if, in fact, I was a first-round pick, I'd be taken 21st (by the Steelers) or 26th (by the Raiders). I didn't know what my chances were of joining either club or even of becoming a first-rounder. Although things had gone beautifully with my April 7 audition, there was no way of telling exactly how confident each team was that my right shoulder could hold up to NFL-type pounding.

I felt like someone about to pull the handle on a slot machine.

The draft began at eight o'clock in the morning. I was in Akron, Ohio, where my agents at the time—Greg Lustig, A. J. Faigin and Ken Weinberger—were based. (I wanted to use another word besides "agents" here, but that's better left for the lawsuit that is currently pending in Texas. My mother always said if you don't have anything good to say about somebody, don't say anything at all.) My parents came over from East Brady to watch the draft with me on ESPN at Weinberger's house.

The first quarterback to go—and first player, period—was John Elway. He was drafted by the Baltimore Colts, who would later trade him to Denver.

The second quarterback to go was Todd Blackledge; he was picked seventh overall by Kansas City. (He never was able to establish himself as a full-time starter with the Chiefs, was traded to Pittsburgh in 1988 and spent a year as a backup there before being cut in 1990.)

Now the tension was really starting to build. As soon as the Chiefs grabbed Blackledge, the ESPN analysts talked about a possible "run" on quarterbacks and said I might be the next player at the position to be taken.

Twelve teams would have a chance to select me before Pittsburgh's turn came. Buffalo would have two chances (twelfth and fourteenth), and I was praying they'd pass on me both times. Everything I ever heard about the team and the city was negative. The Bills had had a 4–5 record in the strike-shortened 1982 season. They had just lost a head coach with a strong reputation, Chuck Knox, who bolted for Seattle. And after spending my college career in South Florida, I just didn't feel like playing in the snow.

I realized Pittsburgh wasn't the tropics, but it was home. I couldn't count the number of times I closed my eyes and saw myself throwing passes for the Steelers in Three Rivers Stadium. Besides, the Bills already had a veteran quarterback, Joe Ferguson, and he wasn't expected to budge for several years. True, Terry Bradshaw was still calling signals in Pittsburgh, but he figured to be out of the picture much sooner. And if I had to sit behind my boyhood hero for a little while, that wouldn't have been such a bad thing.

Philadelphia, Houston, the Giants and Green Bay all avoided taking quarterbacks with the next four picks.

Then came Buffalo, in the twelfth position.

"No!" I yelled to the TV screen. "Don't take me. Noooooo!"

When the Bills drafted Tony Hunter, a tight end from Notre Dame, I breathed a sigh of relief.

The Lions picked next; they took James Jones, a fullback from Florida.

Buffalo was up again, with the fourteenth choice.

"Please!" I said. "Not me. Pleeeease!"

NFL commissioner Pete Rozelle stepped up to the microphone and announced, "Buffalo selects . . . Jim Kelly, quarterback, University of Miami."

I let out a groan. My chin dropped to my chest. I thought, "Why did they have to take me?"

I realize how strange that might sound to some people. How could anyone feel bad about becoming a number-one pick in the NFL draft? But that wasn't the point. I was thrilled to death to be recognized by the NFL as a first-round talent. I just wasn't happy with the idea that, no matter how I felt, I would *have* to play somewhere I didn't want to be. I guess you could say my feelings were similar to those of Elway, who dreaded the thought of playing in Baltimore so much that he forced the Colts to trade him. As the top overall choice—and someone who also could pursue a professional baseball career—Elway had the kind of clout to make a deal like that happen. I didn't.

So the minute I was drafted by the Bills, I began thinking about my options. One was the USFL, where I had already been drafted by the Chicago Blitz. Another was the Canadian Football League, where the Montreal Concordes had a lot of interest in me.

At first, my agents didn't think I was serious about skipping the well-established NFL for a spring/summer league in only its second year of existence or jumping north of the border. The fact was, I had never really mentioned going to another league before. All my thoughts were geared toward playing in the NFL. I had wanted to be an active member of the Quarterback Class of '83, which included a total of six first-rounders. Besides Elway, Blackledge and myself, there were Tony Eason (New

England), Ken O'Brien from Cal-Davis (New York Jets) and, the next-to-last pick of the round, Dan Marino (Miami).

But I was serious about not wanting any part of Buffalo. Dead serious.

"If you can make everything right—get me the right kind of contract, the right kind of money—I will go somewhere else," I told my agents. "I mean it!"

Other than my family and my agents, very few people were aware of my feelings toward the Bills. I didn't mention them in public at the time. I figured, until all my options were explored and I knew exactly which direction I was going, the smartest thing to do was just grin and bear it.

One thing I discovered when I arrived in Buffalo shortly after the draft was that none of its top picks was all that crazy about playing there. Not Tony Hunter. Not Darryl Talley, the outside linebacker from West Virginia who was chosen on the second round. We all shared the same outlook—that we were not being brought into a very pretty picture. And the hardest thing for the three of us to do was stand up and pretend to be happy while being introduced at a luncheon of the Buffalo Quarterback Club.

A short while later, the Bills held their minicamp. I have to admit, just about everyone I met tried to make me feel at home. Kay Stephenson, the head coach, was the nicest guy in the world. He went so far as to loan me his car so I could make the three-and-a-half-hour drive to East Brady and visit my mother, who was struggling with emphysema. Kay had a close friend named Frank Fuhrer, who used to own indoor soccer and professional tennis teams in Pittsburgh, and he asked him to help "recruit" me to Buffalo by working on my father. Fuhrer would visit Dad at the plant, take him out to dinner, anything he could to get him to encourage me to sign with the Bills.

Ferguson was also a great guy, a real down-to-earth country boy from Louisiana. What impressed me the most about him was the arm strength he possessed despite not having a particularly large frame. I soon found out that Joe did a lot of weight lifting, more than most pro quarterbacks. And, boy, did it show.

The Bills' number-two quarterback was Matt Kofler. Apparently, Matt thought that being Joe's understudy also meant being his shadow. I never saw anything quite like it, at least not among teammates. Whatever Joe did, Matt had to do the exact same thing. If Joe faked right before making a throw, Matt faked right. When Joe got up after lunch or a meeting, Matt was right there to pull the chair out for him. I got the feeling that when Joe went to the bathroom, Matt was probably standing there holding the toilet paper. After I got to know Matt better, I discovered he was a pretty good guy. But at the time I thought, "Is he serious?"

The only thing that bothered me about Ferguson was that he wore my college number, 12. That left me searching for a replacement among the available quarterback numbers on the team. I started out minicamp with 14, and I didn't like it. A couple days later, I switched to 18. I didn't like that either.

But the point was moot because I wasn't planning to play in Buffalo anyway.

While I was in minicamp with the Bills, Lustig and Faigin, who handled all the negotiating, were having serious discussions with the Blitz and the Concordes. Their strategy was to get those teams to make their best offers, set the standard, then see if Buffalo could do better.

Toward the end of May, the late John Bassett (God rest his soul), principal owner of the USFL's Tampa Bay Bandits and the most influential man in the new league, invited me, my agents and Mark Rush (who was also represented by Lustig and Faigin) to a Bandits game. He wanted us to get a feel for the quality of play in the USFL. We ended up spending several days at his condominium in Sarasota and being treated like kings. One day when we were cruising around on a yacht, Mark got behind the wheel and almost drove into a steamer in the Tampa harbor. The next day we were having a barbecue on the beach outside the condo. We cooked some steaks, drank some beer and had a lot of laughs. It was supposed to be only an overnight trip, but each day Mark and I found ourselves calling home to say we were going to stay "just a little longer."

Meanwhile, the Bills weren't standing still. They came up with a proposal that definitely got my attention: $2.1 million over four years. It was better than anything we had gotten up to that point from the Blitz or the Concordes. It was so strong, in fact, that Lustig and Faigin were in the office of Pat McGroder, the Bills' seventy-nine-year-old vice president, going over final details and closing in on an agreement. They had even gotten to the point of talking about when to hold the press conference to announce my signing.

Then, all of a sudden, McGroder's secretary walked into the office and said there was "a Mr. Bruce Allen calling from Chicago for Mr. Faigin." Allen, who was the general manager of the Blitz, was on a three-way line with Bassett. They told Faigin to hold everything with the Bills and said that he and Lustig should meet them that night at Bassett's home in Toronto to hear an offer that would knock their socks off. They agreed. And during the midnight rendezvous, they were told that the USFL wanted me so badly, I could have my pick of any of its teams (Allen said the Blitz would gladly trade my rights to wherever I wanted to go) and play for a hell of a lot more money than Buffalo had on the table.

That wasn't the way things worked in the NFL, of course. The Bills would hold my exclusive NFL negotiating rights for four years whether I signed with them or not. And there wasn't anyone powerful enough to persuade them to do the sort of the thing the Blitz was willing to do.

This choose-your-own-USFL-team deal was made available not only to me but also to Mark, who had been drafted in the fourth round by Minnesota of the NFL. Any USFL club was ready to sign us as a package deal. It was unbelievable. We were like kids in a candy store.

We put together our short list of "dream" teams, and not surprisingly, they were all in warm-weather sites—Tampa Bay, Jacksonville and Houston. Shortly thereafter, we received a call from Jerry Argovitz, owner of the Houston Gamblers, an expansion team that would begin play in the Astrodome in the spring of 1984. The name came from the song "The Gambler," sung by Kenny Rogers, who was also one of Argovitz's limited partners. On Tuesday, June 7, Jerry flew Mark and me down to Houston, along with our agents. At that point, the only player the Gamblers had under contract was Kiki DeAyala, a linebacker from Texas. I really wasn't expecting anything to come of the trip; I just saw it as another preliminary session to get a feel for what was out there.

Just as Bassett had, Jerry gave us the royal treatment. He

took us to a couple of great Mexican restaurants. He introduced us to some of Houston's biggest wheels. He gave us tours of the area, including an inner-city park where he wanted to see for himself what kind of shape my throwing arm was in after the surgery. First he handed me an official USFL football and asked me to throw a few long passes. I let go a 70-yarder on the first try, with no warm-up, and that ended that part of the examination.

Then Jerry asked me to throw to him while he ran patterns. I couldn't believe it: the owner of a pro football franchise running pass patterns! The first couple of times, I didn't put too much zip on the ball because I figured it was best to give him a chance to catch it. But then he asked for more velocity. So I thought, if he wanted to be convinced about what my arm could do, I'd better really drill the ball. And when I did, I broke the ring finger on his right hand.

He didn't need any more convincing about my arm.

The next day, Mark and I were looking over some eye-popping contract offers. Mine was worth $3.5 million over five years, including a $1 million signing bonus. That meant that whether the Gamblers fielded a team or not, I was guaranteed at least $1 million. The Bills weren't about to match that amount, which didn't surprise us in the least. The Gamblers and the USFL were treating me the same way the Jets and the American Football League had treated Joe Namath in the mid-1960s. They were going all out to get a "name" player who'd have an immediate impact on a league desperately looking for credibility; the Bills saw me as someone they could bring along slowly as a backup to Ferguson. Whether I signed or not wasn't going to make or break the NFL. Mark was equally ecstatic with his deal for $1.2 million over four years.

But the money wasn't the only thing that made the Gamblers attractive. They'd be playing in a dome, which is a quarterback's dream. No wind. No rain. None of the elements that would make throwing a football in Rich Stadium a hell of a lot more difficult. It would almost be like I never left sunny Miami. Best of all, I'd even get to wear number 12.

I knew it would take time for the league to get going, just as it took time for the Hurricanes to get going. But I figured that the way Americans loved football, USFL games would eventually have as large a TV audience in the spring as the NFL had in the fall. As I saw it, both leagues would have the same caliber of play within the next few years.

We called our families, talked things over and told Jerry we'd sleep on the proposals. My father wanted me to play for the Bills, because Buffalo was a whole lot closer to East Brady than Houston was. But, as with my decision to go to Miami, he told me to do whatever I thought was best and he'd give me his complete support.

On Thursday, June 9, we signed with the Gamblers. I knew a lot of people would question my decision to choose the USFL over the NFL. I knew I'd be subjected to a lot of ridicule from NFL cities, and especially from Buffalo. Bills fans were still upset with the team's failure to sign the top overall pick of the 1979 draft, linebacker Tom Cousineau from Ohio State, who skipped to the CFL. But you've got to take some chances in your life.

Make that gambles.

Of course, I probably wouldn't have taken this gamble by myself. Having Mark with me was very important. We depended on each other so much in college and, if it was at all possible, we wanted to stick together as professionals.

Because we weren't expecting to sign so soon, neither of us had packed the proper clothing for the big press conference the Gamblers called in the main ballroom of our hotel, the Astrodome Marriott. All we had were jeans and sneakers.

So Jerry took us to a friend's clothing store for a little last-minute shopping spree. I picked out a gray suit, and Mark grabbed a brown jacket to go with the cowboy boots he had bought earlier in the trip. As an added touch, we each wore a silk handkerchief in our coat pocket. Wow! Aren't you impressed?

It was all pretty incredible. I mean, there I was, a kid who had very little growing up, Mr. Nobody from East Brady, with a check for $200,000 in my pocket. It was the first installment of my $1 million signing bonus. I never thought it was possible for a person to receive that much money in a lifetime, let alone a day. And I definitely never thought that that person would be me.

After the press conference, our next stop was the bank, to open a few checking and savings accounts and get some cash. Then we returned to our hotel room and began to spread a bunch of hundred-dollar bills across the bed and the table. We also picked the cash up in both hands and started fanning ourselves. We had something like a couple thousand dollars apiece, and we just wanted to look at it and touch it.

Mark had his camera and we took a ton of pictures—the scene was so incredible to us, we felt it had to be captured on film. The one thing we kept saying, over and over, was: "Do you believe all this money?"

To cap off the celebration, we rented tuxedos, top hats, canes and a limo for a night on the town.

I knew I hadn't fulfilled my exact childhood dream of becoming an NFL quarterback. But at least I'd be playing professional football. And I'd be playing as a *rookie*. And because of the spring schedule, I'd have the time to go home for Thanksgiving and Christmas, watch NFL games, watch my college team play, watch my high school team play, and do some hunting. I was also confident that, sooner or later, things would work out for the USFL.

Plus, a large part of my dream was being in a position to take care of my family. I certainly was able to do that now. I bought Dad a new Lincoln Continental. I offered to buy my mother a new house, but she didn't want it. She said she was happy right where she was. I also offered to send her and my father on a Caribbean cruise, but she didn't want that either. So I bought her furniture, carpeting, siding and whatever else was needed to fix the old place up a little bit.

But I think the best money I spent then or at any other time in my life was when I took my father and five brothers on a ten-day trip to Hawaii to celebrate my first pro contract. Mom wasn't up to traveling that far, so she stayed in Virginia with my sisters-in-law, Trish (Pat's wife) and Pam (Ray's wife). I rented three connecting condos, a couple of Lincolns, and we all just kicked back and enjoyed ourselves in the sun, sand and surf. It was an unbelievable time. And the thing that made it so great was the conversation. We learned more about Dad and each other during that one trip than we ever knew before. Although we were already an extremely close family, we all seemed to grow a little closer then.

It was just a case where you'd sit around, have a few beers and all of a sudden your true feelings started coming out. We recalled a lot of fun times when we were kids. We'd tell Dad about some of the things we did behind his back, like sneaking out with his van. And he'd shock us by saying, "Yeah, I remember that." So we'd mention something else that we thought he didn't know about, and, sure enough, he'd say, "Yeah, I remember that, too." We'd keep starting stories, and Dad would keep finishing them.

I probably spent close to $30,000 on that trip, and it was worth every penny. So was the rest of the money I spent on my family. One of the first things I realized after receiving my signing bonus was that all the wealth and fame in the world didn't mean a thing if there was no one to share it with. I also knew that if any of my brothers had the same wherewithal, he'd share it with me. That's just the way we were raised.

I built a 5,000-square-foot house in Sugarland, Texas, a nice area southwest of Houston. Made of brick, it had five bedrooms, seven bathrooms, a gigantic kitchen, weight room, wet bar, den, library, Jacuzzi, double-fronted fireplace and a small forest of plants and trees growing beneath the winding staircase.

Not to mention a swimming pool and hot tub in the back.

I basically designed the house as a place for fun. And it sure was the scene of some great parties. One time, about four hundred people showed up when I was expecting two hundred. Suffice it to say there were a few extra beer runs that night. I always invited my Gambler teammates over because, first, we got along great together and, second, I knew there were some guys on the team who weren't making a whole lot and I wanted to share what I had with them. Especially the offensive linemen. I had those guys over all the time, and I usually wound up cooking around thirty huge steaks on the barbecue.

Mainly, I just enjoyed having a good time. I wanted to live life to the fullest. Like the rest of my family, I've always believed in the "Irishman's Philosophy," which goes as follows:

There are only two things to worry about: Either you are well or you are sick.

If you are well, there is nothing to worry about. If you are sick, there are only two things to worry about: Either you will get well or you will die.

If you get well, there is nothing to worry about. If you die, there are only two things to worry about: Either you will go to heaven or you will go to hell.

If you go to heaven, there is nothing to worry about. But if you go to hell, you will be so damn busy shaking hands with friends, you won't have time to worry.

Soooo why worry?

My brothers Ed, Danny and Kevin moved in with me. Ed worked for the University of Texas Medical Center. Danny enrolled at the University of Houston to finish his work toward a degree in business management; I paid his tuition. Kevin worked for a Miller beer distributor. At the time, we were all single and everybody had a different household chore—Ed cooked, Kevin took care of the pool and spa, and Danny made sure all the bills got paid on time. With a little help from me, of course.

We temporarily had a fifth resident in Ben Bennett, a former Atlanta Falcons quarterback who was trying to catch on with the Houston Oilers. Ben and I had the same agents, and he asked if he could stay for just a week while he looked for a place of his own; he didn't leave until eight months later. He was a good guy, a lot of fun to have around. But after his bedroom started stinking, we told him, "OK, Ben, it's time to move on."

I'd fly my parents to Houston as often as possible. I'd also fly my other brothers and family members down on a regular basis. And I loved to take them all shopping.

"But, Jim, I don't need anything," my mother would always say.

"But, Mom, there must be *something* you want to buy."

Money wasn't the only reward for taking the USFL gamble. My agents worked out a promotional deal with a Houston car dealership which gave me a brand-new Corvette every three months or 5,000 miles, whichever came first.

But I still kept my weatherworn 1965 Volkswagen Beetle, which I parked out in front of the house. I loved that car. I had it in college; it was my first set of wheels. And no matter how many new Corvettes I drove, I refused to let it go. That bug had 265,000 miles on it—most of which came during round trips between Miami and East Brady and a one-way ride from Miami to Texas—and was as battered and beaten as could be. One time in college I made the mistake of giving a ride to one of our 280-pound linemen. As soon as he sat down, the passenger seat crashed to the floor. Another time a couple of us were riding back to the campus after a night out and we were pulled over for going through a red light (although I swore it was yellow). It so happened that we weren't quite finished with the beers we bought just before last call. But thanks to the wonderful condition of that car, we were able to stow our bottles on the ground through holes in the floor and keep them out of sight of the police officer, retrieving them after he gave me a warning and left.

One reason I hung on to my VW was that it still ran. Granted, sometimes it only went as fast as 35 mph. But one trusty can of this special gas additive I bought, called Mix-a-Go, and that thing would start hauling all the way up to 55.

Another reason I kept it was that, even with all the luxuries that came with a big pro contract, it still had a place in my life. It helped give me a sense of perspective, of where I had been—and where I could return to if I ever took my accomplishments on the football field for granted.

At first, I had no idea what kind of offense we'd have. Hell, I didn't even know what kind of team we'd have. When Mark Rush and I signed, the Gamblers consisted of three players (including Kiki DeAyala), the owners and a front-office staff. They hadn't even hired a coach yet.

But it wasn't long before Jack Pardee, former head coach of the Chicago Bears and Washington Redskins, came aboard to guide us. He had a strong reputation for leadership as a player and coach in the NFL, receiving Coach of the Year honors with the Redskins in 1979.

Soon after joining the Gamblers, Pardee named Mouse Davis as his offensive coordinator. Other than the fact that his real name was Darrel but everyone called him Mouse, I didn't know anything about the man. And I had no idea what he was talking about when he told me we were going to use a run-and-shoot attack.

I had never even heard of the run-and-shoot before. When Mouse explained the basic principle of rolling out and throwing a lot of quick, short passes on the run, I thought, "No way! I'm a straight-dropback passer. I don't do any of this sprint-out stuff. It just isn't me."

I soon discovered that sprint-outs were the trademark of Mouse-coached quarterbacks. He used them as offensive coordinator of the CFL's Toronto Argonauts and as head coach of Portland State, where Neil Lomax became the NCAA's all-time passing leader. Still, it wasn't something I had ever done or seen at any level of organized football. It wasn't something that was ever mentioned during the negotiation process with Jerry Argovitz.

Had I known they were planning to change my style, I probably would never have signed with the Gamblers. Now I didn't have a choice. I was under contract. We were going to be a run-and-shoot team. I would have to learn how to be a run-and-shoot quarterback. The only consolation was that I began practicing in July 1983, and the regular-season opener wasn't until February 26.

It took about a month before I began to feel comfortable throwing on the run. Initially, there was a lot of frustration and resistance on my part. All you had to do was check the ugly scar on my right shoulder to see what kind of scrambler I was in college. But the more I did it and the better I got to know Mouse, the more natural I felt. He was very down-to-earth, just the greatest guy you'd ever want to meet. He was also very knowledgeable about football and an excellent teacher. He seemed to know exactly what to say and how to say it to make the game fun and interesting.

The first thing I had to get used to was working with a basic formation that consisted of four wide receivers, a running back and no tight ends. I'd call the play in the huddle, but within that play each receiver had three to five choices. Once the ball was snapped, the whole offense was reading the defense and hoping to come to the same conclusion. Which brings up the next major adjustment I had to make: reading on the run. Like every other quarterback, I always made my reads on the drop. But now I had to get used to reading on the run, and it was a big difference.

When you're taking a three-, five- or seven-step drop, you're going to throw on your third, fifth or seventh step depending on the type of pass you're attempting. The play usually dictates exactly when you're going to release the ball. Generally, it's a case where the shorter the drop, the shorter the pattern and the longer the drop, the longer the pattern. In the run-and-shoot, you're moving out of the pocket, and there are a lot of times where you'll throw on your fourth or sixth step—your off step —because you have to be able to fire the ball the instant you see something you can take advantage of. It's seldom dictated when the ball's going to be thrown.

What the offense amounts to is a modified version of basketball, a run-and-gun game.

Mouse also helped me with all the different mechanics of being a run-and-shoot passer. The biggest was that in sprinting out to the left as a right-handed quarterback I had to remember to keep the ball by my right shoulder. If you keep the ball by your left shoulder, then you have the added motion of bringing it across your chest to the opposite side to throw. Not only is that awkward but it makes for a slower release and increases your chances of being sacked. When you roll the other way, of course, it's no problem because you automatically put the ball by your right shoulder as you assume the throwing position.

Another thing Mouse stressed was foot quickness. I didn't have much to begin with, so he gave me various drills to help me move a little faster. For instance, he had me running X's, like basketball players do, and running and hopping back and forth on a line across the field as fast as I could.

I still had plenty to learn when we began our three-game preseason schedule. But after we finished with a 3–0 record, I came away with plenty of confidence. One relief was that my shoulder, which hadn't been exposed to any serious contact since the injury, held up fine. There were still tinges of numbness in my forearm from lingering nerve damage. But as long as I got in a good, long warm-up, they were usually gone by kickoff.

Another relief was working with the people who'd catch my passes. We called them the Mouseketeers, because of our offensive coordinator's nickname and because most of them stood under 5-10: Ricky Sanders (5-11), Richard Johnson (5-9), Gerald McNeil (5-8) and Clarence Verdin (5-8). They were extremely fast. A lot of times, it was just a case of throwing a five-yard pass to one of those guys and watching him burn 65 yards downfield. The NFL would eventually discover the great talent I had at my disposal, with Sanders going to the Redskins, McNeil going to the Browns and Verdin going to the Colts. Not to mention our running back, Sam Harrell, who scored six touchdowns in our last two exhibition games.

(Naturally, I expected Mark Rush to have a large role in the offense, but it became apparent right away that the run-and-shoot wasn't suited to his skills. He had been moved to wide receiver, but that didn't work out after all the "Mouseketeers" were signed. Mark was eventually released and played for two other USFL teams that year, the Michigan Panthers and the San Antonio Gunslingers. Of course, that did nothing to hurt our friendship, which remains super-tight to this day.)

As far as I was concerned, we had everything we needed for success right away, beginning with great coaches who had us all well prepared. I was very excited. I knew we could be an explosive offense. I knew we could put some points on the board.

The question was: When would we light the fuse?

We certainly didn't in our regular-season opener at Tampa Bay, which we lost to the Bandits, 20–17. I did complete 24 of 41 passes for 229 yards and two touchdowns, but we couldn't put the ball in the end zone as much as I knew we were capable of.

That all changed the following week when we traveled to San Antonio and pounded the Gunslingers, 37–7. I threw for 315 yards and a touchdown, and ran for two other scores.

It was all the spark our offense needed.

Through our remaining sixteen regular-season games, we'd score no fewer than 24 points per game on the way to piling up a league-leading 618. We also would win twelve more times, for a final record of 13–5, and capture the Western Conference championship.

Not that it was all one big walk in the park. We had some turbulent moments, such as after our 31–28 overtime road loss to the Oklahoma Outlaws. Apparently, during our return flight to Houston, Argovitz thought we weren't pissed off enough about the game, which we lost in the last minute. So just before we got off the plane, he blasted everybody, saying he had given us first-class treatment from top to bottom and that we weren't responding.

"I just don't think they realized what had just happened to them," Argovitz later told a reporter. "I was embarrassed for them. The best thing I could do was let them know in my humble way what it takes to go the extra mile. And if there's some character on this team, we're going to bring it out."

It was his team; he could say whatever he wanted. But I didn't think that was the way to go about it. I also didn't think our character deserved to be questioned after a tough loss like that.

My favorite memory of the season was my "homecoming" in Pittsburgh to face the Maulers on May 12. The mere thought of playing my first pro game at Three Rivers Stadium, in front of family and friends who filled a dozen buses from East Brady, made it exciting enough. But I also came up with one of the best performances of my rookie year. After being sacked on the first two plays, I hit 15 of 29 attempts for 367 yards and five touchdowns as we cruised to a 47–26 victory. It meant a lot to me to do well in front of my hometown, especially after all the fun we had during a big family gathering at my Uncle Ed's house in Pittsburgh the night before. It was the best I felt after a game since Miami defeated Penn State in my first college start.

Another thing that made the Maulers game so special was that it fell on the eve of Mother's Day. I told Mom all of those touchdown passes were for her. That is, once I could get her and my father away from the newspaper and television cameras that seemed to follow their every move that night. I loved it.

I loved almost everything about the season except the way it ended, with a 17–16 loss to the Arizona Wranglers in the first round of the USFL playoffs at the Astrodome. It snapped a seven-game winning streak. And it was very frustrating, because, for one thing, we blew a 16–3 fourth-quarter lead after punts of 15 and 13 yards set up a pair of Wrangler touchdowns. For another, we generated our lowest point total of the season despite gaining 415 yards. I threw for 301 yards, but most of them came between the 20s.

It was painful to have to be a spectator for the league championship game, which the Philadelphia Stars won by beating Arizona, 23–3. That should have been Jack Pardee, not the Stars' Jim Mora, getting the shoulder ride off the field in Tampa Stadium that night.

I did receive consolation, though, in being named the USFL's Most Valuable Player. For the regular season, I passed for 5,219 yards and 44 touchdowns and had nine games of at least 300 yards, including five in a row. The TD passes (I threw at least one in all eighteen games) were an all-time record for professional football until Dan Marino threw 48 for the Dolphins that fall. The nine games of at least 300 yards surpassed the record of eight set by Dan Fouts during a sixteen-game NFL season in 1980, but was tied by Marino that fall. And the yardage mark was second to Warren Moon's 5,648 with Edmonton of the CFL in 1983. Ironically, with 98.2 points, I was the third-rated passer in the USFL behind Chuck Fusina of the Stars (104.7) and Cliff Stoudt of the Birmingham Stallions (101.6).

We also had pro football's first two players on the same team to catch more than 100 passes and gain more than 1,000 yards in a season—Richard Johnson (115 receptions, which set an all-time pro mark, for 1,455 yards) and Ricky Sanders (101 grabs, the most ever for a rookie, for 1,378 yards).

Most of the credit for those lofty numbers belonged to the brilliance of Mouse Davis and the run-and-shoot. There was a time when I thought that he was crazy for devising such an offense and that Pardee was even crazier for letting him use it. But once I understood the concept—after Mouse kept pounding it into my skull—and became comfortable with reading and throwing on the run, I didn't even want to think of playing in another system.

Of course, like anything else, the run-and-shoot isn't perfect. From a quarterback's standpoint, the major flaw in its design is that you take one hell of a beating. With no tight ends or fullback, the offensive linemen become more vulnerable in pass protection, because most of the time they're blocking one on one. And there are a lot of occasions when the quarterback rolls directly into the pressure instead of away from it.

Consequently, I was sacked 76 times. But even that statistic only tells a small part of the story. I took at least another 150 hits after I threw the ball. There wasn't a single day during the eighteen-week season that I didn't feel sore. Thank God for Jacuzzis.

I realized my accomplishments were being lost on most of the country because they took place in what was widely regarded as an inferior league. I knew I'd have gotten a hell of a lot more attention had I done the same things in the NFL. But I also knew I probably wouldn't have had a rookie season like that in the NFL. I probably wouldn't have been playing, let alone operating an offense like the run-and-shoot, because no team in the NFL was using it.

Besides, I figured someday I'd get to carry those statistics with me into the NFL when it merged with the USFL. Based on what I heard from almost everyone throughout our league, I believed that would happen.

Entering the second season, I had no doubt whatsoever we could compete with any NFL club. We asked the Oilers to play a game against us for charity, but they said no. I think they were afraid of being embarrassed.

We had already moved ahead of them in attendance. I'm sure part of that was because the Oilers were in the middle of a down period, having won only six games in the previous three seasons. But I think it was also because we were a lot more entertaining. We weren't a dive-right, dive-left team. Ours was a wing-it, gun-it, let's-go-for-it approach.

And the fans loved us. They loved our black-and-silver uniforms. They loved our black helmets. They loved our logo, the big red G with the map of Texas inside and a yellow star denoting Houston. They loved our fighting spirit.

We also worked a lot harder than the Oilers to make ourselves visible. We were aggressive with promotional appearances and commercial endorsements all over town. I even had my own radio show.

For a brief time, however, it looked like that big Gambler balloon might suddenly burst. Mouse Davis, who had become one of the hottest coaching minds in the game, left to become head coach of the USFL's Denver Gold. John Jenkins, who had guided our special teams, took over as offensive coordinator. So the natural question was: Would the change spell the end of the run-and-shoot?

It didn't. And we didn't miss a beat.

In fact, the offense was as hot as could be in our 1985 regular-season opener against the Los Angeles Express at the L.A. Coliseum. So hot that we were able to overcome a 33–13 deficit with about nine minutes left. All we needed were 12 plays, 208 seconds and touchdown passes of 52, 40 and 39 yards. Final score: 34–33.

I finished the day with 35 completions in 54 attempts for 574 yards and five touchdowns. For some reason, the Express insisted on playing man-to-man coverage instead of zone. It made no sense, not against the speed and big-play skills of the Mouseketeers, but we certainly didn't complain. We just burned them.

That touched off a 5–0 start. Through the first four weeks, I threw for an average of 418 yards and four TDs per game. The year before, I didn't have a single 400-yard game. Now I already had two, plus the 500-yarder.

As the victory over Los Angeles proved, most teams had no idea how to defend the run-and-shoot. We just gave them too much field to cover. And if I got the few seconds I needed to throw, I was going to find somebody open. Also, the only time most defenses saw the run-and-shoot was when they faced us, so they usually didn't have the knowledge or the experience to deal with it.

Another highlight of that '85 season was my streak of 120 passes without an interception.

Unfortunately, there were also some low points, like the injury-filled 0–3 stretch that followed our 5–0 beginning. One of the losses was to the New Jersey Generals in what was billed as the "big quarterback showdown" between me and Heisman Trophy winner Doug Flutie. But the star of the show turned out to be Herschel Walker, who rushed for 233 yards to lead the Generals to a 31–25 upset win. In the third quarter, the ring finger of my throwing hand was dislocated after I got it caught between a pair of colliding New Jersey helmets. I looked down at it, saw it was pointed sideways and realized I'd better get off the field. The trainers straightened it out in the locker room. I tested it out by throwing a few passes to Pat and Ray, who had come down from the stands to check on me. Then I went back in the game and threw a touchdown pass.

Too little too late.

We would regroup and win three games in a row. But as the season progressed, it became evident the Gamblers were experiencing the same kind of financial problems that were spreading throughout the league. There were a couple of times when Gene Burrough, our general manager, came into the locker room and announced that our weekly game checks would be late.

"You're all going to be paid, I promise you," he said. "There's just going to be a little delay."

We all looked at each other, rolled our eyes and said, "Yeah, right."

But eventually we did receive our game checks. Other clubs, like San Antonio, stopped paying their players and never started again. Those poor guys were basically playing for free.

In our fourteenth game, against Arizona, I got off to a great start with three touchdown passes in the first two quarters. But on the final play of the first half, I crumpled to the ground after being sacked. I left the field with stretched ligaments in my right knee and missed the final four weeks of the regular season, which we finished at 10–8.

I did return to action in time for our playoff game against the Stallions. Once again, we ended the year on a downer, with a 22–20 loss. Once again, I found consolation in my final numbers. I was the top-rated passer in the league with 97.9 points, completing 360 of 567 passes (63.5 percent) for 4,623 yards and 39 touchdowns.

One thing I will always look upon with pride is the fact that no quarterback in any league has thrown for more yards (9,842) or touchdowns (83) in his first two years.

In August 1985, a month after its third championship game as a spring/summer league, the USFL began preparing for a switch to fall play in 1986. And its first major move to that end was merging the Gamblers with the Generals to form a franchise that would play in the New York metropolitan area.

Donald Trump, owner of the Generals, and New York real

estate developer Steven Ross struck the deal after Ross bought the Gamblers from Jerry Argovitz. Trump made it clear right off the bat that I was his quarterback, and strongly suggested that Doug Flutie was on the trading block.

Harry Usher, the USFL commissioner, called it a "dream team," with me and Walker sharing the backfield. I felt good about that. Now, instead of having a one-dimensional passing attack, we'd have the threat of both the pass and the run, with opposing teams unable to key on either one of us too much.

I was also very excited about the prospect of playing in the Big Apple. Of course, the New York Giants and Jets were already sharing Giants Stadium in East Rutherford, New Jersey, so no one was exactly sure where we would play our home games.

But in the spring of '86, we were in Giants Stadium for mini-camp, which served as the first on-field gathering of the new-look Generals. I took turns running plays with Todd Dillon, my backup for two years in Houston, and Flutie. Everything we used was from the Gamblers' playbook, which gave Todd and me a definite advantage.

A reporter from the New York *Daily News* asked what I thought was a pretty harmless question when he said, "If the Generals keep all three of you guys, could Flutie end up third string?"

I gave what I thought was a pretty harmless answer when I said, "Yeah, he could."

The next day's headline in the *Daily News* read: "Kelly Warns Flutie He Could Be Third String." But that wasn't what I was doing at all. I was just expressing the great respect I had for Todd's strong arm and his experience in the run-and-shoot, which Trump said would be our offense. I had nothing against Doug; I thought he was a hell of an athlete. And aside from the inaccurate headline, we got along well during the week of mini-camp. With that great running ability of his, he even practiced a little bit at wide receiver.

We all had gone into minicamp feeling confident we were going to play in the fall. I spent about a month at a hotel in New York, awaiting details on what we'd be doing next to get ready for our regular-season opener, which was scheduled for September 14 against the Memphis Showboats.

But on July 29, a federal court awarded the USFL a measly three bucks in the $1.69 billion antitrust suit it had filed against the NFL. Some award. Trump and the rest of the USFL were counting on a much larger sum to finance a head-to-head battle with the NFL or at least force the NFL to take them in.

On August 5, the USFL announced it was suspending operations until 1987, but giving all of its players permission to negotiate with NFL teams.

Of course, there would never be another USFL season. Everything we accomplished in those two years in Houston, all the stats and the national recognition that was brought to the run-and-shoot, was gone forever. I was still owed $320,000 of the $1 million signing bonus from my original agreement with the Gamblers (which was part of a lawsuit I'd file later against Argovitz and all the other parties involved).

But I can honestly say that, given the chance to do it all over again, under identical circumstances, I'd have done the same thing—except for the way the contract was structured, of course. No matter how short my USFL career was, I'll always cherish the memories. To all my former Gambler teammates— wherever you may be—thank you for two of the most exciting and enjoyable years of my professional career.

I'd have been content to remain a part of the USFL for as long as it lasted. When the league folded, my stock in the NFL, thanks to the numbers I put up with the Gamblers, was a hell of a lot higher than when I came out of college.

I was in a win-win position.

5

Warming Up to Buffalo

NOW THAT I WAS SET FREE by the USFL, I found myself trapped by NFL rules allowing the team that drafted you to hold your exclusive negotiating rights for four years from the day of the draft. The Bills still had one more year to call me their "own," so that meant I was left with two options: sign with them and play in the 1986 season or not sign with them and miss the 1986 season. Unless, of course, they decided to trade my rights to another team. I could think of two that would have suited me just fine—the Pittsburgh Steelers or the Los Angeles Raiders. When I wasn't wearing a Steelers cap as a kid, the colors on my head were silver and black. I was even wearing a Raiders cap at Super Bowl XX in New Orleans after the 1985 season. And once the USFL went belly-up, the Raiders pushed very hard to get the Bills to make a deal for me. My agents, knowing how badly I wanted to continue my career in a warm-weather site, did their share of pushing, too.

The Bills wouldn't budge.

Not for any price.

"If I were to trade Jim Kelly's rights, this team would no longer be in Buffalo," Ralph Wilson, the Bills' owner, told my agents at the time. "We would get booed right out of town."

As it was, the Bills were on the verge of being laughed out of the NFL. They were in even worse shape than when they drafted me in 1983. After back-to-back 2–14 seasons in 1984 and 1985, average attendance at 80,000-seat Rich Stadium was down to 37,000. Fewer than 30,000 fans showed up four times in 1985, including one crowd of 21,000.

Those numbers might have been OK for a USFL team in its early stages. But they just didn't cut it for an NFL franchise in business since 1960.

When people started driving around with "Bring Pro Football Back to Buffalo" bumper stickers on their cars, Wilson began giving serious thought to moving the club out West or down South. Instead, he gave Bill Polian, whom he had just hired as general manager, the go-ahead to spend the kind of money necessary to bring the team back to respectability.

I knew I was going to like Polian from the very first time we met, which was when we began contract negotiations in Houston. It was on Friday, August 15, the night before the Bills faced the Oilers in an exhibition game. Besides being Irish, Polian was also a hard-nosed sonofagun who didn't take shit from anybody. He was a lot like me.

I wasn't looking for a rah-rah speech about the Bills. I had watched them enough on television to have a pretty good idea of what they had and what they needed to get better. I had even seen them in person once, during the '85 season, when they played the Minnesota Vikings at Rich. I was a guest in the luxury box of Charlie Barcelona, president of a major food-store chain in western New York. It was a dreary day, the stands were about half full and the Bills were on their way to a fourth consecutive loss. Not a pretty sight.

All I wanted to learn from Polian was whether the team was truly dedicated to bringing in the right players, besides myself, to help turn things around. I was talking about offensive linemen and wide receivers. I didn't care about the defense; I figured as long as the offense could put points on the board, the defense would automatically show improvement.

I knew the Bills had a pretty talented running back named Greg Bell, who was also represented by my former agents. But if they were going to enjoy any kind of success offensively, they would have to construct a good enough line to give me time to throw and Greg room to run. I also knew they had a respected veteran named Jerry Butler and a promising second-year man named Andre Reed at wide receiver. But I was looking for a whole lot more. I was looking for a receiving corps with the kind of speed, skills and depth that the "Mouseketeers" gave me in Houston.

"Jim, I guarantee you Ralph is committed to building a winner in Buffalo," Polian said. "But we have to start with you. We have to get you in first before we can do anything else."

He sounded sincere enough.

Joe Ferguson was gone, having been traded to Detroit during the 1985 draft. When the Bills opened their '86 training camp, their quarterbacks were Bruce Mathison, the incumbent starter; Frank Reich, their third-round pick in the previous year's draft; Brian McClure, a twelfth-round choice that year; and free agents Art Schlichter and Bryan Clark. They had been operating a conventional, straight-dropback, pro-style offense. And regardless of whether I signed, the offense would stay the same; no provisions were made, either through coaching or personnel, to switch to the run-and-shoot at the last minute. That just wasn't going to be possible. But it wasn't a problem either, because I had been a straight-dropback passer in college. I could adapt.

I still had the option of sitting out the 1986 NFL season and becoming a free agent in 1987. But I had already been sitting for a year and a half, thanks to the USFL's switch to the fall schedule it never played. To stay away for more than two whole seasons didn't seem to make a great deal of sense. It was a year of development I couldn't afford to lose and a year of competition I couldn't stand to see go down the drain. If I didn't sign with the Bills, Donald Trump would still pay me the $800,000 I was due to receive in the USFL in '86. But giving up the difference from the anticipated pay increase for joining the Bills would have been lost revenue that I'd never recover.

At the same time, I wasn't kidding myself. I realized, even if the Bills found the right players on both sides of the ball, it was going to take a few years to put together all the pieces to the puzzle.

And before they could do anything with this piece, there would be some very intense negotiations.

I watched the exhibition game with Ralph Wilson from the luxury box provided for him at the Astrodome. After the Bills' 23–20 loss, I went down to the locker room to say hello to some of my potential future teammates. Then, later that night, the players and coaches flew back to Buffalo, but Polian stayed behind to try to hammer out an agreement with my agents.

Things really began heating up on Sunday, August 17. Outside, the thermometer had soared into the hundreds. But that was Antarctica compared to the temperature at the negotiating table in a suite at Houston's Intercontinental Hotel. Actually, there were three rooms for the negotiations, which, besides Polian and my agents, also involved two of Wilson's financial executives from his main office in Detroit. In addition to the extra-large suite, there were two smaller adjoining rooms—one for each party to go when they needed to huddle in private . . . or just to cool off whenever things turned nasty.

Suffice it to say those side rooms got a lot of use.

With Polian and that Irish temper of his, the sound coming from behind the closed door of any big negotiation usually resembles that of an erupting volcano. For instance, in trying to make the strongest case for me, A.J. had been especially critical of the Bills' offensive line. He said I was going to take a beating and should be paid accordingly. Polian became enraged and challenged A.J. to drop down in front of him in a three-point stance.

"If you know so much about offensive-line play," Polian growled, "why don't you demonstrate the swim technique against a short-set formation for me? Come on!"

A.J. took one look at Polian's face, which was as red as his hair, and backed off.

I wasn't around for all the fun, though; I had a dinner date. But I did carry a cellular phone with me, and Greg and A.J. called with updates every two hours or so. I know what some people might be thinking: This guy didn't care enough about his own negotiations to be there. It was hardly a case of not caring. Who could have been more interested in how those talks turned out than me?

I didn't involve myself in the actual negotiating process because that was what I was paying my agents for. I hired them to do the research, put together the strategy, fight the fight and get me the best contract possible. There was no need for me to be a part of all the back-and-forth stuff. If I went through that, I might as well have done the whole thing myself.

Plus, it would have been really awkward for me to have sat there and said, "OK, Bill, I'm a great quarterback. Now pay me X amount of dollars." And it would have been just as awkward for him to have sat there and said, "Well, Jim, we don't think you're quite *that* good. So we're going to offer you this amount." You might reach an agreement, but you'd also run the risk of spilling a lot of bad blood that could make things uncomfortable for years to come.

Late into the night, Lustig called me with the most encouraging update of all.

"We're getting close," he said. "Why don't you come over."

So my date and I drove to the Intercontinental. She stayed in the side room that Greg and A.J. had been using, while I joined the action in the suite. At that point, we were down to brass tacks, with both sides in the take-it-or-leave-it mode. Following our strategy, the three of us began to play serious hardball with the Bills. And that touched off more serious arguing between Polian and A.J. They started to scream and yell at each other at the top of their lungs. I thought for sure they were going to come to blows. So did Greg, who stepped between them and suggested they go to their "neutral corners."

They did. Then they came out to talk again. They started to scream and yell, and they had to be separated again.

It was wild.

For all of his toughness, though, the one thing I can say about Polian is that he's fair in the end. Very fair.

And in the wee hours of the morning of August 18, we came to terms on a five-year contract worth $8 million. At the time, it made me the highest-paid player in the NFL.

My first reaction was a mixture of relief and excitement. I was relieved that all the negotiating, all the back-and-forth crap, was finally over. And I was excited that, after nearly two years away from the game, I was finally going to get to play again. I knew it wasn't going to be easy. I knew I was going to take a beating for a couple of seasons.

But, at age twenty-six, this was my one and only shot to continue fulfilling my dream of being a pro quarterback.

I don't know what time it was that I got to my home outside of Houston that night. But it seemed like only minutes after I closed my eyes that the media started ringing my doorbell to find out what had gone on with the negotiations. The Bills weren't planning to make the official announcement until six o'clock that night, so we were all sworn to secrecy until then. But word of the agreement had already leaked out in the *Buffalo News*. After the wire services picked it up, television crews from Buffalo and Houston were camped on my front porch.

My brothers answered the door and said I wasn't home. They were kidding, of course, and I had put them up to it. I figured since I wasn't supposed to say anything, I was better off avoiding the media altogether until the press conference. I was also in dire need of sleep.

Ralph Wilson sent his private jet to Houston to pick me up and take me to Buffalo. I really had no idea what to expect when I got there. In fact, I thought there was a better than even chance I would hear more booing than cheering because of the feelings I had expressed about wanting to play for the Steelers or the Raiders just before I officially severed ties with the USFL. I also made some nasty remarks about Buffalo's weather. Most of that was said for the sake of the negotiations with the Bills. But I figured it was likely people in Buffalo wouldn't see it that way and would hold it against me.

Not to mention the fans who still could have been bitter because I turned my back on the Bills in the first place to sign with the Gamblers.

But what I saw after the plane landed was incredible.

Television cameramen and newspaper photographers were everywhere. One TV station gave me a football to throw to one of its reporters so he could say he caught my first pass as a Bill. I complied, tossing a really easy one so he wouldn't drop the ball and be embarrassed in front of his live audience. Besides, I didn't want my first pass in Buffalo to be incomplete. I also posed with Wilson, holding up my brand-new number 12 Bills jersey.

After that, we climbed into the back of a black stretch limo parked right on the tarmac. A full-fledged motorcade, complete with a police escort, was there to take me to the Hilton Hotel for the press conference. As we pulled onto the freeway heading downtown, the limo driver kept yelling, "Look, Jim! Look at that! Look at what they're doing!"

I looked out my window and I couldn't believe my eyes: People all over the place were waving and holding up signs that said, "We Love You, Jim" and "Welcome Back." I mean, all over. They were along the sides of the road, with their cars parked on the shoulder. They were on the overpasses. They were hanging out the windows of their houses. I was just floored by it all, especially by the fact that I didn't hear one negative thing.

Meanwhile, at Rich Stadium, long lines had formed in front of the ticket windows. A thousand season tickets would be sold by the end of the day. Three thousand more would be purchased by the end of the week. Everyone seemed so excited to have me in their town.

When we arrived at the Hilton, the lobby was jammed with hundreds of people chanting, "Kel-lee! Kel-lee!" and "Go, Bills! Go, Bills!" and "Super Bowl! Super Bowl!" Police dressed in riot gear escorted me through the mob on the way to the grand ballroom, where almost 500 reporters and more fans were waiting. But it wasn't until I saw my parents, just before we went inside the ballroom, that I started to realize something special was unfolding all around me. Especially when I saw my mother. I had expected my father to drive up from East Brady. But Mom's presence was a real surprise because, with her emphysema, she had planned to stay home. I gave her a big bear hug and we both broke into tears.

The Bills had set up a long head table, with seats for me, my parents, my agents, Ralph Wilson, Bill Polian, Mayor Jimmy Griffin and County Executive Ed Rutkowski, a former Bill. As we entered, the ballroom broke into a loud, continuous applause. It really felt more like a testimonial dinner than a press conference.

"I don't have a prepared speech because attorneys have to read those to make sure everything's OK, and attorneys cost a hundred fifty dollars an hour," cracked Wilson, who served as master of ceremonies. "And for some reason, we're kind of low on funds today."

There was a telephone hookup with Governor Mario Cuomo, who had written a letter encouraging me to play for "New York's only professional football team."

"Who knows?" I said. "Maybe I'll be able to take this team to the Super Bowl and get a call from the President next."

There was another loud ovation.

But the last thing I was going to do was stand up there and promise everybody a Super Bowl. We were a long way from being a Super Bowl contender.

"You're only as good as the people around you," I told the audience. "But if I get some help, I think we can definitely take this team to a championship."

Buffalo's three network affiliates had preempted their six-thirty national newscasts to show the press conference live. And because it ran well past seven, one station actually bumped Vanna White and *Wheel of Fortune* in favor of yours truly. Can you believe that?

Before we left, Charlie Mancuso, a car dealer from nearby Batavia, New York, would come up to me with the keys to a shiny new Corvette, duplicating the promotional deal I had in Houston. No one had even talked to him; he had read about my agreement in Houston and just showed up with the vehicle and a big smile under that bushy black mustache of his. Charlie would also become one of my closest friends.

I wasn't the only one receiving new wheels. Among the many ways I celebrated my new contract was buying my parents a thirty-four-foot motor home so they could make the three-and-a-half-hour ride from East Brady to Buffalo in style. It had everything, including a television and VCR. The only problem was that it was a little too long for their driveway.

I also finally convinced my father to retire after thirty-two years of working as a machinist. The thing that swung it was when I pointed out I could pay him twenty times what he would receive from his pension. After that, I gave him the first credit card he ever had in his life.

"And the best part is that you're never going to see a bill," I told him. "Whatever you want, charge it to me. Don't even look at the price."

I took my brothers on a shopping spree at a mall, then gave them each a check for $5,000 to do whatever they pleased.

I just love being a year-round Santa Claus, coming up with all kinds of surprises for my family. Once, we were watching television at my parents' home, and the set, which had been giving them problems, started acting up again. I didn't say a word. I just got up and left. A little while later, a truck pulled up to the house with a brand-new color TV set with a remote control, something we'd never had in our East Brady home before.

They never know what I'll do next; nor do they expect or ask for a single thing from me. And hardly a day goes by when one of them doesn't say, "Thanks, Jim." Which is all I ever want to hear. As long as they appreciate what I do for them, I'll keep on doing it for as long as I live. And I know they'd do anything for me.

I intended to eventually build a new home in the Buffalo area, but I still had the place in Texas. So for that first season, Bell and I rented the home of former Buffalo Sabres star John Van Boxmeer in East Amherst, a nice suburb north of the city.

I got up early the next morning for a few more media interviews. Then it was off to the stadium for the actual signing of the contract. That's when it finally hit me. With one stroke of the pen, I had officially become an NFL quarterback.

Next I made the half-hour trip down to Fredonia, New York, for the Bills' training camp, already in progress. My first stop was the office of Bob Leahy, the offensive coordinator and quarterbacks coach, for my first glance at the playbook. Countless other meetings with him would follow in my crash course on the Bills' offense. I'm talking day and night. And those one-on-one sessions were in addition to the meetings I had with the rest of the team and the rest of the quarterbacks.

Leahy was a straightlaced guy, a born-again Christian, and he didn't like it when his players cussed around him. Because I have a bad habit of cussing whenever I make a mistake—and mistakes by me were many in those early stages—it wasn't long before I managed to irritate Leahy. So he established a rule: For each cuss, I had to pay a fine of ten cents. No wonder I could never find pocket change for the vending machines.

Later that day, I would take part in my first practice with the Bills. I wasn't nervous during the press conference. I wasn't nervous during any of the media interviews. But when I walked into that dressing room and put on that red, white and blue uniform for the first time, that's when I became nervous.

Very nervous.

It dawned on me that, with all the fanfare from the day before—and especially with the publicity over the money I was being paid—I was expected to perform instant miracles. Or at least demonstrate I was capable of doing so.

Thousands of fans lined the fences around the practice area. Reporters and photographers from all over the country were also on hand. "Kelly hounds." That's what Fred Smerlas, our nose tackle and resident comedian, called them.

"Maybe now," Fred told a reporter, "we'll get to play on *Monday Night Football* again." The Bills hadn't appeared in ABC's showcase game since 1984.

As I stepped onto the field, the first thought that entered my mind was: "Don't screw up." Although I hadn't played for quite a while, I knew that neither the fans nor the media would give me a whole lot of leeway. I knew that the moment I launched that first long pass I was going to be immediately judged a success or a failure. That wasn't fair, of course. But like it or not, that was the situation I faced.

Leahy had told me beforehand that, because I had gotten only a peek at the playbook for an hour after lunch, I didn't have to go in the huddle; I could just throw some passes on the sidelines. But that wasn't going to cut it with me, let alone with all those "hounds." I figured if I was going to be playing, I might as well get out there as soon as possible. And before Leahy could blink, I was in the huddle calling plays. Granted, they were pretty basic, but at least I was out there running the offense. And that was a hell (excuse me, heck) of a lot more than Leahy or Hank Bullough, our head coach, expected. I wasn't expecting it myself.

Soon thereafter came the moment of truth.

I took the snap, dropped back, stepped into the pocket and let one fly. Despite a brisk wind in my face, I managed to get off a nice, tight rainbow spiral. Sixty yards downfield, Jimmy Teal, who was running along the right sideline well ahead of the free safety, made the catch. Without breaking stride.

The crowd went nuts. The players and coaches seemed equally excited.

Next!

Hank was a funny guy. As a joke, he told me to purposely throw one pass a mile over Jerry Butler's head, just to see how the crowd would react. I followed his instructions and sure enough, the fans let out a disappointed "Awwww!" Hank even picked up a football and slammed it to the ground in mock disgust. What a card.

As we left the field, about twenty kids on the other side of the fence started screaming for me to throw them one of my wristbands. I obliged, whipping it as high as I could. Much to my surprise, they all went diving for it. Headfirst. After that, they yelled for my towel. I threw that over, too. But this time an older guy actually shoved all the kids out of his way, jumped a couple of feet off the ground and grabbed it. I just shook my head in amazement.

All my new teammates jagged me about my contract. They were saying things like "Here comes the eight-million-dollar man." They were asking me for loans; even Hank asked for one. During those first several days, I realized there was a general attitude of "OK, let's see what this hotshot from the USFL is all about."

But by the end of camp, most of them discovered that I liked going out for a couple of beers and having a few laughs just like everyone else. They started treating me like one of the boys. Especially the offensive linemen. They didn't show any resentment for some of the negative comments I had made in the media about the Bills' blocking. What they showed was they were determined to prove me wrong.

There were two longtime veterans at the tackle spots, Joe Devlin (in his tenth year) and Ken Jones (in his eleventh). One of the guards, Jim Ritcher, was in his eighth season, while the other, Will Wolford, was one of our first-round draft picks in 1986. I already had a friend in the center, Kent Hull, who had spent three years with the USFL Generals and arrived in Buffalo at the same time I did.

I also knew Frank Reich, who would move into the number-two quarterback spot from then on. We had first met at the Penn State football camp in my junior year of high school. Frank, who was from Lebanon, Pennsylvania, was a sophomore. During our many card games at the camp, I wore a bandanna—which Frank thought was the coolest thing around as I took all his money. The next time we saw each other was in 1985, when I was with the Gamblers. Boomer Esiason, the Cincinnati Bengals' quarterback, had invited me to play in his charity golf tournament and stay at his house. Frank, who had become close with Boomer when they were teammates at the University of Maryland, was also invited to the tournament and to stay at Boomer's house. But Boomer didn't tell Frank I was coming, saying only that there would be a "special guest staying with us." Frank, who had just been drafted by the Bills, was shocked when he saw me there.

"Don't worry, Frank," I said. "I will never sign with Buffalo. Your job's secure."

Since then, he has always called me "Special Guest."

We became roommates on the road and formed a bond, on and off the field, that is still strong to this day. I'll do anything I can to help him out, and I know he'll do the same for me. Our personalities make us sort of an unlikely pair. Frank's married and spends a lot of time at home with his wife and daughter; I'm single and constantly on the go. But one thing we both have in common is a great devotion to our families. And we've always had a tremendous mutual respect for each other's skill on the field. I don't know of a smarter quarterback in the game.

Because I wasn't familiar enough with the offense, the coaches decided it would be best for me not to play in our next exhibition game, at Kansas City. I did make the trip, however, so I could watch and learn from the sidelines. I wore my new jersey, minus the shoulder pads, and nearly lost my voice from cheering so loud in our 13–6 victory. I really got into the game. Every time we scored, I went crazy. I felt like doing a backflip or something.

I was dying to be out there.

But my chance came the following week, in our preseason

finale against the Chicago Bears at South Bend, Indiana. The defending Super Bowl champion Bears.

Frank started, and we gave them a pretty good scare, scoring on our first two possessions to take a 14–0 lead. I took over in the second quarter, and directed four offensive series before I left the game late in the third quarter. I connected on my first five passes, for 60 yards, before throwing incomplete on my last four. But we only managed three more points and wound up losing, 31–17.

On a scale of one to ten, I gave myself a six. For its being the first time, I didn't do quite as badly as I thought I would. The offensive line did well, not allowing a single sack, which was quite an accomplishment against those big, bad Bears.

But we still lost. And I hate to lose, regardless of the game's importance. I had never been a part of a losing program before; it was a trend I was hoping very much to avoid.

I knew that getting myself mentally prepared in time for our September 7 season opener at home against the New York Jets was going to be difficult. But I was determined to make it.

Leahy and I began working at an accelerated pace. After each of our one-on-one sessions, I would go back to my dormitory room and study all the material we had covered that day. I would keep reviewing things, over and over, until I had them straight in my mind. It was the most intensive studying I had ever done in my life. But as I learned very early in my college days, preparation was the key to success for a quarterback. You can have the greatest arm in the world, the best offensive line around and the fastest and most sure-handed receivers ever to come along. But if you don't have a clue as to where and when to throw the ball, you'll be an ex-quarterback faster than you can say "Hut!"

The last thing I wanted in the world was to go into that first game and make a bunch of mistakes because I didn't know what I was doing. I could get away with that in practice. Maybe even in an exhibition game. But this time we would be using live ammo.

The media hype that began August 18 seemed to grow and grow as the game drew closer. So did the expectations. This was different than my USFL debut. To most of the fans and the media in and around Houston, we were still just a curiosity at that point. Even though the Gamblers were paying me a lot of money, if it didn't work out it was no big deal to most of those on the outside.

But this was the NFL. I knew that the moment I stepped onto the field against the Jets—after I did my usual pregame vomiting, of course—everyone there would be asking the same question: "Is this guy worth it?" I knew everyone would be watching. Not only the 79,951 in the stands, giving the Bills their first sellout in three years (a franchise record at the time). Not only those within NBC's regional television audience for the game. But the whole country. Those who didn't see it live on TV or hear it on radio were going to check out what I did on the highlights or read about it in the papers.

You wear the label "highest-paid player in the NFL," people take notice.

One sign inside Rich that caught my eye was: "I'm in a Jim-packed stadium." That was neat. But what I didn't like were references to my being some sort of messiah, the savior of a football franchise and an entire community. I wasn't the least bit comfortable with that, because, as I said during the press conference, one player is not going to turn around a team by himself. And to expect me, alone, to do wonders for a community is really stretching it. The most ridiculous sign I saw that day was: "Kelly Is God," painted in red and blue on a bedsheet draped over the wall around the field. Why anyone would write something so absurd is beyond me.

Some people were picking the Jets to go to the Super Bowl that year. The Bills were a team that everybody just picked on— a team in desperate need of a spark. Because the opener sets the tone for your whole season, what better time or place to get the fire started.

I tried as hard as I could to put the pressure I felt to perform well out of my mind. I kept saying, "Just go out there and be yourself." I even thought back to high school—to our big games against Union and Karns City—and how much fun I had back then. That was when I doubled as a defensive player, and the thought of making a huge hit would get me really pumped up. I would be more excited about that than the thought of throwing a touchdown pass. Eventually, I'd be too excited even to think about my nerves.

It worked then; it works now.

Between my arrival and the Jets game, there was only enough time for me to learn about half the offense. I would have preferred going into the game with more, but it was enough to get by. What I didn't know, I improvised. For instance, when it came to reading coverages, I predetermined where I was going to throw the ball much more than normal.

The approach worked well enough for me to complete my first three passes and give us a 7–0 lead on a two-yard touchdown throw to Greg Bell. A muffed punt set up the Jets' first TD, and they made it 14–7 when Ken O'Brien, one of my classmates from the 1983 draft, found Al Toon for a 46-yard score.

The Jets' defensive linemen were so eager to get in my face that sometimes they didn't even wait for the snap. On one play in the second quarter, Joe Klecko, their great nose tackle, came firing through offside, smashed me chest-high and knocked me on my ass. It was one of those "Welcome to the NFL" hits. The funny part was, nobody else from either team moved; they all just watched as this 275-pound ex-tractor-trailer driver sent me flying. But I bounced right back without any problem. As I said, those kinds of hits, where it's just straight-up contact, don't hurt much. I also landed on the perfect spot.

Just before halftime, we got a 19-yard field goal, courtesy of Scott Norwood, and I got a hit to the head, courtesy of defensive end Mark Gastineau. This time, I was left semi-conscious. I went over to the sideline to talk about the next play with Coach Leahy. For some reason, I was thinking about the fact that he used to play for the Steelers way back when and I wondered if we were in Pittsburgh instead of Buffalo. He gave me the play anyway. But by the time I trotted back to the huddle, I had completely forgotten it. So Bell called another play before we got a delay-of-game penalty.

Gastineau nailed me again, late in the third quarter, and put a nice big bruise on my back. But a short while later, in the face of a three-linebacker blitz, I hooked up with Andre Reed for a 55-yard scoring pass to put us in front, 17–14.

O'Brien rallied the Jets to two touchdowns in the fourth quarter to make it 28–17. And just when it looked like we might quit, we came back with seven more points. How we got them, I'll never know. Because after I took the snap, Ritcher stepped on my foot and I fell. (I already had a twisted ankle from tripping over Gastineau a little earlier.) Then I got back up, rolled to my right with a wave of green chasing me, pump-faked and lofted a four-yard pass to the back of the end zone, where Pete Metzelaars, our 6-7 tight end, made the catch.

But we never saw the ball again. Final score: Jets 28, Bills 24.

I finished with 20 completions in 33 attempts for 292 yards and three touchdowns, without throwing an interception. The last Bills quarterback to throw three TDs in a game was Joe Ferguson, who did so in 1983 against (guess who) the Jets. Walking up the tunnel after the game, Gastineau came up to me. At first I thought he might be looking to get in just one more lick for good measure. Instead, he shook his head and said, "Jim, we gave you our best shot today. And you kept getting up."

I appreciated his saying that. But the thought of losing was eating me alive. I think I wanted to win that game more than anybody in the world.

At the same time, I couldn't act as if I was way down in the dumps. I was looked upon as a leader; every quarterback is. And the key to establishing yourself as a leader is building confidence among your teammates. You do it, first, through your performance on the field. You have to prove you have the talent and the toughness to play the game before they'll even begin to take you seriously. Then there's your attitude. If those guys saw too much discouragement in my eyes after one loss, they wouldn't have an ounce of faith in me.

I had to show that the first game was forgotten and I was ready to lead them into another battle.

"Keep your heads up high," I said to everybody as we walked into the locker room. "We played a good team today, but we're definitely going to win our share of games this year."

The following week, we traveled to Cincinnati and wound up losing in overtime, 36–33. We went with a pretty conservative approach in the first half, and fell behind, 21–9. Then we turned it loose for a while in the last two quarters, and I hit Jerry Butler for a 53-yard gain to set up one touchdown and another when I hooked up with Chris Burkett on an 84-yard pass play. But after blowing a 10-point lead in the final 6:27 of regulation, we blew the game when, on the first play of OT, I put the ball right in the hands of linebacker Carl Zander. I never saw him coming as I tried to lead Burkett over the middle. The interception set up Jim Breech's winning field goal from 20 yards. Ouch!

We finally broke the ice in Week Three by beating St. Louis, 17–10, at home. I only threw 10 passes, completing six for 82 yards—all lows for my professional career. My previous low for attempts was 12 against the Memphis Showboats in 1984. But it didn't matter. What mattered was that we got our first victory . . . and a much-needed confidence boost. Sure, I wished I could have put up better numbers that day, but they still weren't going to top the ones on the scoreboard.

We all received game balls for finally breaking into the win column, and I gave mine to my father. In fact, I had the equipment men paint "Dad" on it. He was the reason I had made it that far in my football career and I thought he deserved the game ball more than I did.

Things were even closer the following week, when we hosted Kansas City, but this time we ended up on the wrong end of a 20–17 score. I thought we were on our way to an easy win when, on our first possession, Robb Riddick popped loose for a 41-yard touchdown run. On our next series, I completed six of seven passes to move us all the way to the Chiefs' 2-yard line. But on the last completion, linebacker Tim Cofield, who had blasted me twice before on questionable hits after I released the ball, buried his helmet into my left arm. My wrist swelled up and I thought for sure it was broken. Until the X rays showed otherwise, even our doctor, Richard Weiss, thought it was broken. Unfortunately, right after I left the game, there was a fumble and the Chiefs recovered. End of scoring opportunity.

I returned later in the first half, and the easy win I thought we were headed for was nip and tuck the rest of the way. It was the kind of game that would be decided by a mistake, and it came in the last couple of minutes when I was intercepted by free safety Deron Cherry. Six plays later, Nick Lowery booted a 46-yard field goal for the winning points.

We also lost our next two games, both on the road, against the Jets and Miami.

The Jets apparently felt they didn't put my toughness to enough of a test the first time around. At one point, I was flat on my back and staring down at me was Marty Lyons, the Jets' 6-5, 270-pound defensive end. He just lay there on top of me, and I was getting angry. So I told him to get off, only not in those words. He said something back to me, I said something back to him and the next thing I knew both of his hands were around my throat. I shoved back and, all of a sudden, I ended up on top of him, with my hands on his face mask. Somehow, one of my fingers went through and I cut his eye. He was furious.

By that time, my teammates from the bench joined the ones on the field in coming to the rescue. Even mild-mannered Frank Reich came out, although he probably should have been wearing a helmet instead of a baseball cap. The Jets emptied their bench, too, and it took a couple of minutes before order was restored. Marty had made the mistake of trying to intimidate someone who, with three older brothers, had learned from a very young age the meaning of taking shit and giving it right back. He also cost the Jets a 15-yard roughing penalty. Well, that was the official infraction. Referee Ben Dreith made NFL blooper-film history when he switched on his wireless mike and, while punching downward a couple of times, announced that Lyons was "giving him the business down there."

We were all punished later, however, when Pete Rozelle handed out fines to everyone involved in the fight. The way I saw it, $800 was a small price to pay to keep myself from getting bullied. Because if you allow it to happen to you once in the NFL, it's going to keep happening. But to this day, I can't figure out why Rozelle fined me for being a punching bag.

After our loss at Miami the following week, there was a lot of speculation that Hank Bullough was on his way out as head coach. The defeat was his twelfth in the fourteen games since he replaced Kay Stephenson.

Beating Indianapolis at home after that, for our second win of the year, was a small bright spot—very small, considering the Colts hadn't won a game. And it was quickly doused seven days later when New England pounded us, also at home, 23–3. It was the longest day of my pro career up to that point. I was sacked five times and forced to leave the game with 8:28 remaining after suffering a twisted back. The Patriots pressured the daylights out of me; it was like they were all taking turns getting their shots in.

The end for Hank finally came on November 2, after our 34–28 loss at Tampa, the Bills' twenty-first in a row on the road. We had a chance to pull it out in the final seconds when, on fourth down at the Buccaneers' 3, I threw over the middle to Riddick, who was wide open in the end zone. But Robb was wearing a cast for a fractured wrist. The ball hit the cast and bounced away.

Would a touchdown have saved Hank's job? From what I was told afterward, the decision had already been made that Hank would be sent packing the next day—and Marv Levy would become our new head coach.

The thing that bothered me at the time was hearing people, both on and off the team, say that *I* was the reason Hank was fired. The assumption was that, because of my salary, I was in a position of power to force such a move. And nothing could have been further from the truth.

The weird part was that I didn't receive blame so much as credit. Hank wasn't too popular with a lot of players, especially those on defense. His personality didn't mesh with theirs, and vice versa. I mean, I actually had people thanking me for going up to Bill Polian and Ralph Wilson and demanding that they fire Bullough.

"Don't look at me," I told them. "I didn't walk up to Bill or Ralph and say, 'I can't play for this guy anymore; get rid him.' Ralph owns the team. He calls the shots."

That's not to say I didn't agree with the decision. The way things were going, there had to be a change of some kind. As far as I was concerned, Hank was an outstanding defensive coordinator; he had an excellent mind for coaching defense. But I didn't think he was the best head coach in the world. He just didn't seem to have a good grasp of the big picture, in terms of overseeing the whole team, which is what a head coach needs.

Marv had an immediate, positive impact on the team. But it wasn't a case of coming in and running everybody into the ground, the way some new head coaches feel they have to do when they take over a losing program.

In fact, the first thing Marv did was shorten practices, saying it was quality that mattered, not quantity. He emphasized that more than anything. We ran as many plays as when Hank was there; we just ran them in less time. With Hank, there was a feeling that a lot of things we did during workouts didn't seem necessary—that we were out there sometimes just for the sake of being out there. After a while, that sort of approach wears on players. It drains them, physically and psychologically.

Overall, Marv brought new life back into all of us.

And it showed in our next game, when we faced the Steelers at Rich. To me, it wouldn't have mattered if we were 9–0, rather than 2–7; I was going to be sky-high for this one. Sharing the same field with the team I grew up loving was yet another dream come true. Just as they did for my USFL game against the Maulers at Three Rivers Stadium, almost all of East Brady climbed on buses and headed up to Orchard Park to watch me play. I'm sure, even though they rooted for me individually, a lot of them wanted the Steelers to win. As it turned out, I didn't do anything spectacular. With wind gusts up to 50 mph, it certainly wasn't a day for passing. We just used a lot of short routes, like the one that went for a three-yard touchdown pass to Andre in the first quarter, and ground out a 16–12 victory. It would go down as one of the most satisfying wins of my career.

Although I liked a lot of the things he did and said in his first week on the job, Marv's coaching style took a little getting used to. I had always played for men who were big on motivating their troops. In high school, there was Terry Henry, a rah-rah type who knew just what to say and how to say it to get his players pumped up for every game, regardless of the opponent's record. In college, there was Howard Schnellenberger, a very brash, take-charge kind of guy who commanded your respect just by glaring at you with those bushy eyebrows. In the USFL, there was Jack Pardee, a former NFL linebacker who had toughness written all over him.

Marv came across as more of a college professor than an NFL head coach, using a lot of big words and talking about a lot of historical figures whom most of us had never even heard of before. It's the same now. His approach is to let you play your own game. The way he sees it, if you can't motivate yourself to do the job you're being paid to do, then you shouldn't be out there.

That isn't to say Marv doesn't do a lot of talking during the week. He talks plenty. But the things he says are meant to educate you and get you mentally prepared for a game. He does an excellent job of analyzing why a team wins or loses, whether it's his own team or the opposition. He also does a great job of pinpointing the things we can expect from an opponent, what to watch out for and what we have to do to beat them. After that, he pretty much leaves it up to your own skills and desire to succeed.

All that really concerns him is the bottom line.

Now, there are always going to be some players who need more than that. At the beginning, I thought I needed more, too, because I was so used to those other coaching techniques— to having someone stand up in front of the room and talk about kicking ass and taking names. I had never really heard it from that perspective before. But after a while, a lot of the things he said started making sense. I realized, "Hey, this is my job. It's up to me to want to do it the best I possibly can. I don't need someone telling me I should."

After losing again to the Dolphins and Patriots, we managed to get another victory, beating the Chiefs at Kansas City, 17–14. When Nick Lowery's 44-yard field-goal attempt with 19 seconds left sailed wide left, the Bills ended a twenty-two-game road losing streak. Ironically, the team's last win away from home was also against the Chiefs, on December 4, 1983.

But that would be our fourth and final triumph of the season. The last three weeks were a disaster as we lost to Cleveland at home and Indianapolis and Houston on the road.

From the moment I arrived in Buffalo, I discovered that, despite the poor attendance of the '84 and '85 seasons, the fans were really behind the team. And they started showing their support at the gate, with the average crowd soaring from 37,893 in the previous year to 66,476. I also was made to feel very welcome by the people I met around town and those who called my radio show.

The only time I ever had a problem with the "twelfth man" was during the Cleveland game. It was played in December, so naturally there was snow on the ground. And after we fell behind, 21–10, some fans among the 42,000 on hand threw snowballs at us in the final eight minutes. We had just taken possession and were moving downfield with a chance to score a touchdown that would have put us right back in the game, and we were being pelted with snowballs. I couldn't believe it. And it got even worse when the drive stalled at the Cleveland 18 and we were heading back to the bench. One snowball hit a security guard smack in the face. Another landed at my feet.

So I lost it. I turned and walked toward the stands, yelling at the jerks who thought it was cool to use us for target practice. Joe Devlin then came over to calm me down and get me back to the sideline.

"Jim, no matter how hard you try you aren't going to straighten them out like this," Joe, who had seen more than his share of Rich Stadium snowballs through the years, told me. "That's just the way it is here sometimes. Get used to it."

I knew he was right. But it just pissed me off that there were a few people who had to act in a way that was totally unreasonable. And it was a shame that they were giving a bad rap to the loyal majority who were freezing their butts off to watch us play. I wanted everybody across the nation to respect and know about the kind of great fans we had in Buffalo rather than think that the only thing they knew how to do was show how ugly they could get.

When reporters asked me about the snowballs after the game, I said the people who threw them were low class. And I wasn't alone in my feelings. As one column in the next day's paper said, "It may not have been wise for Kelly to take on the fans, but it is completely understandable. Their behavior was imbecilic. Moronic. Doltish. To say nothing of disloyal."

During our embarrassing 24–14 loss to the Colts, defensive end Donnell Thompson body-slammed me to the artificial turf at the Hoosier Dome and I suffered a mild concussion that sidelined me from early in the second quarter until late in the third.

I took more punishment in the season finale against the Oilers, in my "homecoming" at the Astrodome. I was sacked six times, I fumbled twice and I was pressured into an interception.

I guess the Oilers hadn't forgiven me for stealing their thunder with the Gamblers.

The most disturbing thing I saw through the course of that first year was that the team didn't have a winning attitude. And it was something I spotted early on. It just seemed like, after suffering through so many losses over the previous two or three seasons, some of the veteran players didn't know how to win anymore. They had forgotten what it was like to be a winner and approach each game with the confidence that they could and would come out on top.

And we had some guys, who are no longer with the team and shall remain nameless, who came into the season not really caring whether we won or lost. They wanted to win; everybody wants to win. But at a certain point, they lost track of the difference between winning and losing. You'd walk into the locker room after a loss and hear just a tad too much laughing and joking around. Something didn't seem right about that. I'm not saying everybody had to carry on like it was a funeral, but a true competitor should feel a certain amount of anger and frustration in defeat. I know I felt a lot. Of course, I couldn't allow myself to get too far down because that also would have a negative impact on the rest of the team. But losing should hurt enough to dampen your sense of humor for a little while.

Unfortunately, some players had gotten used to having the "I don't give a damn" attitude. Their main concern was picking up a paycheck Monday morning, because they knew, regardless of the previous day's outcome, the numbers on the check would all be the same. They'd go through another week of practice, play in another game, shrug at another scoreboard and collect another paycheck. I had never seen anything like it before, at any level of organized sports, let alone football. It was a bad habit they just couldn't shake. And, next to smoking, it was the last one I ever wanted to start.

The funny part was, we weren't getting blown out. We were playing everybody tough and losing in the final couple of minutes. We weren't that far away from being a good team. And I figured that between Marv's arrival and the assistant coach and player changes he was likely to make for the 1987 season, the losing mentality would start to disappear.

I also knew there was more I could have done, as a quarterback, to help us win. There were plays I could have made and mistakes I could have avoided, and it was up to me to learn from those experiences. My final numbers were decent. I completed a team record 285 passes in 480 attempts for 3,593 yards and 22 touchdowns, while throwing 17 interceptions. I got sacked 43 times, which was no fun. But at least there was improvement as the season progressed. After throwing only nine touchdowns and 12 interceptions through the first half of the year, I rebounded with 13 TDs and only five pickoffs through the second half.

At one point, I completed 104 straight passes without an interception. My completion percentage of 59.4 also broke a club record, and the yardage total was the second highest for a single season in Bills history.

"I couldn't be higher on a player than I am on Jim Kelly," Marv told the media. "Never in my recollection has there been a quarterback who has performed as well as Jim has in his first year in the NFL. He's better as a first-year player than Dan Marino was or Joe Montana or Terry Bradshaw or Johnny Unitas or Bert Jones or any of them. He's had a lot of statistical accomplishments with a team that is not a strong team."

Still, I knew I was going through a transition period. I was coming off a long stretch of inactivity. I was working without the benefit of a full training camp in an offensive system that was far different than the one I had used in my previous two seasons. And I was facing much better competition than I had faced in the USFL. It was going to take time.

It was also going to take a few more players. We needed help in the offensive line. We needed another big-play receiver besides Andre and Chris Burkett. And we needed defensive help. Bruce Smith, the number-one overall pick of the 1985 draft, was just coming into his own as a dominant defensive end. But there were plenty of holes around him.

More than anything, we needed to start winning so everyone could get back the feeling of what it took to be a winner. I could see that on the horizon.

6

Respecta-BILL-ity

MARV LEVY didn't waste any time putting his signature on the Bills for 1987. As soon as the 1986 season ended, he fired five of the assistant coaches he had inherited from Hank Bullough, including Bob Leahy.

Marv immediately hired Bobby Ross to be my new mentor. I had heard many great things about him from Frank Reich, who had played for him at Maryland. But before Bobby ever set foot in Buffalo, he resigned from the job to become head football coach at Georgia Tech. I tried not to take it personally.

Next, Marv hired Ted Marchibroda, who had been an assistant coach with the Philadelphia Eagles and spent five years as head coach of the Baltimore Colts. I didn't know anything about the guy, but a lot of people told me he had a reputation for being conservative on offense, which I didn't like to hear. I worried that there might be too much conservatism considering that Jim Ringo, our offensive coordinator/offensive line coach, was also more run-oriented in his thinking. But I figured it would be best to give Ted the benefit of the doubt and form my own opinions.

I hadn't learned a great deal from Leahy, although some of that was because there really wasn't a chance for me to receive much detailed instruction in the preseason. There was barely enough time for me to learn the plays. And once you get into the regular season, preparing for a new opponent each week, detailed instruction pretty much goes out the window.

Now I would have an off-season of looking at the playbook and a full training camp under my belt. Plenty of time to work on the finer points of my game.

As it turned out, however, I wound up having fewer chances to apply anything new, thanks to the strike called by the NFL Players Association after the second game of the regular season. At that point, we were 1–1, having lost the home opener to the Jets, 31–28, and defeated Houston at Rich, 34–30.

Against the Jets, I threw for 305 yards and three touchdowns, but it just wasn't good enough. Against the Oilers, we were down 30–20 and I led us to two scoring drives in the final five minutes. The second ended with a 10-yard touchdown pass to halfback Ronnie Harmon, one of our two first-round picks in 1986, with 57 seconds left. For the day, I was 26 of 43 for 293 yards and three scores, giving me my first NFL Player of the Week honors.

The strike couldn't have come at a worse time. Our offense had definitely showed a spark in those first two games and I could sense that it was ready to explode.

I could also sense a lot of confidence among the fans. They had watched us double our win total from 1985 to 1986. And in 1987 they only had to suffer through one loss—as opposed to eleven in 1984, six in 1985 and two in '86—before seeing our first victory of the season. In one section of Rich, fans were even hanging a line of "K" cards for my touchdown passes, celebrating them the way New York Mets fans celebrated Dwight Gooden's strikeouts.

Actually, the Bills continued to play games after the strike began. But they did so with almost no "real" players. We were walking the picket lines while "replacement" squads (we called them scabs) took over. The majority of those guys were pulled away from jobs as bartenders and construction workers and suddenly given "an opportunity of a lifetime" to play in the NFL. No training camp, no tryouts. They were just signed and issued uniforms and helmets.

I hated the whole idea of being out on strike. Most "real" players did, because, for one thing it cost us money—money we were never going to get back. I was losing about $70,000 per week. Second, nobody really agreed with the reason we were striking in the first place—to get unrestricted free agency. That was probably last on everybody's list of demands. And never in a million years did I expect a work stoppage to force the owners to give up something like that, because it would cost them too much money. Salaries were already pretty high, and giving players more freedom of movement would make them climb even further out of sight. A court ruling might accomplish what the Players Association was after, but not a strike.

Besides, the NFL Management Council had every intention of going on without us, which was another thing that really upset me. We're talking about the country's most popular and prestigious sports league, and in one week it went from fielding some of the greatest athletes around to guys who wouldn't survive past the first cut in training camp. And those players received first-class treatment from their teams, being bused to and from practices and games under super-tight security. I guess the Management Council was afraid that those of us honoring the strike just might try to "pick" a few of those scabs. For the most part, though, all we did was shout nasty things at them, and some threw eggs at the bus as it crossed our line.

Unfortunately, the scab games counted toward our overall record. With Willie Totten at quarterback, *we* ended up winning one (against the New York Giants) and losing two (against Indianapolis, which had a "real" quarterback in Gary Hogeboom, and New England), and our overall record fell to 2–3.

Probably the most fun I had during the strike was when we picketed outside Rich before the "Counterfeit Bills" took on the Colts. Some guy came over and started heckling us pretty good while holding up a big sign that said, "Down With the Players!" He kept screaming and yelling and it wasn't long before we all got tired of his act.

So I came up with a little plan to silence the guy. First, I walked around behind him, whistling nonchalantly and looking the other way so he wouldn't notice me. Then, just as the guy was in the middle of saying something obnoxious, I grabbed the sign right out of his hands and smashed it into about a million pieces.

He was too shocked to do any more heckling or, for that matter, even utter a sound. He just stood there with his eyes and mouth wide open for several seconds, then quietly walked away.

Obviously, everyone could have just kept playing and not lost a cent. But we Bills players decided we would stick together and do whatever the majority wanted to do even if we didn't agree with the strike. The majority wanted to strike, so we struck. The most important thing was staying unified as a team in any action we took because we all knew the whole silly thing would end at some point and we'd all go back and play. And if we became too divided while we were on the outside, that could make things pretty tense and uncomfortable once we were inside again.

Our slogan was: "Everything we do, we do as a team. We went out as a team; we'll go back as a team."

Two of the older veterans, Joe Devlin and Fred Smerlas, took it upon themselves to organize meetings, picketing and, most important, the practices that had to be held away from Rich Stadium. They had gone through the 1982 players strike, which also began after the second week of the regular season. They remembered that the Bills had gotten off to a good start, just as we did in 1987. And they remembered that, as soon as the strike began, everybody went their separate ways. Some teams just completely forgot about football and acted as if they were on vacation for about eight weeks. Then, when they came back to work later in the season, they weren't prepared to play again and wound up collapsing at the end. Meanwhile, the teams that had stuck together the whole time and worked out on a regular basis made the playoffs.

We were so determined not to collapse that we practiced an average of four times per week. Everybody, including yours truly, showed up on a regular basis. I tried to take as active a role as possible to help us maintain unity. If I was going to be an effective team leader for the whole season and years to come, I couldn't very well turn my back on something that involved the majority of players. There were a lot of people who speculated that I might lose interest or, because I was losing so much money, I might just cross the line. Then a bunch of guys would follow and a bunch wouldn't and all hell would break loose.

I'd be lying if I said I didn't think about going in. But I knew I wouldn't be doing the right thing for the team and our hopes of turning the corner. A couple of veterans who did cross were running back Robb Riddick and fullback Carl Byrum. They were followed by two rookies, tight end Keith McKeller and defensive end Leon Seals.

It pissed me off to see those guys break from the ranks. They said they had their reasons—that they did it because they were losing too much money and had too many bills to pay. But we all were losing money. We all had bills to pay. And the money I was losing and the bills I had to pay were a hell of a lot more than theirs or anybody else's on the team.

Everybody who stayed out on strike was pissed off at those guys. We kept saying, over and over, "Stick together . . . Do everything as a team . . . Everybody stays out or everybody goes in." We said those things until we were hearing them in our sleep.

And they weren't being said just to be said. They had meaning. The guys who decided to leave the group to play just so they could get a paycheck were being selfish. They weren't thinking about the feelings of everyone else on the team.

Luckily, the rest of us didn't have the same sense of panic and desperation at that point. Of course, had the strike lasted longer than four weeks, who knows what would have happened?

After the strike ended, some of the scab players wound up staying with the team. Although I didn't like seeing those guys take our jobs, I realized they were just capitalizing on an opportunity that probably wouldn't have come their way otherwise. Unlike the players who had been on strike, then walked in early, they didn't make any commitments or break any promises with the rest of us. I even ended up becoming good friends with one of them, an offensive lineman named Tony Brown from the University of Pittsburgh.

There were a couple of other players who had stayed out for the duration who didn't have the same understanding when it came to the replacement players. And like me, they were upset with the guys who had gone back in on their own.

Sensing that little bit of tension still lingering in the locker room, Devlin and Smerlas called everybody together for a players-only meeting to clear the air. And the main point they made was, "There aren't any more scabs on this team. We're all Buffalo Bills now. So let's bury the hatchet and get going in the right direction."

I looked around the room and saw a lot of heads nodding. Along with mine. I had every intention of doing all that I could to help us maintain our team concept, which meant not allowing the strike or anything that had happened during those four weeks to affect my performance.

I still considered some of the players who crossed the line my friends. But deep down, I'll always remember what they did.

Our first game after the strike was against the Dolphins at Joe Robbie Stadium. Before we knew what hit us, we were behind 21–0 in the second quarter. We didn't get on the scoreboard until Scott Norwood hit a 41-yard field goal in the final second of the first half.

But at halftime, the talk was upbeat. We knew it wasn't a fluke that we had scored a combined 62 points against the Jets and Oilers. We knew we were a much better offense than we had shown through those first thirty minutes that day. We weren't convinced that all the effort to make sure we had remained in one piece over the previous three weeks had been a waste of time.

And we went out and proved it. Third-quarter touchdown drives of 67 and 45 yards pulled us to within four points before the Dolphins got a field goal in the fourth quarter to make it 24–17. After Miami's Scott Schwedes lost the ball on punt and kickoff returns, Riddick scored his second and third touchdowns of the game to give us our first lead, 31–24. Just when I thought I could enjoy our second-half revival (in which I went 18 of 23 for 244 yards and two TDs), Dan Marino found Mark Clayton for a 12-yard touchdown in the last minute to force overtime. From that point on, I knew that anytime Marino was on the other side, the game was never over until the last tick of the clock.

We won the coin toss, giving us first crack at bringing sudden death to the Dolphins. I threw 18-yard passes to Chris Burkett and Andre Reed on the first and third plays of our eight-play drive to quickly move into Dolphin territory. After three runs by Riddick and one by Harmon, Marv decided to go for the field goal on second down. Scotty connected from 27 yards and, at 3–3, the Bills had their best start since 1983.

Boy, did we ever need that!

We also needed what we received the following weekend, when Bill Polian pulled off one of the biggest trades in NFL history to acquire Cornelius Bennett from the Colts. The star linebacker from Alabama had been the number-two overall choice of the 1987 draft, but the Colts wouldn't come up with the money to sign him. The Bills would. And that led to the amazing three-way deal that unfolded like this: (1) We gave the Colts our first-round draft pick in 1988, first- and second-round picks in 1989 and my housemate, Greg Bell; (2) the Colts gave us Cornelius, then took all our choices, combined them with their own first- and second-round picks in '88 and a second-rounder in '89, Bell and running back Owen Gill, and shipped the whole thing to the Los Angeles Rams; (3) the Rams sent running back Eric Dickerson to Indianapolis. Got that?

Bennett was the third part of a rookie defensive face lift that began when we made another linebacker, Shane Conlan, our first-round pick from Penn State, and a cornerback, Nate Odomes, a second-round choice from Wisconsin. Shane had already established himself as someone who could stuff the run. Now, with Cornelius, we had a great pass rusher to complement Bruce Smith.

Biscuit (Bennett's nickname going back to his healthy appetite for biscuits and gravy when he was a kid) wasn't quite ready to play the day after the trade, when we hosted Washington. And he was lucky. The Redskins dogged us, 27–7.

The following week, Biscuit was on the field when we faced Denver at home. This time, we were the lucky ones. On his first play, he blitzed John Elway into throwing incomplete. On his second play, he forced Elway to run for his life out of bounds. On his third, the Broncos ran a sweep away from him. On his fourth, they were penalized for holding him. And on his fifth play, thirty minutes into his pro football career, Cornelius was drawing the ultimate compliment for a pass rusher: double-team blocking.

He finished the game with four tackles, including a sack in the fourth quarter. We raced to a 21–0 lead and hung on for a 21–14 win.

After losing at Cleveland a week later, we beat the Jets at New Jersey, 17–14, and the Dolphins at home, 27–0. The win over the Jets snapped a seven-game losing streak to them. In pitching a rare shutout against Miami, our defense ended Marino's string of consecutive games with a touchdown pass at 30. It also held him to only 13 completions in 28 attempts for 165 yards, and picked off three of his passes. Danny's extra-long day ended in the fourth quarter, when Don Strock took over.

If any game indicated how far we had come as a team, that was it. The whole defense was performing so much better than at any point since the beginning of the 1986 season. And the reason was clear: With players like Conlan and Bennett disrupting everything and drawing more attention from blockers, that opened things up for everyone else. It also pumped everybody up, including those of us on offense.

Now we had a 6–5 record and we were feeling very good about ourselves. We knew, without a doubt, that Ralph Wilson was committed to winning. He was delivering on his promise to get those "right" players necessary for us to be a Super Bowl team. He was determined to build a champion.

The Raiders took away some of that joy when we traveled to Los Angeles and suffered a 34–21 defeat. But after we rebounded with a 27–3 victory at Indianapolis—with our defense stuffing the Colts' running game and not allowing them to convert a single third down in ten tries—we were in a position not only to make the playoffs but also to win our first AFC East title since 1980. All we had to do was win our last two games of the season, against New England at Rich and the Eagles at Philadelphia.

We had the talent to get the job done. The question was: Did we have the maturity?

The answer flashed on the scoreboard seven days later: Patriots 13, Bills 7. We couldn't get anything going on offense. Our only points came on a 14-yard fumble recovery and return by defensive end Sean McNanie. We had a chance to score in the last five minutes with a fourth down at the Patriots' 4-yard line. But free safety Fred Marion, my former Hurricanes teammate turned NFL nemesis, intercepted me at the goal line. That snapped a streak of 141 consecutive attempts without an interception. Also ended were my streaks for consecutive USFL/NFL games in which I completed at least 50 percent of my passes (60) and for consecutive NFL games with at least one touchdown throw (18).

The loss, coupled with wins by Miami and Indianapolis, kept the Bills out of the playoffs for the sixth straight year.

We also lost the season finale to the Eagles, giving us a 7–8 record. The one bright spot that day was Cornelius. He made 17 tackles, sacking Randall Cunningham four times and forcing three fumbles. It was further proof of his tremendous impact on our defense. Through the four nonstrike games without Cornelius, we gave up an average of 30 points per contest; in the eight games with him, we allowed only half that amount. Through the four nonstrike games without Cornelius, we only had eight sacks; in the eight games with him, we had 22.

I was happy with my own progress, too. Ted Marchibroda had a positive influence on me and won my respect with his knowledge about the mechanics of quarterbacking, which helped me complete 59.7 percent of 419 passes for 2,798 yards and 19 touchdowns while throwing only 11 interceptions. The completion percentage broke the team record I set the year before. But there wasn't a whole lot Ted could do about our offensive *philosophy;* that was controlled by Jim Ringo. And what bothered me about our philosophy was that we were becoming too predictable. We'd run on first down, run on second down, throw on third down.

Every single time.

I loved Jim Ringo. I thought he was one of the greatest guys around. But we didn't see eye to eye in terms of our offensive philosophies. I believed you should mix things up, you should always try to keep the other team off balance and guessing at what you'll spring on them next. But as long as Ringo was calling the shots for our offense, I was going to do things his way. He was the boss.

Still, I had no doubt about our continued growth into a playoff team. We were turning the corner. After years of being the butt of a lot of jokes, the Bills were finally gaining some respect.

In the 1988 draft, Bill Polian and Marv Levy found more pieces to the championship puzzle we were trying to assemble.

The Bennett trade left us without a number-one pick, so they used our second-round choice wisely and took running back Thurman Thomas from Oklahoma State. Greg Bell was gone, Robb Riddick was getting older and Ronnie Harmon had yet to emerge as a major force in the backfield. So, after a great college career, Thurman was expected to have a big impact right away.

Two other draft picks who had the coaches excited were eighth-rounder Jeff Wright, who was seen as Fred Smerlas's eventual replacement at nose tackle, and ninth-rounder Carlton Bailey, an inside linebacker with a lot of promise.

Then, just before training camp, we got another break when we acquired defensive end Art Still in a trade with the Chiefs. Art was thirty-two and entering his eleventh season in the league. He had played for Marv when Marv was the head coach in Kansas City. He had been to the Pro Bowl four times. And Marv and Walt Corey, our defensive coordinator, who had also coached Art in Kansas City, thought he had enough good miles left to help our run defense in a big way at left end. If they were right, considering the players already on our roster, we would have the makings of a pretty strong defensive team—maybe one of the strongest in the NFL.

Offensively, we were leaning toward the conservative approach that Coach Ringo favored. The idea was to stop teams with a dominating defense and keep the ball away from them with a run-oriented, ball-control offense. I loved to throw the ball, of course. I wanted to throw it as often as possible. But winning was, is and always will be my top priority. So if he and Marv believed at that time that a run-oriented philosophy would help us win more games, I was all for it.

A lot of people thought our regular-season opener at home against Minnesota was a preview of what they'd see at Miami five months later in Super Bowl XXIII. The Vikings were considered the top guns of the NFC. We were picked by many as a contender for the AFC crown.

Two days before the game, we received what looked like a major blow when it was announced that Bruce Smith would be suspended for the first four games for violating the NFL's substance-abuse policy. It had started out as a normal Friday, with everyone showing up for meetings, to be followed by practice— everyone, that is, except Bruce. As the morning progressed, whispers could be heard around the locker room about what had happened to him. But no one was saying anything official.

We walked out to the practice field, and there was still no official word. But the whispering continued and became more widespread throughout the team. Finally, Coach Levy called all of us into a circle at midfield and confirmed the bad news: Bruce wasn't going to be with us for the Vikings game or the next three after that.

Even though some guys had already overcome the initial shock, there were still a few comments like "Oh, shit!" and "I don't believe this!"

By the time we started practicing, however, I noticed a different attitude. Now guys were saying, "He's only one player. Hey, if we have to play without him, we have to play without him." I didn't see us getting down at all. In fact, I saw us getting even more pumped up about the game. Going against a tough opponent while missing one of our key players, we knew we were all going to have to work a little bit harder. And just as when a starter suffers an injury, it was up to the next man on the depth chart to step in and do the job. In this case, the man was Leon Seals.

Once Bruce's suspension became public later that day, media and fans were quick to jump all over his case, saying he had been selfish and was letting the team and the whole city down at a critical moment. But I wasn't mad at Bruce. I didn't get a sense that anybody on the team was angry with him or accusing him of letting us down or anything of the sort. In a situation like that, people are sometimes dealing with a disease and need help. If being out for four weeks was what it would take for Bruce to get help, then that was fine. We all wanted to see him get through the suspension, get back into the lineup and do his part to get us to the Super Bowl.

At that moment, though, someone else had to pull Bruce's load. Soon after Coach Levy's announcement, player after player walked up to Leon and gave him a reassuring pat on the back.

"This is your big opportunity to show what you can do," I said to him. "We know you can do it, we're behind you a hundred percent. Now let's go for it!"

Filling Bruce's cleats at right end wasn't going to be easy; everybody understood that. At the same time, one of the things that make a team a champion is having more than a few backups who can hold their own as starters. And Leon and the rest of the defense truly rose to the occasion against the Vikings, beginning with an interception by Bennett that set up a Scott Norwood field goal from 27 yards.

Thomas ran five yards for a touchdown to give us a 10–0 lead late in the first quarter, then Chuck Nelson hit a 30-yard field goal to make it 10–3 at halftime. A mishandled punt by Bucky Scribner set up a 26-yard Norwood field goal to put us in front, 13–3, in the fourth quarter. But things got a little hairy after the Vikings drove 74 yards for a touchdown, cutting our advantage to 13–10. They got the ball at their 24 with three minutes left and, after picking up 12 yards on first down, they were stopped on three straight pass attempts, including a big sack by my good buddy Hal Garner that forced a punt. That gave us six sacks for the day, with Still and Smerlas getting two apiece. Leon also played well, moving and hitting everything in sight.

After the punt, Thomas ripped off a 28-yard run to help kill the clock and preserve our three-point victory. We paid a price, though. Tim Vogler, our veteran right guard, suffered a knee injury that would sideline him for several weeks. As a result, there was some major shuffling up front, with Will Wolford moving from left tackle, which was where he was destined to play as a rookie guard, to right guard and Leonard Burton, a backup with little experience, taking over for Will. Again, it was time for someone to step to the fore when we really needed it.

In Week Two, Norwood provided all of our points and the defense stonewalled Marino on four consecutive passes late in the game in a 9–6 victory over Miami at Rich. Then we traveled to Foxboro, Massachusetts, for what figured to be another tight contest; the Bills hadn't beaten the Patriots since 1981. And the Pats thought they were going to extend that winning streak after taking a 14–3 halftime lead. But Norwood hit a 44-yard field goal late in the third quarter. And early in the fourth, I led us on a 66-yard drive that ended with a three-yard touchdown pass to Riddick to make it 14–13.

The Patriots punted and we got the ball at our own 48 with two minutes left. A couple of passes and a couple of runs moved us to their 23, then I heaved the ball away to stop the clock with 11 seconds left. Out came Scotty for a 41-yard field goal to pull out another one for us, 16–14.

Our defense was strong, but it became even stronger two days after the New England game when we picked up Leonard Smith, a hard-hitting strong safety, in a trade with Phoenix. He brought the intimidation factor to our secondary that would give opposing wide receivers something to think about while running their patterns—something besides catching the ball. They always had to look around to see if Leonard was lurking somewhere, ready to take their heads off.

Next we were home to face my boys from Pittsburgh again. And after our 36–28 victory over the Steelers, we had a 4–0 record. The Bills hadn't won their first four games since 1980.

Our credibility was as strong as ever. But we knew it could get a hell of a lot stronger if we beat the Bears, who were 3–1, at Soldier Field. We had Bruce back, so there was a lot of confidence that, as well as we did without him, we'd do even better with him. Unfortunately, the Bears had other ideas. After they jumped to a 7–3 lead in the first quarter, they scored the next 17 points and sent us home with our first loss of the season, 24–3. Jim McMahon was fantastic, completing 20 of 27 passes for 260 yards and two touchdowns. Between Vogler's injury and the body shuffling it caused, our offensive line had a long day against Dan Hampton and Richard Dent. I had an even longer one, being sacked six times.

As we walked off the field, some Bears players told us we were the best team they had faced all year. But that was small consolation. We really wanted to win that game and convince the rest of the NFL to take us seriously as a Super Bowl contender.

In worrying about that, however, we forgot to take the Colts seriously when they visited Rich in Week Six. Watching them build a 17–7 halftime lead did wonders for our memory. With Bruce and Tim Vogler back in the lineup (and Will back where he belonged at left tackle), we knew there was no excuse for us to have fallen that far behind. So did the fans. And, boy, did they let us know it! I hadn't heard booing that loud during any of our previous home games, including the six we lost in 1986. But I guess we deserved a little grief.

The locker room was not a happy place at halftime. We had lost a big game the week before to a top-level team. Now, we were looking like a bunch of stumblebums against the Colts. Maybe it was because we were thinking too much about the previous week's disappointment. Maybe it was because we weren't pumped up or excited enough to play against a team that came into the game with a 1–4 record.

Whatever the reason, we had thirty minutes to make it change. So I thought it was time to speak up.

"We're playing like shit," I said. "We're picking up where we left off against the Bears. So let's get our asses in gear and wake up. We're a hell of a lot better team than we've been showing here today."

I definitely knew I was a better quarterback.

Ted Marchibroda came up to me with Polaroid snapshots of some of the things the Colts had been showing defensively and giving us problems with in the first half. Nine times out of ten, we'll look those over and Ted, working with the help of the bird's-eye view of the camera lens, will point out the things we need to adjust in the second half. But this time I told him, "I don't need to look at the pictures. I know what I'm doing wrong."

And what I was doing wrong was trying to force too many of my passes to make the big play rather than going to the receiver I was supposed to go to. The more mistakes I made, the harder I tried to force the issue and the deeper I fell into a rut. I knew it was just a matter of settling myself down. I also knew that once I got my game straightened out, everyone else on offense and defense would probably do the same. It has to start with the quarterback.

Sure enough, the struggling I had gone through the first two quarters stopped. I went on to have what would be my best day of the season, completing 21 of 39 passes for 315 yards and three touchdowns. The defense also turned things around. After allowing 229 yards in the first half, it gave up only 79 in the final two quarters and we won, 34–23.

We saw our ability to bounce back like that as a definite sign of the kind of maturity that was lacking in '87.

The first reward for the improvement we showed the previous season came on October 17, when we appeared on *Monday Night Football*—something the Bills hadn't done since 1984—to face the Jets at the Meadowlands. I couldn't have been more excited. From the time I was a kid, you could always find me parked in front of the television set for ABC's NFL game of the week. I even liked Howard Cosell. *Monday Night Football* was a big deal around our house, and now I was actually going to play on it.

My long-standing pregame ritual of throwing up just before we took the field had continued through the '86 season and the first three quarters of the '87 season. But late in '87, it stopped for some reason. I don't know why, but it just wasn't happening and still wasn't happening through the first six games of '88. I was a little bit uncomfortable about that, because usually after I threw up, I'd have a great game.

When the coach called us together for the team prayer just before we took the field that night against the Jets, I suddenly ran to the bathroom. As I did, Kent Hull turned to Frank Reich and said, "Well, I think we're going to have a big night tonight."

He was absolutely right.

It turned out to be one of those games that we grabbed by the throat from the opening kickoff and never let go. I shocked the Jets early with a 65-yard touchdown pass to Andre, followed by a 66-yard TD strike to Flip Johnson. We knew it was going to be our night when Flip made the catch after the ball was tipped right into his hands by the intended receiver, Riddick. We scored on all of our first five possessions, Bruce Smith made 2 1/2 sacks and we rolled to a 37–14 triumph.

Watching the game on film the next day was even more unbelievable. You'd see plays where Jets defenders weren't even blocked and Thurman would still be able to rip off huge gains. It was just one of those nights that was the complete opposite of Murphy's Law—everything that could possibly go right for us did.

After that came another toe-to-toe game with New England at home. And as in the last one, Norwood's toe made the difference, as he kicked a 33-yard field goal with 13 seconds left to give us a 23–20 victory. Then, while hosting Green Bay seven days later, our defense got into the scoring act. Free safety Mark Kelso returned an interception 78 yards for one score and Seals returned a fumble seven yards for another as we defeated the Packers, 28–0. The defense came up big again the week after that when we traveled to Seattle for a 13–3 win over the Seahawks. It was the second game in a row in which we didn't allow a touchdown.

With six weeks left in the regular season, we had a 3½-game lead in the division and a 9–1 record. All we had to do was beat our next two opponents—the Dolphins and Jets—and the AFC East championship was ours for the first time in eight years.

My passing arm hadn't been an overwhelming factor in the three previous weeks. Through that stretch, I averaged 19 throws per game and had completed only two for touchdowns. Even the "K" cards disappeared.

But I wasn't complaining. I always considered myself a team player. You start complaining when you're 9–1 and you've got some serious problems. As long as we're winning, there's nothing to complain about.

"Even though he has some ego and it sometimes shows," Marv said of me, "he's a very unselfish football player."

We made the Miami game look easy, scoring a 31–6 win on Monday night at Joe Robbie Stadium. That marked the first time the Bills ever won four straight against the Dolphins, who had once held a 20-game winning streak against Buffalo. It also set up the showdown six days later against the Jets at Rich with an eight-year drought for the division title on the line.

Unlike the first time the teams met in the '88 season, this was a game where both teams scratched, clawed and punched for every inch. The Jets weren't going to give us a thing that day; we were going to have to take it from them—by force. Both teams were playing so hard and it was such a physical game that neither offense could ever get anything going beyond four or five plays. It just seemed like we were constantly running into a brick wall. After a while, when we came off the field, I could see that the wear and tear was starting to get to our linemen. Those guys were just thoroughly exhausted.

And when the fourth quarter rolled around, we were tied, 6–6.

After that, we blew two chances to move in front. On the first, Scotty hit the crossbar on a 47-yard field-goal attempt. On the second, I connected with tight end Pete Metzelaars for a 35-yard gain that put us at the New York 25. But on the next play Thomas was separated from the ball and the Jets recovered at their 30. Ten plays later, they were on our 23, setting up what would have been the winning field goal by Pat Leahy from 40 yards with 25 seconds left.

But Smerlas, hardly known for his leaping ability with that jukebox-like body of his, managed to jump high enough to get his left forearm in front of the ball. My first thought was that we still had a few seconds left to try to win the game in regulation. We were at our own 30, I took the snap and when I couldn't find anyone open, I started to run with the ball. The clock had expired, but I was still looking to make something happen. So around midfield, I turned to lateral to Will Wolford, our 300-pound offensive tackle. But Will didn't catch it, and after the ball hit the ground, he pounced on it—and about eight Jets pounced on Will.

When he finally got back on his feet, I got in his face.

"Why didn't you catch it?" I yelled. "What's the matter with you? You catch that ball and run for a touchdown and this game's over."

Will looked at me like I was crazy.

"You've got to be kidding," he said. "You really expected *me* to run fifty yards for a touchdown? I think you've been watching too many films of California versus Stanford."

But I was serious. No matter how much time is left or how far away we are from the end zone, if we need points, I'm going to try to get them any way I possibly can. Who knows? Maybe, if Will had caught the ball, he could have run with it a little bit, then lateralled to somebody else. And that guy could have lateralled to somebody else. And maybe we'd have been in the end zone—just like California in that incredible comeback win over Stanford in 1982 when, as time expired, the Golden Bears lateralled five times while fighting their way through the Stanford band for a touchdown. You just never know.

The Jets had possession first in overtime, but lost it when

fullback Roger Vick was stripped by cornerback Derrick Burroughs. Bennett recovered at the Jets' 32, I handed off to Riddick four times to move us to the 20 and Scotty hit one of the biggest field goals of his life, from 30 yards, to give us a 9–6 victory.

The moment the ball sailed through the uprights, thousands of fans were over the wall and on the field, looking for some goalposts to take home. "Fan-demonium" had broken out everywhere. And a lot of players ran for the tunnel as fast as they could before the crush of bodies broke one of them.

I had never seen anything like it. I mean, it was like a human sea out there. And some guys got caught right in the middle of it. Those who had the hardest time reaching the tunnel were the ones who had been on the field for the winning kick and spent a little too long jumping up and down in celebration. Will was among them. By the time he started heading toward the tunnel, the crowd was at its thickest. And as large as he was, Will couldn't avoid being swallowed up by it. In fact, he was so packed in, he lost control of his own movement. For almost twenty seconds he was caught in the wave of bodies, and it actually started taking him in directions he didn't want to go.

With the temperature rising, it became harder and harder for him to breathe. So Will kind of flipped out and started grabbing people and throwing them out of his way. That allowed him to regain control and get to the tunnel to join the rest of us, who were just standing there and watching in amazement as a thick layer of fog—from the cold night air mixing with all that body heat—formed over the stadium.

I already had a pretty good idea of how important the Bills were to Buffalo, but that scene told me something else. It told me that the fans weren't happy just to have a pro football team in their town. They wanted a team they could be proud of. They had waited a long time for something to celebrate—something besides the end of the season. Finally, they had a legitimate reason to sing the club's theme song, "Shout!," which echoed throughout the stadium.

But we also had a larger goal in mind, like playing in Super Bowl XXIII.

The next step was to clinch home-field advantage through the playoffs. With four games left, we felt pretty good about our chances. That is, until we took the field at Cincinnati without two of our defensive starters, Conlan and Burroughs, whose foot and ankle injuries were casualties of our war with the Jets. As if that weren't enough, a third key member of the defense, linebacker Darryl Talley, limped off the field on the first play with a thigh bruise.

Trying to fill one hole was one thing. Trying to fill two was another. But three? That was asking a lot. As it turned out, it was asking too much. We fell behind, 21–0, in the second quarter. From there it became a scramble that we ended up losing, 35–21, to a Bengal team that was playing at the top of its game.

In Week Fourteen, we were off to Tampa Bay to face the 3–10 Buccaneers. Despite their record, they had a defense that, when hitting on all cylinders, was good enough to play with anybody. On this day, it was hitting on all cylinders. And it definitely was good enough to play with us.

The Bucs mounted a pair of long drives to build a 10–0 half-time lead. We could only manage five points the rest of the way, as I was intercepted twice and Riddick was stopped on three plunges for the goal line. Besides the game, we also lost Vogler for good with the same knee trouble that sidelined him earlier in the year.

People began to wonder whether we were headed for trouble at that point, whether we were taking a late-season dive that would cost us a chance to reach our ultimate goal. But there were still two regular-season games left, which meant it was too early to raise any white flags. I certainly wasn't giving up on anything.

A week later, the Los Angeles Raiders visited Rich Stadium. The temperature was 11 degrees, with a windchill of minus 14, making it the coldest day the Bills ever played. Before I joined the Bills, I had talked about wanting to maintain the warm-weather career I began in college, and, of course, the Raiders were my top choice on that count. But the more time I spent in Buffalo, the more I came to realize that freezeball was perfect for us. In fact, I like to call what we were having that day "Bills weather," because it's something we're used to and it's something that warm-blooded opponents from the West or the South usually can't handle.

The Raiders were in trouble the instant they reached the end of the tunnel and grabbed a breath of our nice, fresh December air. That, plus a powerful running game that saw us rush for 255 yards, resulted in our 37–21 win.

"Bills weather" applies to our fans, too. They aren't the least bit afraid of the cold and snow. If anything, they thrive on it. They like the opposing team and the few opposing fans brave enough to buy a ticket to know that they're tough enough to sit through anything Mother Nature can dish out. In fact, the crowd for the Raider game was 77,438, which gave us 622,793 for the year and allowed us to break the NFL's single-season attendance record. When you consider the climate and that Buffalo is the second-smallest market in the league, it was an amazing accomplishment to say the least. Congratulations, fans.

The final regular-season game was against the Colts, who had already been eliminated from the playoffs, at the Hoosier Dome. It looked like we had things pretty well in hand when I threw a six-yard touchdown pass to Andre to give us a 14–3 lead with 12 minutes left in the game. But after Gary Hogeboom took over for injured Chris Chandler at quarterback, the Colts drove 80 yards for a TD to cut the margin to 14–10. After that, we were forced to punt, and Hogeboom took the Colts on a 75-yard scoring march to move them ahead, 17–14. With 1:10 remaining, we got the ball back and drove as far as the Indianapolis 46. But on fourth down, I was sacked.

So were our hopes of gaining home-field advantage throughout the playoffs.

It was easy to take a negative view of our season. We lost three of our last four games. We were beaten by one team (Tampa Bay) that we had no business losing to, another (Indianapolis) that we led by 11 points in the fourth quarter. We put ourselves in the difficult position of having to go through someone else's backyard to get to the Super Bowl.

But we also had a 12–4 record. That placed us among the three winningest teams in the NFL that year and gave us almost as many victories as in the three previous seasons combined. We were division champs. We had the No. 1-ranked defense in the AFC.

Our offense? Like I said, we were winning, so it was hard to bitch. And it wasn't a matter of my not liking the fact that we ran a lot; that didn't bother me as much as the fact that we were too predictable.

Although we would likely be on the road for the AFC Championship Game, the divisional-round match was at home, on New Year's Day 1989, against Houston. It was the first postseason football game in Buffalo in twenty-two years. And it felt like the whole city was going to pop. Everywhere you went around town that week, that's all people talked about: the Bills versus the Oilers. It seemed like no matter where I drove, I'd look out my window and see a Bills flag, a Bills banner or a Bills sign. Not just in front of homes, but businesses and schools as well. The entire area was caught up in playoff fever. It reminded me of the way Louisville gets just before the Kentucky Derby (which I try to attend every year). For that one week, there just wasn't anything else around Buffalo that came close to being as important as the Bills versus the Oilers. Even the New Year celebration seemed to take a back seat.

If a player walked into a restaurant or a bar, the red carpet was always rolled out for him. People—either those who ran the establishments or other customers who were there—wouldn't let us pay for a thing. The linemen would go into Denny's for breakfast, and the waitress would pile extra food on their plates and smile and say, "This is on the house—we want to make sure you're well-nourished enough for the big game." Great as the hospitality had been from most Western New Yorkers since I had arrived in the area, it seemed to be even greater that week. It was unbelievable.

At the same time, because it had been so long since the Bills were a winning team, you could sense—listening to some of the radio call-in shows and the way the media was talking—a little bit of doubt as to how far we would actually go in the playoffs. People were excited that we had won the division and were still playing past Christmas. But it was almost as if they were prepared for the party to come to an abrupt end, saying things like, "Hey, no matter what happens from here on out, they've given us a great season" . . . "They've given us our money's worth" . . . "They're a young team that's only going to get better" . . . "Wait 'til next year."

But that wasn't the attitude of the players at all. We believed in ourselves. We were convinced we were in the postseason for the long haul. We weren't satisfied with anything we had accomplished at that point.

Jerry Glanville was the Oilers' coach at the time and he had them playing that chippy, dirty style he likes so much, especially on defense. Several of us reminded the officials of that before the game. Either they would keep the Oilers in line . . . or we would take matters into our own hands. The last thing you ever want to do in a football game is allow the opponent to intimidate you. Once that happens, you don't have a prayer. They've gotten inside your head and they'll never come out. What you always have to remember is that cheap-shotting is a two-way street, and whatever one team starts, the other can finish. But cheap shots should not be a part of any sport.

We weren't going to have Conlan, which was a big loss. But we didn't let it become a distraction. In fact, we immediately grabbed momentum when Leonard Smith blocked a punt to set up a one-yard touchdown run by Robb Riddick that gave us a 7–0 advantage in the second quarter. Big special-teams plays have a way of lighting a fire under everyone's butt. Six minutes later, Tony Zendejas hit a 35-yard field goal, but when he tried another just before halftime, from 38 yards, Bruce Smith got in front of it. We increased our lead to 11 points in the third quarter on Thurman Thomas's 10-yard touchdown run. And an interception by Mark Kelso set up a 27-yard Norwood field goal to put us up, 17–3, early in the fourth. After that, the Oilers could manage only one more score, a one-yard TD run by Mike Rozier. And that was it.

For my first NFL playoff action, I was pleased with my performance. Surprisingly, we didn't play it too close to the vest. I threw 33 times, connecting on 17 for 244 yards. I couldn't deny that I was happy about the more wide-open strategy and the confidence the coaches showed in our passing game to loosen things up in a do-or-die situation. It looked like we were turning aggressive at just the right time.

Next was the AFC Championship Game at Riverfront Stadium, site of our embarrassing loss to the Bengals in November. I'll never forget how excited we all were—players, coaches, fans —about being one step away from the Super Bowl. It was the first time we had ever traveled to a city two days beforehand. Ordinarily, we arrive the night before and leave immediately after the game. But this was no ordinary trip. The NFL wants the visiting club in town forty-eight hours in advance so it can hype the game to the hilt in the media.

I had to appear at a Friday night press conference in the ballroom of a hotel that was jammed with hundreds of reporters. It was the largest media gathering I had faced since the press conference for my arrival in Buffalo in 1986. Being in the national spotlight for the first time was exciting. So was the thought of standing on the doorstep of the Super Bowl. We were getting our first taste of what it was like to be an elite team in the NFL.

It was delicious.

It was also our first experience with having our hotel packed with Buffalo fans. On most of the road trips before then, we pretty much had the hotel to ourselves. This time, however, we were joined by all kinds of Bills supporters. They were everywhere—the lobby, the restaurants, the gift shops, the elevators, the escalators—and it made getting around the hotel a little hectic. After a while, I did the best I could to stay in my room and only go out when I had to, like for meetings, practice and the game.

But it was great to know we had that kind of support in "hostile" territory.

Actually, Boomer Esiason tried to ease some of that hostility by inviting me to his house, along with Frank and a few of our teammates, for dinner the night before the game. We had gone there the night before our regular-season meeting with the Bengals that year, and had a lot of fun. His wife, Cheryl, had cooked a great pasta dish, then all the boys went downstairs and played cards and pool until it was time to get back to the hotel for the eleven o'clock curfew.

Because of our embarrassing loss to the Bengals the next day, I decided to turn down the second invitation. It was nothing personal against Boomer; he was still one of my good friends and I appreciated being invited over for a nice home-cooked meal. But the way things turned out on the field the last time, I just thought it would be better to try something different and stay at the hotel. On our way to the airport in Buffalo for the chartered flight to Cincinnati, Frank called Boomer from my car phone to confirm the time and other details about the dinner because he and the others were still going. Then I grabbed the phone and, pretending to be mad, I told Boomer, "You can forget about me this time; thanks but no thanks." We joked back and forth a little, but he knew where I was coming from and was cool about it.

Looking back, maybe we were too excited for the game. Maybe we were a little too caught up in having advanced further than any Bills team since the AFL and NFL merged.

The first indication of that was when several of us headed over to the stadium about five hours before kickoff. Normally, most guys show up three hours before the moment of truth, which is always plenty of time for ankles and knees to be taped as well as for all the other standard pregame stuff. I could just tell that everybody in that locker room was really uptight. A lot of times that isn't such a bad way for a team to be before a big game, but only if you're able to control it and make it work to your advantage. If used correctly, it can help you keep your edge and avoid getting mentally lazy, which can happen when fatigue starts to set in.

But if it controls you, then you've got a serious problem because your concentration is shot. You're either too aggressive and end up making mistakes because you're not thinking about what you're doing, or you become so worried about not making a mistake that you forget the things you're supposed to do—and you end up blundering because of it.

Being a fairly young and inexperienced team, with no player having been in a game of that magnitude before, we definitely were letting our emotions control us that day.

I know I was overexcited. And I showed it in the first quarter by throwing two interceptions. The second resulted in a one-yard touchdown run by Ickey Woods to give the Bengals a quick 7–0 lead.

I did manage to keep my poise for the next possession, though, when I led us on a 56-yard drive that saw me hit four consecutive passes. The last throw was a nine-yard rollout to Andre to tie the score at 7–7 early in the second quarter. Soon thereafter, the Bengals ground out a 74-yard march that ended with Boomer's 10-yard TD pass to James Brooks. However, after a 39-yard field goal by Norwood, the margin was down to a hopeful four points at halftime. Hopeful, that is, until we went out for the second half and couldn't get a single thing going offensively. Our third-quarter output was a pathetic minus 12 yards. Even with Shane back in the lineup and performing well, the added pressure we, as an offense, placed on the defense was just too much for those guys to handle against a high-scoring team like Cincinnati.

Meanwhile, the Bengals used a fake punt to pick up another first down and proceeded to drive for seven more points to send us home with a 21–10 loss.

I didn't play well, completing only 14 of 30 passes for 163 yards and throwing three interceptions. The Bengals played us tough defensively. They weren't huge, but their guys loved to hit and they were very aggressive that day. David Fulcher, their great strong safety, was punishing receivers and making it hard for me to complete a pass. During pregame warmups, he had come up to me and said, "Come on, Jim. Quit being so greedy and throw me one today." Unfortunately, I complied and he killed our last drive by picking me off in the end zone on fourth down.

But their defense only stopped us to a certain point. Most of the time we stopped ourselves, with big mistakes. Because I didn't keep my composure the whole way, I forced a couple of passes that I normally wouldn't have forced. I was just trying to make the big play too many times. We had guys open and I wasn't making the throws when I had to make the throws.

I was embarrassed. I was disgusted. It was a horrible feeling to come out of a game of that magnitude with the knowledge that you didn't do anything to help your team win.

I wasn't alone, of course. And the loss itself wasn't the only nagging thought. In the end, we knew we hurt our chances for success by not securing home-field advantage when we had the chance. The fans at Rich would have been a tremendous plus, just as they were in our building a nine-game regular-season/postseason winning streak at home. You could just picture Boomer out there, struggling to hear himself think over the roar of 80,000 voices—and the rest of the Bengals' offense unable to hear his signals and audibles.

By the same token, all that noise does something incredible to us. We feed off of it. We begin to think we're invincible, unbeatable. The whole personality of the team is just so much more aggressive at home than it is on the road.

But crowd support isn't the only advantage to playing at Rich. There's also the psychological comfort of being in your own house for the weekend—except the night before the game, which we spend at a Buffalo-area hotel—with all your family and friends around. You don't get that feeling in a different city. Traveling throws your whole routine off.

Still, the bottom line in that 1988 AFC Championship Game was that maybe we didn't know yet what it took for us to go the distance. Maybe we didn't have quite as much maturity as we thought. One thing Marv always tells us is, "Champions win on the road."

7

Shouldering
the Load

WHEN I BUILT MY HOUSE in Orchard Park, my main concern was that my family would have a nice place to stay when they came to visit. I didn't want them checking into any hotel. The idea was to have them with me, not near me. I also wanted to provide them all the comforts of home—and then some.

With a family as large as ours, comfort begins with space. So that was why the house I built just before the 1988 season covered 7,500 square feet, including eight bedrooms, six bathrooms, a sauna, a steam room, two Jacuzzis and a finished basement. Not to mention the bocce court in the back designed by former pro wrestler Ilio DiPaolo, who owns a restaurant outside of Buffalo and is a great friend of just about everyone connected with the Bills.

Besides holidays, it usually takes a weekend home game to get all twenty of us in the Kelly clan together. Mom and Dad come up from East Brady, along with Uncle Ed and Aunt Toni from

Pittsburgh. My brothers Pat and Ray come up from Richmond, Ed from Texas. (Dan lives with me; Kevin has his own home in the Buffalo area.)

Everyone arrives by Friday, which, for a Sunday game, is our last full day of practice. Saturdays are always light—mostly special-teams work and review of a couple of basic plays—and some of the players bring their sons with them. Without a wife or children of my own, I've always brought along my oldest nephew, Pat's son Sean, who's nine. Now his brother, Brian, five, also comes with us.

We're at the stadium for an hour, maybe an hour and a half, and after that I go home. Dad, my five brothers and Uncle Ed are usually in front of the television watching college football. Mom, Aunt Toni and my sisters-in-law can usually be found cooking, if they aren't out shopping. Overall, it's just a day to sit back and relax. Of course, if there's enough snow on the ground, you can bet my brothers and their wives will head out to the Orchard Park tree nursery of our friends George and Debbie Schichtel and ride snowmobiles.

I'll join the boys to watch the games or shoot the breeze around the bar in the basement. The only bad part is, while everyone else is drinking beer, I'm drinking ice water; alcohol does not pass these lips within three days of a game.

"Kelly's Irish Pub" is etched on the large mirror behind the bar, which is wide enough for fourteen stools. After home games during the '88 season, I began inviting all my teammates and their families and friends, as well as other guests, to party in the "pub." I make sure there's plenty to eat and drink, and depending on the kind of shape I'm in from the game, I usually tend bar until about seven o'clock, when the bartenders arrive. Music blares from the four speakers of my sound system, and the two most popular spots—besides the bar—are the pool table (where there's always a challenge tournament that lasts well into the night) and a big-screen TV (where that day's game is shown on videotape).

All the players decided it was better for everyone to gather at my place after games than go out on the town and take the unnecessary risk of getting into trouble. Plus, it helps promote team harmony. The players can kick back, have a few laughs and spend time as friends rather than co-workers. It's the best way to get to know each other.

Our Saturday-night family ritual includes dinner, either at the house or at Ilio's restaurant, managed by his son, Dennis. After dinner, I leave my relatives at the house and head over to the Bills' hotel, where I spend the night with my teammates, coaches and club officials. The reason they want us at a hotel on the eve of a home game is that it allows us to have our usual Saturday-night team meeting and the coaches can make sure we're in our rooms by the eleven o'clock curfew.

For a couple of years, I would have breakfast at the hotel the next morning, drive back home to make sure my family was all set for the game, then leave for the stadium in a separate car. I'd make sure everyone had their tickets (and would make the necessary phone calls if any were missing). I'd also see to it that everyone was out the door early enough so they could get their parking spot for the pregame and postgame tailgate parties around the motor home; I only show up for the postgame edition. You could almost always count on the motor home getting ready to pull out of the driveway with at least one straggler somewhere in the house.

Once they were gone, I was left with barely forty-five minutes of peace and quiet to gather my thoughts for the game.

It wasn't anyone's fault but my own, of course. No one asked me to do it that way; I just took it upon myself to worry about all these other details on top of the responsibilities that go with leading a pro football team into battle. We Kellys put a lot of work into having fun, and tailgating takes a lot of planning to do right. We do all the cooking for the parties, which include not only family but friends, such as Father Phil Oriole from our church in East Brady.

After a couple of years, I changed my game-day routine. Now, after breakfast I go back up to my hotel room, relax in front of the TV for a while, then drive straight to the stadium. All the family hassles regarding tickets and whether everyone gets out of the house on time are left in the capable hands of my brother Danny and Tommy Good, a friend from Pittsburgh who handles odd jobs for me around the house and for the company I formed in 1988, Jim Kelly Enterprises.

Nevertheless, my main concern is to do everything possible to make my family happy. I worry about doing right by them, just as they worry about doing right by me. Even during games, we stay connected. After every touchdown pass I throw at Rich Stadium, I always point up to the luxury box I rent for my family or to our season seats in section C, aisle 2 and say, "That one's for you!"

If I ever get too full of myself, I can count on them to bring me back to earth. If I'm down, I can count on them to lift my spirits.

They are everything that a true family is supposed to be. And more.

After the 1988 season, Jim Ringo retired and Ted Marchibroda took over as our offensive coordinator.

As I've said, there was nothing wrong with the basic stuff in our playbook. It was just a question of how we used it. And by going with the approach we took with Coach Ringo, opposing defenses knew what to expect and were often exactly where they had to be to stop us. Despite his conservative reputation, Ted recognized this, too. He realized we had to mix things up in our play calling to get the most out of our offense, and he intended to have us do just that in 1989.

For me, it was the next-best thing to calling the plays myself.

I knew it was going to take a little time before we started to mesh completely as an offensive unit. But I also knew the wait wouldn't be very long. It was a matter of everyone staying poised—just keeping your patience while younger players continued to develop and a few holes were filled here and there. I felt very good about the direction our offense was headed.

We opened the 1989 preseason at the Pro Football Hall of Fame in Canton, Ohio. It was only the Bills' second trip there ever and my first since the summer after my junior year of high school, when I watched my brother Pat play in the annual Hall of Fame game. Just as I had hoped while sitting in the stands on that Saturday afternoon in 1977, my next visit to Canton was in an NFL uniform.

Although we got our butts whipped by the Redskins, 31–6, it was still a great experience to fulfill yet another of my dreams. Besides, Coach Levy doesn't place much emphasis on winning in the preseason anyway. That's why starters see limited action and we don't do any real game-planning. All he wants is to get through those meaningless games with everyone healthy and well rested for when we play for keeps.

We opened the regular season with a rare early road game at Miami. Usually, the NFL sends the Dolphins to our place at the beginning of the season, so they won't turn into "fish sticks," and it sends us to South Florida late in the season, when our bodies aren't prepared for the climate change. Chalk up another one to the power of Don Shula.

Anyhow, with 4:17 left on the clock, we were trailing, 24–13, and had the ball at our 18-yard line. Time for the two-minute drill.

Before I stepped onto the field, Marv Levy offered some advice on what plays I should run, but I told him he didn't have to bother.

"Coach, I've got it all," I said.

And I did know every call I would make because Ted had told me beforehand exactly what to do in certain situations. I kept that information in my mind and quickly moved us to the Dolphins' 26, from where I hit Flip Johnson for a touchdown to make it 24–20 with 2:50 remaining. On the ensuing drive, Dan Marino, faced with a third-and-10 from his 39, tried throwing for the first down. But Nate Odomes came up with his second interception of the game to give us the ball at our 49.

With 1:44 showing and no time-outs, I continued to call my own plays and passed us deep into Miami territory. After I connected with Andre Reed at the 2, there were a couple of seconds left, just enough time for one final snap. The play I signaled to the rest of the offense was a throw to Ronnie Harmon in the flat to my right. But we were in shotgun formation, and in shotgun the first key I read is the free safety, which in this case was a rookie named Louis Oliver. At first he was up by the middle of the line, but out of the corner of my eye, I noticed him drop back and drift to my left. And before the play even began, this giant hole, where Oliver once stood, was staring me in the face.

"I'm going for it," I said to myself.

Without ever looking for Harmon or any other receiver who might have been open in the end zone, I caught the long snap from Kent Hull and took off for that hole. Because I was lined up so deep, I had about eight yards to cover, which for me is like running a marathon. As I got closer to the goal line, I saw Oliver, who had a reputation for being a hard-hitter, closing in on me. I knew it would be a case of my putting my head down and fighting my way into the end zone. Somehow, I managed to cross the line as Oliver and linebacker David Frye rammed their helmets into both sides of my hip. (In fact, Oliver hit me so hard, he wound up leaving the field on a stretcher with a concussion.)

The next thing I knew, a pile of my teammates, with a combined weight of about 2,000 pounds, was on top of me celebrating the winning touchdown of our 27–24 victory. I was happy, too, having run for the first touchdown of my NFL career. I was sore as hell, especially on my sides, but happy. And I enjoyed sharing that great moment with them.

"Now, would you guys please get the hell off me!" I yelled. "I can't breathe down here."

The play shocked everyone in Joe Robbie Stadium, including all of my teammates and coaches. They were convinced I was going to throw, just as I had called beforehand. The linemen were even blocking for a pass, and the receivers flooded the end zone with the thought that one of them would have a chance to catch the game-winning ball. If I hadn't seen Oliver drop back, I definitely would have looked right for Harmon. But my instincts told me to run. I never thought about doing anything else.

I heard that after the game Shula walked into the Miami locker room with tears rolling down his face. That defeat was especially painful to him and everyone else on the Dolphins, because they were certain they had us beaten. Everyone was— except yours truly.

Afterward, some of my teammates were saying I had brass balls for taking it upon myself to try to run it in with the game on the line. I'd say that was a pretty accurate way of putting it. Because if I didn't score and we lost, I would have gone down as one of the all-time bums in Bills history. Throughout Buffalo, all you would have heard was: "He should have thrown it . . . He had a guy wide open in the end zone . . . What made him think he could run for a touchdown?"

A quarterback always walks that fine line between bum and

hero. On a single play, you can look like a genius because something you decided to do worked. By the same token, you can make the right decision, but if you or anyone else doesn't execute properly and the play fails, all of a sudden you're an idiot. I mean, if my body had been just a little bit higher as I approached the goal line, I probably wouldn't have gotten in. I scored, so I was the hero.

Not that you can worry about which way those decisions will go. Making them is part of what I'm paid to do as a quarterback. But at least, in those situations, there's a chance to be right.

Off the field, there are decisions I make that put me in a lose-lose position, such as when I'm out in public. At a very young age, I promised myself that if I ever made it big as an athlete, I would try to fill as many autograph requests as would come my way. That was because I remembered how terrible I felt whenever a pro player I approached refused to sign. I pride myself on staying mostly true to that promise, especially when it comes to kids. For instance, I've never taken the back door out of the dressing room at training camp—when hundreds of kids are waiting outside the front door. (Except on those very rare occasions when I'm in a hurry to get home for a night off from meetings and curfew.)

But when I'm having dinner at a restaurant and someone comes up to ask for my autograph in the middle of my meal, my standard answer is: "I'll be happy to after I'm done eating." And the standard response I get, either to my face or behind my back, is that I'm a jerk or a snob or a few other choice things.

Of course, I could always sign the autograph. But as soon as I do, everyone else will see it, and the next thing I know, a line is forming at the table. I certainly can't say no to the rest of them when I've said yes to one. Meanwhile, the food I had started eating is getting cold and the good time I was having with the person or people with me comes to an abrupt halt.

Or if I'm out at a bar, having a few beers, and I don't spend ten or fifteen minutes with everyone who comes up to meet me, I'm automatically branded an ass. But I can't possibly spend that kind of time with everyone. If I did, I would have to stay in the place for a week. And then everybody would call me an alcoholic.

Don't get me wrong. I appreciate the fact that people *want* my autograph and *want* to shake my hand and *want* me to pose with them for a picture. It's when they don't care to have anything to do with you that you have a reason to complain. As hard as I worked to get where I am, I hope that day never comes.

But I just wish people would be a little more considerate—particularly adults, because kids don't always know better. And I love kids.

Beating the Dolphins was important on three counts. Number one, it was an AFC East game and the first goal of any season is to win the division championship. Number two, it was a victory that came when it looked like we were sure losers, so it figured to build confidence. Number three, it was the opening game.

Unfortunately, none of those factors added up to much in Week Two, when we faced Denver in our home opener on *Monday Night Football*. Unlike our two prime-time routs over the Jets and Dolphins in 1988, this time we were the ones who were humiliated. After our fullback, Jamie Mueller, was tackled in the end zone for a safety midway through the first quarter, it was pretty much all downhill from there. Final score: Broncos 28, Bills 14.

Our biggest problem against the Broncos was that we were as flat as could be the entire game. I'm talking from the opening kickoff until the final gun. And the funny part was, I think everyone on the team knew we were flat but there just wasn't anything we could do to pick ourselves up.

It didn't make sense. For one thing, the game was on Monday night, and that alone should have been enough to have had everyone psyched out of their minds. For another, we were playing in front of a super-charged home crowd for the first time that year. For still another, Denver had been in two of the previous three Super Bowls and was again considered a Super Bowl contender in 1989.

But it was something that you could sense in the locker room before the game. Usually, you can look around and see the excitement or lack of excitement in everyone's eyes. Looking around that night, there just wasn't any spark. None.

Explaining why that happens sometimes—and it happens to the best of teams—is hard. The only thing I can think of is that maybe, after winning eight regular-season games and one play-off contest at Rich, we started to feel we could do no wrong at home, as if all we had to do to win was put on our uniforms.

I guess we found out how wrong we really were that night.

On top of the loss, Shane Conlan suffered a knee injury that would keep him out of action for six weeks.

But we got our act together six days later at Houston. And it didn't look anything like any of those low-scoring, ball-hogging, defense-dominated games we played in '88. It was your classic shoot-out. We scored, they scored; they scored, we scored.

All of a sudden, we had a 41–38 lead with less than two minutes left in the fourth quarter. But the Oilers, with Warren Moon leading the way, came back in the last three seconds with a 52-yard Tony Zendejas field goal to tie the score and send us into overtime.

Zendejas had a chance to win it in OT, but was wide left from 38 yards. After that, I found Andre for my fifth touchdown pass of the day, on a short hook pattern that he turned into a 28-yard gain, to improve our record to 2–1. I finished with 17 completions in 29 attempts for what would be a regular season high of 363 yards, including what would be the longest regular-season TD pass, a 78-yarder to Reed.

We used the two-minute drill a lot in that game. And we used it well beyond the normal times you see it, such as in those final desperate moments when you're trying to rally. As was the case against Miami, I felt so comfortable running it, so natural. I really felt I was at my best when we got away from the conventional approach of huddling before every play. I liked being on my own.

The only downside to that Houston game was the injury to cornerback Derrick Burroughs that ended his career. After Derrick crashed helmet-first into wide receiver Curtis Duncan, he was on the ground for about ten minutes. Derrick was motionless. He couldn't feel anything from his neck down.

I remember having an empty feeling in my stomach. And I remember looking around and seeing that nobody from either team was moving or saying a whole lot. Everyone was just standing right where they were. Standing and staring and waiting for Derrick to move his legs or his arms or his hands. Anything.

When you witness an injury like that, it puts things in perspective.

I definitely knew the potential for him being paralyzed was there. They kept showing the replay on the big-screen TV in the Astrodome, and you could see that when he made the tackle, his chin was tucked in and his head was down as low as it could go. That's the number-one safety lesson you teach a kid about playing football—never tuck your chin in, always keep your head up. When you see something like that, you fear for the worst. You just can't help it.

Luckily, Derrick's paralysis was only temporary. But the shot he took revealed a spinal condition that wouldn't permit him to play anymore.

The offensive fire we showed against the Oilers was still burning strong in our next game, against the Patriots, at Rich. We rolled to a 31–10 victory. I was 12 of 17 for 278 yards and three touchdowns, the last a 74-yarder to Thurman Thomas, who was wide open on the sidelines. That performance helped me move to the top of the AFC quarterback ratings.

At 3–1, we were feeling good about ourselves as we traveled to Indianapolis to face the 2–2 Colts. That is, until the Colts took the opening kickoff and drove 80 yards for a touchdown. They scored another touchdown in the first quarter and two field goals in the second, and before we knew it, we were behind at halftime, 20–0.

The Colts would get one more field goal in the third quarter before we would finally score our first points of the game, on a 16-yard touchdown pass I threw to Andre. After I released the ball, Jon Hand, a 300-pound defensive end, wrapped me up, lifted me off the artificial turf and threw me down on my left shoulder as hard as he could. I knew, the very instant I hit the ground, that my shoulder was separated. I remembered what my right shoulder felt like when I hit the ground in that Virginia Tech game in my senior year of college. It's a feeling you never forget.

Once again, there was sharp pain, that major-league pain that rips all the way down to your stomach.

When the trainers, Ed Abramoski (we call him Abe) and Bud Carpenter, and our doctor, Dick Weiss, came out to the field, they knew it was serious before they even started examining me. They knew because, number one, I didn't get up; ninety percent of the time, after I get knocked down in a game, I bounce right back to my feet. Number two, when they asked me how much it hurt, I said, "Big-time!" And when I say something hurts big-time, they know they aren't dealing with a hangnail.

Doc Weiss could tell right away that it was a separation. X rays would later confirm as much.

"Why me?" I thought. "Why do I deserve this?"

It seemed like I had asked myself that question before. If there was any consolation, it wasn't my throwing shoulder this time.

Although he was not penalized for a late hit, when Hand unloaded on me he realized I didn't have the ball. Without a doubt, he was looking to bury me into the ground. I couldn't say, if I was a defensive player, I wouldn't have done the same. On that side of the ball, the object of the game is to hit someone as hard as you can. You don't want to intentionally hurt anybody, but if you have a shot to do it legally, to plow a guy into the ground, then you're going to take it. I always did when I played linebacker in high school.

At first, I had no idea how serious the separation was. If I had a bunch of torn ligaments in my shoulder, like the last time, I would have to undergo surgery and be out for most or all of the remainder of the year. But it wasn't as bad as that; I'd only be out for three weeks.

Obviously, between the injury and the fact that we went on to a 37–14 loss, I wasn't in the best of moods. But I coped with it. You have to cope with an injury, because there's nothing else you can do about it. Injuries happen in football, some more severe than others. You just have to be able to come back from them, and I had every intention of coming back from this one.

During a news conference the next day, somebody asked me about the play that resulted in the separation. Standing at the podium with my arm in a sling, I mentioned that our 320-pound right tackle, Howard (House) Ballard, had missed his block, which allowed Hand to be right on top of me just as I let go of the ball. Then I went on to tell the reporters, "It should never have happened. Hand should have been blocked. Watching film, I don't know what Howard was thinking. It seemed like he was looking outside to see if a guy blitzed or something

. . . and not at the guy over him." I also made a reference to the line being solid in every place but one, and although I didn't mention any names, the media took it from there and instantly created an issue: Jim Kelly versus Howard Ballard.

The way they blew it up, you'd think I hated House's guts and wanted him off the team. And as soon as it was reported that way, everybody began to accept it as fact. But nothing could have been further from the truth. I spoke with Howard shortly after the news conference. By that time, he had heard what I said to the media and he told me he knew where I was coming from. Beyond that, the conversation we had was just between the two of us and I want it to remain just between the two of us. I will say, however, that Howard and I were friends beforehand and we were still friends afterward.

Of course, that wasn't going to change the opinions being formed about me outside the team as a result of my remarks in the media. That wasn't going to stop all the negative things being said on radio and television and written in the newspaper. Kelly-bashing seemed to be the popular thing to do at that time. And I was getting hit from all sides. I was used to being blitzed on the field. I knew how to handle that. But this was a whole new experience for me.

What I heard and read were a lot of things I knew I was not. I was being described as someone who put himself before the team, as someone who wasn't a team player. From the moment I first put on a helmet and shoulder pads, I always saw football as a team game. I always prided myself on being a team player.

Anyone who had ever seen me play knew that my putting myself ahead of the team could never be close to the truth. For most of my first three seasons with the Bills, we were a run-oriented, ball-control team—especially in '87 and '88. And I kept my mouth shut. We were winning, the coaches felt that was the best way for us to go, so I went with it. Why? Because it was good for the team. The same goes for my willingness to stay in the pocket as long as possible to make the big play, and my never-say-die attitude when we're behind.

I do those things because they're good for the team.

The media also said I was receiving favorable treatment and, because of that, that I felt I could do and say anything I wanted. Without a doubt, a quarterback gets way too much credit for the things that go right. He also gets a hell of a lot more blame than he deserves for the things that go wrong. But saying that I thought I was entitled to privileges my teammates didn't have was ridiculous. They used, as an example, my being able to drive a golf cart around at training camp. The thing that made that so stupid was that the golf carts could be rented by any player at any position. Rented, not given away by Bills management.

On top of that, people were trying to make my remarks about House into a black-white issue. Much to my surprise a *Buffalo News* columnist, whose views I haven't always agreed with, won a little of my respect by pointing out that I wasn't a racist.

As time went on, I realized there was nothing I could do about all that criticism except sit back and take it.

Unfortunately, there were a few people around Buffalo who had been waiting for a chance to take their shots at me in public. Some of them had never been able to accept all the fuss that had been made over me since I arrived in town in 1986—fuss that I didn't invite on myself—and they were jealous. They resented what I was and what I had accomplished. So my "attack" on House opened the way for them to give me a big black eye. They could say, "He's not Mr. Perfect after all."

I'm sure there are still some people out there who feel that way, because no matter what town you're in, there are always going to be those who enjoy seeing so-called stars fall from their perch. But I know the majority of people in Buffalo appreciate what I do for the Bills and for the community, and I am grateful for the outstanding support they've given me all these years.

The whole incident was just another reminder that everything I say and do is listened to and watched and analyzed very closely. That time, it came up and smacked me right in the face.

It also reminded me to be a lot more careful about what I said to reporters. And the first rule is: Don't leave any room for people to misinterpret your words. When you speak, say exactly what you mean. Even if you're being recorded by a television camera, you have to remember that the tape is always edited and only a small part of what you say actually goes on the air. Sometimes in that tiny segment your point doesn't come across the exact way you had wanted it to. Then someone else adds what he or she thought you meant, and you've got a problem.

Which isn't to say that I'm afraid to speak my mind anymore. When I have something that I feel needs to be said, you can bet I'm going to say it. It might not be what everyone wants to hear.

But it comes from the heart.

The worst part about being sidelined with an injury is having to attend practice. I hate standing around at practice. It's the most boring thing in the world. You spend all your time trying to find something productive to do, and you keep coming up empty.

The first couple of practices after my shoulder separation, I would always pick up a football and want to throw it. But each time I did, I remembered my other arm was in a sling and that the mere twisting motion of my good shoulder could aggravate the injury to the bad one.

Finally, I realized the only thing I could do was watch the other guys practice.

Frank Reich, who had never made an NFL start because I had never missed one, would debut as a starter against the 5–0 Los Angeles Rams in our second Monday-night game of the season at Rich. I knew a lot of fans and media wouldn't give Frank much of a chance for success, and they didn't. After watching him struggle in preseason games, they were all quick to say, "He can't play in this league." But what they never considered was that when Frank was out there, he usually had second- and third-string players around him. A lot of times, his blockers and receivers were guys who weren't even going to make the team.

I had a great deal of confidence in Frank. He might not possess the strongest arm in the world, but he always knows where to go with the ball and what to do with it in any given situation. There are a lot of quarterbacks who have strong arms but can't read defenses. Those guys throw all kinds of nice-looking passes —and most of them are caught by the other team. God gave Frank a great gift of intelligence and awareness. Frank's also as tough as they come.

I knew that on smarts alone he could go in there and get the job done for us. It was just a matter of getting his feet wet as a starter and getting used to working with the other starters. There was no doubt in my mind he would succeed.

Frank knew he had my full support and cooperation. He

knew I would do anything I could to help him. And one of the first things I did on that count was to stop talking to the media while Frank was our starter. I felt it was the best way to avoid creating a distraction for him and the rest of the team. I also didn't want to take away any of the focus from Frank. It was his turn in the spotlight, so any questions about the Rams or the other teams we would face with him as the starter should be directed to him, not me. I had every intention of talking again after I returned to the lineup.

Through the first three quarters of the Rams game, Frank was having a rough time. He had connected on only 10 of 24 passes, and some of his throws were a little wild. The crowd was getting on him, but Frank refused to let it get to him.

Sure enough, in the fourth quarter, he settled down and played the way he was capable of playing. He completed 11 of his next 13 attempts, and was perfect on all of his last seven. Frank's final pass was an eight-yard touchdown to Andre with 16 seconds left to give us a 23–20 victory. I couldn't have been happier for the guy.

I've also never been more nervous during a game.

Watching from the sidelines, I see things in a completely different way than when I'm participating on the field. When I'm out there, actually taking part in the game, I'm really not nervous at all. I'm just concentrating on what I have to do and what's going on around me. I also expect to make every play that I'm supposed to make; I'm not just hoping and praying everything will turn out right. But it's an entirely different perspective when I'm on the sidelines and I can't control the things that are happening on the field. I'm yelling and screaming like a fan in the stands.

"Come on! You've got to go for it! You've got to make this, Frank! Come on!"

I can see how my family loses it when they watch me play.

Frank's fourth-quarter hot streak continued the following week against the Jets, also at home. He threw for three touchdowns to lead us to a 34–3 victory and boost our record to 5–2.

When we returned to the practice field, I was miserable again. I wasn't as mentally involved in the workouts or meetings as I would have been if I was playing. When you're not preparing yourself to play, even in an emergency, your mind has a tendency to wander. And when you take the approach, as I do, of trying to improve yourself as a player every day, you feel that you're stagnating because there's absolutely nothing you can do to make yourself a better player. And when you get that urge to pick up a football, which happens about every second, all you hear from the trainers, Abe and Bud, is: "Don't throw, don't throw. You're not ready."

It's just a frustrating, helpless feeling.

Our third straight game at Rich was against the Dolphins. With Thomas and fullback Larry Kinnebrew each running for 100 yards, we coasted to a 31–17 win, our sixth straight over Miami. Frank chipped in with a 63-yard touchdown bomb to Don Beebe, a speedy wide receiver we had drafted in the third round that year—and first overall for us, because we didn't have a first- or second-round choice—from tiny Chadron State in Nebraska.

By the time my shoulder healed and I was ready to return to action, Frank's NFL record as a starter was a perfect 3–0. In only a few short weeks, he went from a guy everybody wanted to cut in the preseason to the toast of the town.

I'd say my injury added at least five years to Frank's career. (Oh, by the way, Frank, you're welcome. Ha! Ha!)

My first game back wasn't quite what I had hoped it would be. We went down to Atlanta and were defeated by the surprisingly strong Falcons, 30–28, on a 50-yard field goal by Paul McFadden with two seconds left. Although I was still a little rusty, I managed to complete 17 of 22 passes for 231 yards and two touchdowns.

Seven days later, the Colts came to Rich. This time, we were the ones putting the hurt to them, 30–7.

That was followed by a 33–24 loss to New England at Foxboro. The Patriots had been torn to shreds by injuries, yet they somehow overcame a 10–6 third-quarter deficit and scored 20 points in the final 8:46. On top of that, on the first play of the game we lost Cornelius Bennett to a knee injury that would knock him out of the lineup for the rest of that day and the next four games.

Our eleven-month wait to get revenge for our AFC Championship Game loss to Cincinnati ended in Week Twelve, when we dominated the Bengals, 24–7, at home. I mentioned earlier that Marv wasn't big on trying to motivate us, and he wasn't—not with the things he said. But a lot of times, he'll clip out newspaper articles in which a player or coach from the other team says something bad about us and tack them up on the bulletin board in the locker room. Or he'll do what he did the night before the Bengals game—show us a videotape that was supposed to fire us up. It contained shots of Cincinnati players celebrating after that AFC title game and making all sorts of negative comments about us. I guess it worked.

I only threw 15 passes against the Bengals, but I completed 10 of them, three for TDs. The defense did a great job of shutting down Boomer Esiason and Cincinnati's no-huddle offense. It finally looked to me like we were going to put an end to our inconsistency and get serious about our run at Super Bowl XXIV.

My thoughts couldn't have been more premature.

We went on to lose three games in a row—at Seattle (17–16), at Rich against New Orleans (22–19) and at San Francisco (21–10)—and watched our record fall to 8–7. We were looking less and less like a Super Bowl team every day.

To make matters worse, there was more off-the-field controversy when Thurman Thomas appeared on a cable television show and took me to task because of the comments I had made about House ten weeks earlier. Once that happened, people in the media began referring to us as "The Bickering Bills." They began portraying us as a team divided, with everyone at each other's throats.

They were wrong. Dead wrong.

The problem was the constant rehashing that took place in the media. When Thurman made his remarks, everyone took it as a cue to bring up the "Kelly criticizes Ballard" story again. And pretty soon every player on the team was being asked about both incidents. And if what they said wasn't juicy enough, their answers would be twisted and words would be put into their mouths. I mean, a day didn't go by when someone didn't bring up those questions or call us "The Bickering Bills."

The media just killed us that year. They couldn't get enough of the back-and-forth stuff between the players, because it was exactly what they wanted. They didn't care about our team.

They didn't care about the players. They wanted to keep "The Bickering Bills" alive because it gave them something to ride with—something that was a hell of a lot more interesting than the boring truth about what really goes on in an NFL locker room.

And they rode with it for a long time.

If you believed the picture being painted on the outside by the media, Thurman and I either weren't talking to each other or were constantly at each other's throat. Both pictures were as distorted as could be. In fact, not only were we talking, but the few times the "The Bickering Bills" issue came up in the locker room, we were actually laughing about it. We all knew what the media was up to, and we just couldn't take them seriously.

More than once, Thurman and I would look at each other and ask, "I wonder what they're going to come up with this week?" It almost became a running joke between us.

What people on the outside failed to realize was that Thurman and I had to work together every day in practice. We had to face each other, we had to communicate, we had to do our jobs. You're talking about two professionals who want to win and who won't allow anything to stand in their path.

Thurman was on his way to leading the NFL in combined yards from scrimmage, a 1,000-yard rushing season and his first Pro Bowl. I was happy to help him achieve those great numbers by feeding him the ball as often as possible. And I was happy to see him excel. He was the one picking up the slack when I wasn't at the top of my game.

If we were going to have any hope of reaching Super Bowl XXIII, that was exactly what we needed.

Media people can say what they want when they read this. They can say it's all bull or any other word they'd like to use. They have the right to their own opinion. But deep down, they know that they loved every minute of the "Bickering Bills" garbage and they did everything possible to make sure it wouldn't go away. Not just local media but national as well. For all the wrong reasons, "The Bickering Bills" put Buffalo on the map more than anything else we had ever done up to that point.

But I don't agree with those who say it brought us closer together as a team. For one thing, we were never that far apart. I don't deny that we had our problems, but every team does.

You can't put forty-seven people in any place of business and expect them all to get along great. Winning or losing, it's just unrealistic to think we're all going to be best buddies. Clashes occur because of different personalities, skin color, religion, you name it.

That's just part of being on a professional football team. That's just part of being in society.

You're better friends with some guys than others, but the bottom line is that we're all supposed to be professionals and we have to be able to work together. No matter what you heard or saw on the outside, we were definitely working together on the inside during that '89 season. Maybe we didn't always look that sharp, but it wasn't because no one wanted to be in the same locker room or on the same field with his teammates.

There were other factors, including the injuries to Shane and Cornelius, that took away from our performance. And there were some guys who just weren't playing up to their capabilities.

With three interceptions against the Saints and three more against the 49ers, I was at the top of that list.

For the first time in my career, I didn't feel complete confidence in myself as a quarterback. Something in my game was missing, and after we suffered those three losses in a row, I was feeling pretty down. I guess every professional athlete goes through that. You just hit a low point when it seems like everything is going wrong. Everything that had come so easy for you suddenly seems very difficult. You're not making the passes or the reads that you've made a thousand times before. You're not coming up with big plays.

I needed help to pull me out of that rut.

And, of course, I knew right where to turn—to the only six people who were capable of getting me back in the right direction. I'm talking about my father and my five brothers.

One day after that awful stretch of games, we all gathered in the master bedroom of my house to talk things over. Actually, a couple of my brothers had talked to me earlier and said I wasn't playing or acting like myself. So when we all got together, the first thing they did was remind me of something a Kelly never does—and that I had never done before—and that was give up on anything he sets out to accomplish.

When I went from a tiny high school to the bottom of the depth chart at a major college that was about to throw football out the window, I didn't allow that to stop me from becoming a Heisman Trophy candidate. When I tore up my passing shoulder in my senior year of college, I didn't allow that to stop me from becoming a pro quarterback. When I joined a league and a team that were starting from scratch and was thrown into an offense I had never seen before, I didn't allow those things to stop me from putting up some of the best statistics in pro football history. When I joined the Bills after consecutive 2–14 seasons, I didn't allow that to stop me from leading them to the AFC Championship Game.

Now, when I wasn't feeling so sure of myself, my family was there to tell me that I shouldn't allow anything to stand between me and my ultimate goal—to lead the Bills to the Super Bowl.

"Things will get better for you," Dad said. "Every quarterback goes through some bad times, and you're no exception. But no matter what happens, you'll always have the support of your family. We're not going to let you go through this alone."

"And I don't want to hear any more of that talk about you losing your confidence," Pat chimed in. "Just go back out there and show them what a Kelly's made of."

That was really all I had to hear. Just knowing I had them to lean on, once again, was enough to give me the greatest boost of confidence I had ever received. I don't know of a closer family than ours, and it's something each of us draws strength from.

The reason I'd rather talk to my father and my brothers more than anyone else is because they're not going to bullshit me. They're going to say things exactly as they are. And when we talk after a game, they don't mention the touchdown passes or any of my other big plays. The first thing they bring up is a mistake—regardless of the outcome. There are always plenty of people around to tell you that you're the greatest quarterback ever to walk the face of the earth and that you can do no wrong. But I don't get that from Dad and my brothers.

For instance, after one big victory Ray and I happened to be sitting down together, each with a beer in front of us. Without ever looking me in the eye and in a low voice, he said, "Great game, Jim."

Just the way he said it, I knew something else was coming.

"OK," I finally said. "Before you take another sip or another breath, tell me what you want to tell me. Get it off your chest right now so we can both relax."

Ray never hesitated for an instant.

"What the ———— were you looking at with that one pass?" he growled.

The "one pass" he was talking about, of course, was an interception. So I had to give him an explanation. Ray's like another coach to me. He grades all of my performances. First he points out the things I did wrong. Then he points out the things I did right—and how I can do them better.

Listening to Ray, my other brothers and Dad in my bedroom now, I realized the most important thing I had to do was focus. I had to channel all my thoughts toward getting my game back in order and getting us to the Super Bowl. Nothing else mattered.

One major step I took in that direction was to stop talking to the media for the rest of the season. And the thing that made it so easy was that the first question just about every reporter asked was about my least favorite subject, "The Bickering Bills."

"I'm here to play football," I said. "If that's all that you're going to ask about, then I have nothing else to say."

And it was one of the best things I ever did for my career. With those kinds of questions popping up all the time, I didn't need the added pressure of worrying about whether I would say the right thing or the wrong thing. When practice ended, I just showered, changed and, instead of attending the usual twenty-minute media session across the hall, went straight home, where I could relax and forget about unimportant things.

All I worried about was being a football player.

The day after the San Francisco game, we held a players-only meeting. In fact, Coach Levy gave us permission to hold it even before the assistant coaches began showing us the film of our loss to the 49ers. Watching film is usually the first order of business the day after a game. But it was obvious that we were down as a whole, down and sinking lower by the minute.

So the feeling on that Monday morning among the players—especially the veteran leaders such as Joe Devlin and Fred Smerlas—was that airing things out after three losses in a row was more important than taking another look at the things we did wrong. Besides, we knew *what* we had done wrong. The bigger question was *how* were we going to go about correcting our mistakes?

We hoped that the meeting, as well as a second one on Friday, would help provide a few answers and get us on the right track as we prepared for our 1989 regular-season finale the following Saturday against the Jets at Giants Stadium. Both days, Joe and Fred made the point that everyone was just going to have to take it upon himself to wake up and do his own job on the field.

"It's a team sport, but if you're not doing your job as an individual, you're not helping the team," Joe said. "If you're not pulling your own weight, you'd better start or get the hell out of the way. It's gut-check time, guys. It's time to take a long look in the mirror and make sure that you're doing everything that you can to help this team win."

I stood up and said, "We as an offense haven't been pulling our share of the load and I'm part of the reason for that. But we still have to remember that this is a team game. During the course of a season, the defense is going to have to come up with some big plays and win some games and the offense is going to have to do the same. We're all going to have to share in it. Don't worry about what the other guy does on this team. If everybody concentrates on their own assignments and what they're supposed to do, we'll be all right."

When those meetings ended, it wasn't a case of us having been worked into a wild frenzy and charging out of the room yelling, "Let's go get 'em!" In fact, it was a pretty calm atmosphere.

Yet everyone seemed to get the message.

The Jets had a 4–11 record. They were on the verge of firing Joe Walton as their head coach and starting over with Bruce Coslett. But getting motivated to play the game wasn't much of a problem, because as bad as things might have been, a victory would still give us a 9–7 record and our second straight division championship. We wanted that title and the first-round playoff bye that went with it to rest and heal.

I did, however, give my offensive linemen a little added incentive just before the game when I said, "I'll give each of you $2,500 cash if I'm not sacked today." They gave me a look of determination that said, "Consider that money as good as spent, Jim."

I also knew that our fullback, Larry Kinnebrew, was close to reaching a performance bonus in his contract for total rushing yards that season. Wanting to give him an even larger goal, I said to him before the game, "Larry, if you run for 50 yards today, I'll give you $500 cash."

Along with everything else we packed for our trip to New Jersey was an ample supply of "Bills weather." The windchill that day was minus 11 degrees.

Given all the Jets' problems—which made ours seem minor by comparison—our 37–0 victory wasn't exactly a shock. But it gave us a chance to redeem ourselves in the playoffs. I had an OK day—13 for 21, 208 yards, two touchdowns. I wasn't throwing the ball particularly well, but at least I cut my interceptions from three per game over the previous two weeks to one. I wasn't sacked so I gladly paid the $12,500 in bonuses to my linemen. And Larry rushed for a game-high 91 yards, so I happily gave him his money.

Because of our mediocre record, we would have to travel to Cleveland for our divisional-round playoff game. Which already put us at a disadvantage, because we'd be dealing with their "Dawg Pound" instead of them dealing with our wild and crazy fans.

One thing I knew for sure, though: My confidence was all the way back. I was at ease. I had total peace of mind.

For the first time in a few weeks, I went into a game fully expecting to play well. And I had no doubt in my mind we were going to beat the Browns. Call it a gut feeling or whatever you want, but I never felt better in my life about our chances of winning a game than I did that day.

I guess Bernie Kosar, my former college teammate and the Browns' quarterback, was feeling pretty good himself, because it wasn't long before Bernie and I were involved in a full-fledged shoot-out. I should have known I'd be in for a battle with him. Anytime I play against a quarterback as good as a Bernie Kosar or a Dan Marino, I always expect a sixty-minute ordeal—if not longer.

I fired the first shot with a 72-yard touchdown pass to Andre late in the opening quarter. Early in the second, Bernie connected with Webster Slaughter on a 52-yard scoring pass to put the Browns up, 10–7. A couple of minutes later, I threw a 33-yard TD to James Lofton, whom we signed early in the year after he was cut by the Raiders. Then, just before halftime, Bernie gave our secondary a great play fake and tossed a three-yard touchdown pass to Ron Middledon to give the Browns a 17–14 lead.

Bernie struck again early in the third quarter, but I came back with a short touchdown pass to Thomas to make it 24–21. I knew Thurman was going to be open all day because Clay Matthews, Cleveland's veteran linebacker, was going to try to cover him one on one, which is impossible. And when the Browns played zone, I would just dunk the ball to Thurman six yards downfield and watch him turn it into a 10-yard gain.

We would fall behind by 10 points twice before I hit six of seven passes to move us to the Browns' 3, from where I hooked up with Thurman for another score. Unfortunately, Scott Norwood slipped during his extra-point attempt and, instead of cutting the Browns' lead to three, we were down by four, 34–30. That meant our only chance for victory was to score a touchdown.

Scotty had always been Mr. Automatic, so I had taken for granted that he would make the kick. But the field was icy—that is, if you can call that stuff inside Cleveland Stadium a field. It is the worst surface I have ever played on in my life. (It's worse than my high school field, and we had practiced on that every single day.) There's no grass to speak of; it's mostly sand and dirt. Any green it has probably comes from paint. Now, put ice on top of it and you've got a real mess. Hockey players probably would have loved it. So I could understand why Scotty had a problem with his footing.

After Cleveland went three downs and out, we had 2:41 to get from our 26 to the end zone. With one time-out and the two-minute warning, I would take over the play calling in our hurry-up attack.

I had only one thought in my mind, and that was winning. I wanted to win so badly, it was unbelievable. I couldn't recall another game that I had wanted to win more up to that point of my career. My concentration level was as high as ever. And when we got in the huddle, I had all the confidence in the world that we were going to score a touchdown. I just knew it.

Two quick passes to Ronnie Harmon gave us a first down at the 42 before the clock stopped at the two-minute warning. Then I converted a fourth-and-10 with a 17-yard throw to Don Beebe, giving us a first down at the Cleveland 41 and forcing the Browns to call a time-out with 1:16 left. A couple of plays later, I hit Thomas for a nine-yard gain, and that caused the Browns to use their second time-out with a minute remaining. I converted another fourth down with a 10-yard pass to Andre to the 22, then quickly got everybody to the line and spiked the ball to stop the clock at 34 seconds.

I picked up another first down with a completion to Thomas to the 11, then spiked the ball again to freeze the clock at 14 seconds. On the next play, I called a flag pattern to Ronnie to the corner of the end zone. He runs that pattern better than anybody in the league and he catches that pass more often than anybody in the league. Nine of ten times that we had run it before that day, it had been successful. I thought for sure it was going to work again as I threw to my left while Ronnie cut across the back of the end zone all by himself. The ball hit him right in the hands . . . but bounced away. That was a killer to watch, but there was no time to dwell on it. We still had one more chance.

On my 16th straight pass of the drive, I looked for Thurman to break across the middle on a post pattern. I found Clay Matthews of the Browns instead.

We were out of the playoffs, but there was no denying it had been a great game. Personally, it was my best NFL performance —28 completions in 54 attempts (40 in the second half) for 405 yards and four touchdowns. You always hear about John Elway's miracle comeback to beat the Browns for the 1986 AFC Championship. If Ronnie catches the ball, we might have had a miracle of our own. It was the ninth drop of the day and every-one was saying afterward how much better my numbers would have been if the receivers did a better job of hanging on to the ball. But drops aren't always the fault of the receivers. There are times when I don't put the ball in their hands quite right, when it gets to them a little too slow or a little too fast, so I share the blame. After we failed to hook up for the touchdown, Ronnie supposedly came back to the huddle and told Thurman that if I had gotten the ball to Ronnie quicker, he would have been able to score. He said I had looked a little too long to my right and by the time I turned to the other side, Ronnie was almost out of the end zone and was therefore concentrating more on where his feet were than on the ball. Ronnie didn't say anything directly to me about it. But maybe he had a point. Like I said, the receiver isn't always to blame for a drop.

The walk off the field seemed to take forever, especially with all those "Dawgs" in the stands yelping at us. I felt a lot of disappointment, a lot of frustration. I had geared myself so much for victory that I never even considered the possibility of a loss. I wasn't braced for it at all, which was probably what made it so damn painful.

I remember Thurman saying in the locker room he'd rather lose a game 34–0 than 34–30.

"Because when you lose like that, you know you never had a chance," he said. "But we had a chance today."

I hadn't spoken to the media at large before the game, and even though the season was over, I intended to stick with my policy, then begin a fresh start with them in the off-season. That went for everybody, including NBC, which had broadcast the game. But producers from the network, as well as other reporters, kept bugging our PR guys to get me to talk that day. The PR guys, in turn, kept bugging me. And I kept saying no.

As I was knotting my tie behind a curtain in our cramped dressing room, Denny Lynch walked up to take one more crack at me. Finally, I just blew my top.

"Noooo!" I yelled. "I said I'm not talking. How many times have I got to say it? That makes about thirty guys who've asked me now, and the answer is still no . . . NO, damn it!"

I think Denny finally got the message.

Even though we lost, I thought a lot of good came out of that game. I thought it was a good confidence builder; not only for myself but for the entire team. Sometimes, all it takes is one game to turn a team around, and I felt us making the turn that day—especially the boys up front.

Who knows how far we would have gone had we won?

8

The Corporate Game Plan

IN MARCH 1990, I signed the third contract of my pro-football life. Actually, most of the terms were worked out late in the 1989 season, but to avoid creating a distraction during our drive toward the playoffs we decided to wait until the following spring to make it official: I would be with the Bills through 1996 thanks to a $20 million six-year extension of my original five-year agreement.

I looked at it as a deal that would allow me to finish my career in Buffalo. The longer I stayed in western New York, the more it grew on me—to the point where I couldn't see myself playing anywhere else. I was also very determined to play in my first Super Bowl, and I felt that with the kind of talent we had, my best chance of getting there was in a red, white and blue Bills uniform.

Signing the new contract was a major milestone. It told me that I had truly arrived as an NFL quarterback. Regardless of those lofty statistics I produced in the USFL and regardless of the lofty salary the Bills agreed to pay me in 1986, I still had a lot to prove. Quite a few skeptics wondered if all the success I enjoyed with the Gamblers resulted merely from the fact that there wasn't a defensive back in that league capable of covering his grandmother one on one. They were predicting that I would have a much tougher time completing passes once I started to face "legitimate" competition.

So I took a lot of pride in performing well enough through my first four NFL seasons to convince Ralph Wilson and Bill Polian that I deserved to continue to rank among the highest-paid players in the game.

This was something I had wanted for a long time—something I had worked very hard for all my life. Once again, I was being rewarded for all those countless hours of practice, film study and rehabilitation; all those bumps, bruises and dislocations; all the blood, the sweat and the tears.

And the best part was that the Bills came to me first; it wasn't anything I had to ask for. Not that I was trying to be cocky and acting like the mountain had to come to Muhammad. Not for a second. It was just that I had enough respect for Ralph and Bill to know that they would be able to recognize when the time was right to talk to me about a raise. I also knew they had an equal amount of respect for my performance and dedication to my job. And from the first day I set foot in Buffalo after the USFL folded, they had given me nothing but fair treatment.

That isn't to say the extension was simple to come by. You can never say that about a negotiation involving those kinds of numbers, or a general manager as tough as Polian. My representatives—my brother Dan, Roger Trevino and Roger's brother Dan Trevino behind the scenes—busted their asses for everything they got. There were items the Bills wanted in the agreement that we didn't want, and vice versa. But with a little give-and-take, whatever differences we had were taken care of and both sides were smiling afterward.

I also felt I earned every cent I was being paid. People will look at the money and say nobody can possibly be worth that much. But my attitude is that I'm worth the going rate for a top NFL quarterback, whatever that may be. It just so happened, in

1990, the going rate was $3 million per year. If it were $75,000, I would have gladly signed for that, too.

I didn't feel any extra pressure because of the new contract. I have always believed that no matter what you make, you have to perform at the highest level possible every time you step onto that field. Money is a concern up to a point, but it isn't the main reason I play the game. You can't participate in something as physically and emotionally demanding as pro football just because it's a job. Guys who try to take that approach usually don't last long. There has to be something in your heart that makes all the risks you take worthwhile and pushes you to outperform the people on the other side of the line.

I can say, with a completely straight face, that the main reason I play is because I enjoy the game. It just so happens I get paid very well to do something I enjoy. And if I wasn't playing pro football, I know I'd be constantly searching for other ways to compete. You'd probably find me in East Brady, doing the things I still love to do today—playing softball, shooting some hoops, hunting and fishing and quenching the terrific thirst I'd build with a couple of cold Iron City beers.

As for my teammates, I didn't sense any resentment at all from them after word of the extension got out. In fact, a lot of guys were quick to come up and congratulate me. Besides, they knew that whenever you have an increase at the top of the pay scale, everyone else moves up, too. A lot of the agents representing other players on our team were doing backflips when they heard about my raise. They couldn't wait for their turn at the negotiating table, which is the way it is in all professional sports. In general, pro athletes share a "get what you can today" attitude. Because we all realize it could be over by the time we wake up tomorrow.

I also took my share of razzing about the new contract. The offensive linemen were probably the hardest on me. They were quick to point out that at the time, I was making ten times more than the highest-paid member of their bunch. So I reminded them about all those dinners I had treated them to on the road (you haven't seen a restaurant bill until you've seen the one that shows up at the end of a meal with five 300-pound guys) and the nice gifts I had given them for their great protection.

"Which reminds me," Kent Hull said. "Remember those cowboy boots you bought for each of us at the end of last season?"

"Yeah," I said.

"Well now that you're making three million dollars a year, you can buy a new pair of boots for each of us."

"That's all?"

"That's all . . . only this time, Jim, we want our names engraved in them in real gold. And we want real gold heels. And we want as much real gold trimming as they can fit on those things."

"Sure, Kent, anything you say."

I'd still rather clothe those guys than feed them.

Although I've spent most of my life preparing for and working to maintain a successful pro-football career, I haven't kidded myself into thinking I can play this game forever. And as focused as I am in striving to become one of the best quarterbacks in the NFL, I haven't developed a bad case of nearsightedness where my future is concerned.

When I'm not playing or practicing, I spend a lot of time looking down the road. That was the main reason I formed Jim Kelly Enterprises in 1988. I'm the chief executive officer, Danny's the president and Roger, whom I met while I was in Houston, is the vice president. Dan Trevino is a former investment banker from Houston. We have our own offices just outside of Buffalo, with a total of ten full-time employees as well as several lawyers, accountants and financial advisers whom we keep on retainer.

We're involved in real estate transactions, youth football camps and—the thing that gives me the most pride and pleasure of all—charitable work that has raised in excess of $500,000.

My other off-the-field ventures include the NFL Quarterback Club, a division of NFL Properties that I helped form. Besides yours truly, it features Dan Marino, Boomer Esiason, Bernie Kosar, Warren Moon, Randall Cunningham, Troy Aikman, Phil Simms, Jim Everett and Bubby Brister.

I've done product endorsements for Nuprin, Domino's Pizza, Wheaties, *The Sporting News* and NFL Pro Line. I have weekly TV and radio shows in the Buffalo area during the season. I make motivational speeches. I've even done a little acting, with a couple of small parts in movies (including the football comedy *Necessary Roughness*) and appearances in two episodes of the soap opera *General Hospital.*

On my off days, I sit down with my "coaching staff" at JKE and we go over a dozen of the approximately fifty proposals that cross my desk each month. Then we determine which ones we should pursue. With a bachelor's degree in business management, as well as my own instincts, I feel I have a pretty good eye for what will and won't work. In fact, the best investment I ever made was one I did by myself in 1987. That's when I formed a partnership with a close friend of mine from college, Jeff Peck, to run a company that repairs freight cars coming into the Port of Miami.

But we are very, very cautious with each new proposal we receive. You get some ideas that are solid, but you also get some that are way off the wall. Like the guy who wanted me to invest in a casino in a ghost town somewhere in Colorado. He was calling it the "deal of a lifetime," a "sure home run." Usually, when someone offers you the chance to become part of a "sure home run," more than likely it's a sure strikeout.

I learned my lesson the hard way about whom to trust and whom not to trust in business. I had had complete faith in my first agents, Greg Lustig and A. J. Faigin. Before signing with them out of college, I talked to a bunch of other players they represented and they all said Lustig and Faigin did a good job on their contracts. Even Jack Lambert, the former Steeler great, gave them a strong recommendation.

Then Danny and the Trevino brothers started taking a closer look at my business affairs. And the more they looked, the more they didn't like what they found.

Finally, I saw the light. In 1988, I fired Lustig and Faigin and put my brother and the Trevinos in charge of all my business dealings. Then I filed a major lawsuit against my former agents, as well as the former owners of the Gamblers for defaulting on the payment of my signing bonus.

Fortunately, I was able to catch the problem before it was too late, which made me luckier than a lot of other pro athletes. When you come out of college, you're so trusting, so vulnerable when it comes to finding people to handle your money. I'm just glad that I had a brother and a couple of close friends who cared enough to slap me upside the head and get my attention.

The funny thing is, my mother never liked Lustig from Day One. There was something about him that told her he couldn't be trusted.

I should have followed Mom's intuition.

One of the first things I established after arriving in Buffalo was the Kelly for Kids Foundation, which, with the support of local industry, raises money for a variety of youth-oriented charities. The biggest fund-raiser we have is my annual celebrity golf tournament, which attracts all kinds of big pro-football names from the present (Marino, Elway, Esiason) and past (Namath, Simpson, Payton).

Getting those guys to show up isn't a problem, because they have charity golf tournaments of their own and I make it a point to show up at as many as my schedule allows. I guess you could say it's a case of one club washing the other. We also have a great time together. We might be fierce competitors on the field, but there's a great camaraderie among us. You can't beat the idea of having a lot of laughs and doing something nice for kids in the process.

The business that I have the most fun with is my instructional football camp for youngsters 10 to 18 years old at St. Bonaventure University in Olean, New York. It has been going strong since 1988. In fact, we've had such great success—with enrollment skyrocketing from 300 in 1990 to 700 in 1991—that the NFL is using ours as a model for similar camps around the country.

At a lot of them the main celebrity shows up the first day for a token appearance and then he's off to another appointment. I'm there every single day, from sunrise to sunset. I have breakfast with the campers. I lead them through stretching and calisthenics. I throw my face in the grass and bounce back up to show them how an up-down drill is supposed to be done. I circulate through all the practice sessions, which are overseen by high school coaches, other Bills players and players from around the NFL. And I make bed-check rounds at night—curfew is 10:30 p.m. for the bantams (10–12 years old), 11 p.m. for the juniors (13–14) and seniors (15–18).

Football's a rough sport, but one thing I won't tolerate at my camp is bullying. Dormitory rooms must be kept spotless; if I find a room that's messy, then those kids have to scrub the bathrooms that they share with the other campers. And curfews are strictly enforced. The kids also never know who I'm going to bring along with me on my bed-check rounds. For instance, on the first day of our 1991 camp, I introduced them to the guy who'd be helping me that night—Reggie Rogers, our former 6-6, 280-pound defensive end. He came up with the meanest scowl he could give, and the bantams just sat there, wide-eyed and stone silent.

What happens to those who continually break the rules? They're gone. You've got to start disciplining these guys when they're young. At my camp, I want them to be where they're supposed to be when they're supposed to be there. No excuses. Any kid who arrives late for practice gets the "grab-a-leaf" punishment. That means he must hike at least five hundred yards to the nearest tree, pull off a leaf, and hike all the way back to deliver it to me.

You can see right away that some of the kids don't have a lot of athletic ability. But you try to teach them something. And by the end of the week, you see them feeling proud that they learned an aspect of the game that they didn't know before. Which, in turn, makes you proud.

Seniors are easier to work with because they're a little more experienced and more mature than the rest. With juniors, we concentrate on fundamental work. And with the bantams, you just try to make sure they're having fun and learning the basics of what football's all about.

What's really gratifying is to see kids who were there in the first couple of years coming back to work as counselors. I don't know if we're ever going to launch a great NFL career. I'd love to see it, but that isn't why I have the camp. And I'm not in it for the money either. Believe me, with all the work involved and all the responsibility of having that many youngsters in your care and all the hassles that come up—you always have about a dozen bantams who get homesick within the first couple of days —it's not worth doing just for the money.

The reason I do it is because I want to help kids improve. Not only as football players but also as human beings. I'm not out there just to show them how to throw a nice spiral. They learn about hygiene and manners and nutrition and, most of all, the importance of staying off drugs and staying in school. And I always tell them the best part of the week, besides getting to catch a pass from Dan Marino or Boomer Esiason, is the chance to make new friends.

In 1990, we ran a contest in Buffalo that offered the winner free board and tuition at the camp. The lucky entry was held by Matt Robinson, a thirteen-year-old with Down's Syndrome. His father called me to explain Matt's handicap.

"Don't worry about a thing," I told him. "Just bring your son to the camp. And you can stay with him, too."

As I wheeled around from practice session to practice session in my golf cart, Matt would always be sitting right next to me. Other times when we saw each other, we'd exchange hugs, high-fives and the Hawaiian sign for "hang loose"—wiggling a hand with an outstretched thumb and pinkie. I called Matt my special camper.

I love kids. I always have. I could be in a lousy mood, but put me around a bunch of kids and it automatically cheers me up.

One of these days, I'll have a few of my own. Of course, I have to find a wife first. So far, Mrs. Right hasn't come along.

9

"K-Gun"

THE WEEK BEFORE our 1990 home opener against Indianapolis, we planned a little surprise for the Colts. The first time we touched the ball, we were going to go immediately to our two-minute drill.

My eyes grew as large as silver dollars when Ted Marchibroda made that announcement a few days before the game in a meeting with me and our two other quarterbacks, Frank Reich and Gale Gilbert. All of a sudden, the offensive attack we had used only late in the first half or when we trailed in the fourth quarter was moving to page one of the playbook. For the entire opening drive, we would go without a huddle and I would get to call all my own plays.

I couldn't wait.

We won the coin toss, always a great way to start a new season, and received the kickoff. Sure enough, the Colts' defenders—not to mention the 78,899 fans in the stands, the reporters in the press box and everyone else watching—didn't know what hit them when we came out looking like the Runnin' Rebels of Nevada–Las Vegas. In rapid-fire succession, I threw on our first three plays and we proceeded to race from our own 11-yard line to the Indianapolis 13.

The Colts' coaches were so stunned that after I completed my seventh pass in a row, they had to call a time-out like a basketball team on the wrong end of a big point run. Their defenders, struggling to keep up as we hustled to the line to begin each play even before the previous one ended, needed to take a breath and regroup.

I wound up going 9 for 9 on that first series. We didn't put the ball in the end zone, but we did get a 29-yard field goal from Scott Norwood. Because it is so important to get the year off on the right foot, how you score those first points doesn't matter—just as long as you score.

I don't know why, but we never used the no-huddle the rest of the day. That was disappointing to a certain extent, but Ted was the offensive coordinator (in his next-to-last season before becoming head coach of the Colts) and someone I respected very much. Whatever he and Marv Levy decided was best for us to do, I did. No questions asked. (Well, maybe a couple.) And it wasn't as if we really needed to use any exotic strategy to beat the Colts anyway. We had the upper hand in overall talent and we were playing at home. That combination alone was enough for a 26–10 victory.

We also used the no-huddle the following week when we traveled to Miami to face Marino and the Dolphins. But by then, we were already staring up from the bottom of a 30-point hole in the fourth quarter. This time, it did produce a touchdown—our only score in a 30–7 loss.

There was a lot of commotion over my being taken out of the game, along with other starters, with almost eight minutes left because Coach Levy didn't want to risk an injury in a lost cause. First, Bruce Smith started screaming and yelling about it to Coach Levy on the sidelines, telling him that we should leave everybody in because we still had a chance. I think Bruce was feeling a little bit of that South Florida heat and humidity, and a lot of frustration. The coach just told him to sit down, and Bruce gave in. Soon after that, Marv started pulling a bunch of defensive starters out of the game. But Nate Odomes, Kirby Jackson and Leonard Smith wouldn't budge at first, then came off the field a short while later.

In the next day's paper, Bruce was quoted as saying that "we just gave up." Coach Levy then fined him, along with the other three guys, and that was the end of it.

I never want to leave the field a second sooner than I have to, especially when we're losing. But that was another coaching decision and it wasn't my place—or anyone else's—to question it. I was always taught that coaches are supposed to coach, players are supposed to play.

Besides, we let that game get away from us before we ever left Buffalo. We had a terrible week of practice, one of the worst I had seen since joining the Bills. I guess we all thought we were so good that we could just show up at any stadium in the league and play well.

That time, the surprise was on us.

Coach Levy had constantly told us, "In order to play like champions, you have to practice like champions." And we had treated those words like any other football cliché, letting them go in one ear and out the other. But after that awful showing at Joe Robbie Stadium, we realized we should have taken them to heart. It finally dawned on everybody that if our concentration was good all during the week, it was likely to be good on game day. We had to get into the habit of pretending each practice session was the real thing.

The other plus that came out of being embarrassed by the Dolphins was that it served as a reminder of the bad things that happen when you play like forty-seven individuals, with each guy doing his own thing to try to win, rather than as a team. We had to get back to the great unified effort we showed in our playoff game against the Browns—minus the ending, of course.

The mistakes were all correctable. And we had them corrected by the following Monday night at Giants Stadium, where we buried the Jets by the same score as the Miami game, 30–7. Our line was opening huge holes all night, and Thurman Thomas found all of them to pile up 214 yards, the best performance by a Bills running back since 1984.

Once again, the no-huddle hadn't been part of our game plan. I would joke around with Ted about the idea of going with it not only for the first series but through an entire game. But he would shake his head and say, "I don't know about that, Jim."

At the time Coach Levy, and to a certain degree Ted, worried that using the no-huddle more than just occasionally would expose me to too much punishment. They thought the linemen would get too tired trying to maintain such a fast pace for four quarters and, as a result, their pass protection would suffer. Which meant I would *really* suffer. Marv was especially concerned about that because he remembered, from when he was coaching the Chicago Blitz in the USFL, how often I had gotten nailed using the run-and-shoot with the Gamblers.

The next two games saw us make miraculous comebacks that, to this day, have me shaking my head in disbelief.

The first was against Denver at Rich Stadium. We were behind, 21–9, with less than 11 minutes remaining when David Treadwell came on to try to sink us with a 24-yard field-goal attempt. But over the next five plays and 77 seconds, we would score an incredible 20 points. The first seven came when Nate Odomes blocked Treadwell's chip shot and Cornelius Bennett took the ball 80 yards for a touchdown. Two plays later, John Elway was intercepted by Leonard Smith, who ran 39 yards for another TD (although Scotty's extra-point try was no good). Then, with the roar of our crowd threatening to break his eardrums, Elway dropped the next snap and Bennett recovered at the Broncos' 2-yard line. One play after that, Kenneth Davis, whom we had picked up as a Plan B free agent from Green Bay in 1989, barreled in for the score to give us a 29–21 lead with 9:10 left.

Denver managed only seven more points in what had to be one of the most exciting fourth quarters ever played. That is, until we faced the Raiders the following Sunday night, also at home. This time, we were trailing 24–14 in the fourth quarter. And this time, we exploded for 24 points in a span of 6:03.

I got the fireworks started with a 42-yard touchdown bomb to James Lofton, who was facing his ex-teammates for the first time, to cut the margin to three. Next, Steve Tasker, one of the best special-teams players the NFL has ever seen, got his left forearm in front of a Jeff Gossett punt. Rookie cornerback J. D.

Williams pulled the bouncing ball out of the air and ran for an easy 38-yard TD to give us our first lead, 28–24, with 6:52 left.

After that, Bennett sacked Jay Schroeder, forcing him to fumble, and beat him to the recovery at the Raiders' 21, setting up a 23-yard field goal by Norwood. On the third play of the next series, Schroeder completed an 18-yard pass to Willie Gault. But Odomes—and I still can't believe he did this—just yanked the ball right out of Gault's hands and sprinted 49 yards for the first touchdown of his NFL career to clinch our third straight victory, 38–24.

The one thing I didn't see in either the Broncos or Raiders games was panic on our part after we fell behind. I know I wasn't panicking. In fact, both times, I walked up and down the sidelines telling everybody, "Don't worry about it. We're going to come back. All we need are a couple of breaks, and we're going to be right back in it."

And after we'd get our first break, and we'd get into the huddle, I'd say, "OK, that's one break. Let's make the best of it and wait for another. We're not out of this thing yet."

I'm not saying I predicted those incredible things would happen. Definitely not in the Denver game. I've never seen a football game turn around so quick or one team score so many points in such a short time as we did that day.

But part of what having a winning attitude means is expecting your teammates—in this case the guys on special teams and defense—to make something happen. Not to mention the crowd. To this day, every single one of us who was part of that Denver game attributes everything that happened after that blocked field goal to the fans. It was unbelievable. The fans just absolutely took that game into their own hands.

A week later, we found ourselves in yet another tight spot at Rich. The Jets had us down, 27–24, with 2:46 remaining. Four passes and a run moved us from our own 29 to the Jets' 29. After a couple of incompletions, I found Andre for the eighth time of the day on a 16-yard curl pattern before calling our second time-out with 48 seconds left. Just enough time for one crack at the end zone, and if we missed, a field-goal attempt to force overtime.

On second and 10 from the Jets' 14, we came out in a four-wide receiver set, with our fullback, Jamie Mueller, as the lone man in the backfield. Jamie's first responsibility was to pick up any linebacker blitzing from the weak side. If no one came, he'd drift out of the backfield to find a seam in the coverage, just in case I needed someone to throw to in a pinch. No one blitzed, so Jamie became my third choice after Andre and running back Don Smith. When I saw that neither Andre nor Smith was open, I scrambled to my left and looked for Jamie, who hadn't caught a touchdown pass since joining the Bills as a rookie in 1987. I waved him one way, then another. And after what seemed like eternity, I hit Jamie for my fourth TD throw of the game (the most since the Cleveland playoff loss) in the last 19 seconds to give us a 30–27 win.

Everyone said we were lucky in those games, and maybe there was some truth to that. The Broncos and Raiders beat themselves to a certain extent. But in all three cases it came down to this: If you play 100 percent of the game, go all out on every single snap for four quarters, you always have a chance to win. A team that falls behind and just says, "Hey, we're out of this thing," doesn't have a prayer. I've always believed that a lot of your "luck" is created rather than found.

As tough as those games might have been emotionally, you couldn't help but feel good about the things that were happening to us as a team. When you look back and think about how some championships have been won, you recall some pretty wild plays, such as Franco Harris's Immaculate Reception that allowed the Steelers to beat the Raiders. In all sports, some things happen that are just not supposed to happen. And when they do, you stop and say, "Wow! Maybe we've got a date with destiny."

We proceeded to win four more games in a row—at New England (27–10), at Cleveland (42–0), Phoenix at home (45–14) and the Patriots at home (14–0). That gave us a 9–1 record and sole possession of first place in the AFC East over the Dolphins, who had been running stride for stride with us the whole season.

But we weren't alone at the top for long. The following Monday night, we lost to the 5–5 Oilers at Houston, 27–24, and again found ourselves tied with Miami.

• • • •

Except for that opening drive against the Colts and the usual two-minute situations, we had pretty much put away the no-huddle for safekeeping through those first eleven weeks of the season. Again, as long as that was what Ted and Marv thought was best, it was good enough for me. Besides, who could argue with our 9–2 record?

But in preparing for our twelfth game, at home against Philadelphia, the coaches decided it was time to bring the no-huddle out of storage. The actual term we use for it is "K-Gun." No, the "K" is not for Kelly; it's for our tight end, Keith McKeller, who everyone on the team knows as "Killer," and whose receiving skills make him a threat along with the three wide-outs (Reed, Lofton and Don Beebe). There's only one running back, Thurman, and he's every bit as much a pass catcher as the rest. "Gun," of course, comes from the fact that we usually run it from shotgun formation, although sometimes I am under center.

Anyway, in studying past games, the coaches saw that whenever we needed to score, the no-huddle was virtually a surefire way for us to do so. Then they said, "Why not see if that trend would hold up through an entire game?"

Actually, it was more Ted than Coach Levy who arrived at that conclusion. Coach Levy prefers to leave a lot of those type of decisions to the assistants on his offensive and defensive staffs. The one area where he chooses to have direct, hands-on involvement is on special teams. Which only makes sense, because he broke into the NFL as a special teams coach and knows the ins and outs of every aspect of the kicking game.

Of course, if Coach Levy didn't agree with an idea that Ted or any of the other assistants presented to him, he could always veto it. But he had a lot of confidence in Ted. He knew Ted wouldn't come up with something that wasn't sound.

As I said, Coach Levy's biggest objection to going with "K-Gun" full-time was the problems he thought it would cause in pass-protection. But Ted and I kept assuring him that we could and would run the ball just as much as we had in our regular offense, which would help keep pass-rushers honest. Coach Levy was finally convinced it was worth a shot.

Another reason the coaches picked the Eagles game to unleash the no-huddle was they felt that having first-strike capability was the best way for us to gain an edge over what everybody had been calling one of the best defenses in the league. And the Eagles' defense was good, with dominant linemen such as Reggie White, Jerome Brown and Clyde Simmons and a great outside linebacker in Seth Joyner.

On that day, however, we played like one of the best offenses in the league. We were clicking right from the first snap. In fact, after taking the opening kickoff at our 34, we needed only two plays and 45 seconds to grab a 7–0 lead—I handed off to Thurman for three yards on the first play, then bang! I threw a 63-yard touchdown pass to James on the second.

Soon after Scotty made it 10–0 with a 43-yard field goal, we got the ball back at our 35. This time, we needed only 27 seconds to score a touchdown in two plays—a nine-yard run by Thurman followed by my 56-yard scoring pass to Andre.

It wasn't long before the Philadelphia defenders, who were blitzing from the start, began to suck wind.

"Come on, slow it down, bro'!" Jerome Brown said, between huffs and puffs. "What are you trying to do, kill us?"

I guess he didn't get the point. But we sure did.

"This is fun," I thought to myself. "What a great feeling!"

The feeling got even better after we began our fourth possession with 2:45 remaining in the first quarter. On third down, I hooked up with James for a 71-yard gain to the Eagles' 4. And on the next play I found Thurm for my third TD pass, giving us a 24–0 lead with still more than a minute to play in the opening period. By that time, I was already 8 for 8 for 229 yards.

We knew Buddy Ryan, the Eagles' coach at the time, didn't have any respect for what our offense could do. We knew he came in there thinking his big, bad defenders were going to pound the crap out of us. But like Elijah Pitts, one of our offensive assistant coaches, said afterward, "Yeah, Buddy Ryan can say what he wants. But before I even had a chance to put on my headset, it was 24–0."

Looking around the locker room at halftime, with us holding a 24–16 lead, you saw everyone trying very hard not to smile too much. It wasn't easy. We all knew something incredible had happened to us in those first thirty minutes and we were all feeling pretty giddy about it. Besides the quick points, we kept our mistakes to a minimum. The Eagles would blitz and, bang!

I'd hit the open receiver. Or I'd shake off a blitzer and find someone for a big play. We were just on a huge roll.

But we also knew we had another thirty minutes to go, and one thing you try to avoid at all costs is celebrating too early. You do that, and most of the time you'll be crying later.

With Randall Cunningham coming up with a bunch of big plays of his own—including an amazing 95-yard scoring pass just before halftime—the Eagles came back to make the game interesting. But we still ended up with the victory, 30–23. I also finished with my first 300-yard output of the season, hitting 19 of 32 passes for 334 yards. I owe most of that to my offensive linemen—Will, Jim, Kent, John and Howard—who kept me from being sacked the whole game.

And their shutout was enough to convince the coaches that the concerns they had had over the kind of punishment I'd take because of the no-huddle were unfounded. If pass protection was going to be a problem in any game, that figured to be the one. And if someone had told me beforehand that—with or without the no-huddle—Reggie White or any of those other All-Pros on Philadelphia's defensive front weren't going to sack me, I'd have thought he was goofy.

We stuck with "K-Gun" throughout our next game, at Indianapolis, and it worked every bit as well as the previous week. I connected on seven of my first nine passes, including two for touchdowns in the first quarter, on the way to our 31–7 rout.

Without a doubt, using the no-huddle on a full-time basis agreed with us. Averaging 18 to 20 seconds between snaps definitely agreed with me, because I'm the type of person who's constantly on the move. It drives my mother crazy. All my life I've heard her tell me, "Please, Jim. SLOW DOWN!" But when I'm awake, I'm on fast-forward. That's just me.

I also loved the idea of being in total control of the offense, of having complete freedom to call whatever play I wanted when I wanted. If I thought that throwing seven passes in a row was the best way to attack a team, then that was what I called. If running the ball down their throat looked like the answer to me, then that was what I called. Or maybe we just had to keep mixing things up.

Whether we scored points or didn't score points was in my hands. And that was right where it belonged. The quarterback is the field general, and field generals are supposed to make all the key decisions that determine the outcome of a battle. Sure, you set yourself up for extra criticism from fans and media that most other quarterbacks don't have to worry about. Now, instead of just bitching about your interceptions and incompletions, they can also add poor play selection to the list. That buck stops right here.

Most coaches aren't like Marv and Ted, who believe the quarterback, because he's out there under the gun, is in the best position to call plays. They think they're in a better position to handle the chore by listening on the headsets to someone with a bird's-eye view of the field. And they'd just as soon not put that kind of pressure on their quarterbacks.

But ever since midget league football, I've readily accepted the responsibility of having everything ride on my performance. It was the same way in high school football and basketball. If I made the big plays, we were usually successful; if I didn't, we usually lost.

But no matter who you are in a team sport, you're not going to accomplish anything by yourself. You're only as good as your supporting cast. During the 1990 season mine had become one of the strongest in the NFL, beginning with our offensive line. Despite all the concern over whether those big studs would have enough stamina to run the no-huddle full-time, they ended up loving the concept right away. The biggest reason was that it helped slow down the pass rush. Never quite knowing what type of play was coming at them next, the defensive linemen automatically lost a little of their aggressiveness because they couldn't expect a pass all the time; they had to respect our running threat. And the faster pace seemed to tire them out more than it did the offensive linemen because the defenders had the extra burden of chasing the ball.

Sometimes Kent Hull will say, "Slow it down just one beat, Jim, so we can catch our breath." Or if we've just run five quick plays, picking up a first down on the fifth, I'll purposely move it a little slower so everyone has a chance to revive himself. But thanks to the great work of Rusty Jones, our strength-and-conditioning coordinator, everyone's in pretty good shape. Plus, we usually score so fast, you aren't out there long enough even to get tired.

Andre Reed and James Lofton emerged as one of the NFL's better receiving duos in 1990. Name the pattern and Andre runs it: five-yard in, 10-yard in, flag, post, streak. He does it all, and that's why he became my favorite receiver through the years. James? On his way to the Pro Football Hall of Fame, he has treated us to the magic he showed as a youngster in Green Bay. It just seems like he's always in the right place at the right time. In his mid-thirties, he might not be quite as quick as Andre, but he has that long stride, which allows him to pull away from just about any defensive back on a deep route. And James has some of the greatest hands you'll ever want to see.

As a receiver, Thurman Thomas can do just about anything he wants out there, and I try my best to take advantage of all his talents. He runs a lot of option routes, meaning he'll go out six yards, drawing one-on-one coverage from a linebacker, with the option of breaking out or breaking in or flying right past the guy for a long one. As I said, there isn't a linebacker in the league who can cover Thurman one on one, I don't care who he is. But if you want to double him and leave Andre single-covered, no problem.

Then there's Keith McKeller, who can run any pattern the receivers run with a lot more grace than your average tight end. So take your choice; if you want to double this guy, I'll just go to that one.

And when I want to run the ball, I've still got Thurman or Kenny Davis ready to motor. You can be so successful running the ball in the no-huddle because there are more opportunities for us to run when teams expect us to pass. A defense sees the no-huddle and automatically thinks pass, but a lot of times I'll come to the line, see that the linebackers are deep and audible to a run—either a handoff or a direct snap to Thurman or one of our other backs.

Having someone like Thurman in the backfield, I'm not the least bit concerned about calling a run on third and eight. I wouldn't do that with most guys, but I'd take the chance of him getting the first down, or even a touchdown, anytime.

When things really click for us in the no-huddle, we're scoring fast, our defense is forcing the other team to go three and out and we're right back on the field looking to score again.

There is a big difference between the way we run our no-huddle and the way the Bengals ran theirs while establishing themselves as the no-huddle kings of the NFL in 1988 and 1989. The Bengals were basically just trying to catch defenses changing personnel so they could get a five-yard penalty for too many men on the field. That's not our goal. Our goal is to keep the same defense on the field as long as we can.

Of course, if you try to substitute on a regular basis, we're probably going to catch you, too. But the thing we're really after is to create mismatches, hoping to force the other team to keep its best defenders against the run out there when we're throwing the ball and vice versa. We tend to get a lot of them.

The only time in "K-Gun" when we usually huddle is before the first play. I already have a pretty good idea of what my first two or three calls will be, but I only give the first one in the huddle. For the rest of the series, my decisions take into account down, distance and what the defense shows.

I look at the contour of the secondary to see what kind of coverage they're in—a three-deep zone, with three deep safeties; a two-deep zone, with two deep safeties; or man-to-man. Even if we have a running play called, I still check out the coverage. I try never to get in a frame of mind where if it's a running play I just look at the line and if it's a passing play I just look at the secondary. For one thing, I like to confirm whether they're showing the same looks I had seen on film. For another, I might find something we could exploit by audibling.

Before calling the play in that first huddle, I always try to say a little something to set the tone for the rest of the day. Something like: "All right, guys. This is what it's all about. This is what we've been practicing for all week long. It's finally here, so let's go out, have some fun . . . and kick some ass!"

After that, most of what comes out of my mouth during the drive is signals. I call the plays, the formations, the blocking schemes, the pass patterns and the snap count. I might be warning the offensive line that a blitz is coming. I might be switching from a pass to a run. We have between thirty and forty different plays, and about ten formations. So it's not something that the other team can easily key on.

I make up all my own terminology, which changes from week to week and year to year. I use colors, names of people, cars, anything I can think of. You wouldn't believe how much information I'm able to dispense just by yelling "Chevy! Chevy!" or "Buick! Buick!" I've even made calls using words that don't exist in any language, such as "Coby Oshi Maroo, on two." That's from my college and USFL days. All it meant was: "Let's go for it, long."

Remembering signals is never a problem for me, because, as a quarterback, everything you do over the years becomes second nature. I can even remember plays I called in high school, such as a "T.A. Slant." That was a quick slant pattern to the man with those initials, Tommy Andreassi. This worked like a charm almost every time.

I also have a set of dummy audibles so the defense can't pick up a play by remembering what we did the last time I used a particular signal. Every time he hears me make a dummy call, Howard Ballard starts to laugh. He can't help himself. He takes one look at the defensive lineman, who thinks we've just tipped him off to what we're going to do, and he laughs out loud. Right in the middle of the game.

Whether they're dummy calls or the real thing, the key is to keep them as simple as possible. For instance, we have one play that's called an "All Go." That's where you have every receiver running an up route, with Andre and Keith inside, James and Don Beebe on the outside. One of them will take the free safety to one side of the field, and I'll throw in the opposite direction. Or I'll have a receiver take the free safety to where I don't want him to be, and I'll look back the other way, trying to bait him with my eyes. When he's hooked, I throw to the guy he has left open. Some quarterbacks like to use pump fakes to get the safeties chasing ghosts. But it's been my experience that, more often than not, they try to read the quarterback's eyes. Pump fakes sometimes work, but I still prefer using my eyes.

After calling the signals, there really isn't time for me to say much else out there, although there are times when I might say things like: "Come on, guys, let's keep it going! We have them on the ropes!" Or: "Come on, guys, we have to pick it up a notch!" Or: "We have to establish the running game more!" Or: "We're going to really open things up now, so give me some time to throw!"

When you take the field, you have to have a firm command of

everything around you; there can't be any uncertainty about what you're doing or you're going to be headed straight for a disaster. Everything has to flow naturally. And that's even more important in the no-huddle because things are moving so fast, you don't have time to stop and think. You have to know exactly what you're doing at the snap of a finger. In a standard offense, you can casually walk up to the line, patiently read the defense and then decide what you want to do. In the no-huddle, once you get everyone set, you have to be ready to go. There just isn't time to go through your cadence and study every little thing. And, by design, there should be less to worry about. In most cases, the defense you see is the defense that's going to be run against you because they won't have time to switch too many guys. So you have to take one good look, scanning left to right, and know instantly where you're going with the ball.

Through studying tendencies on film, you have an idea of what defenses to expect against certain plays you call. But you also can't assume anything. There's always the possibility they will change things up on you at the last second, which they usually do. Because of that, I try to call plays that work against both zone coverages and man-to-man.

I also make it a point to remind the receivers to change their pass routes. If one of them runs a deep-square pattern exactly the same way every time, the defense is going to start catching on. They'll either pick it up during the course of the game or on film. So I tell the receivers to adjust what they're doing, even if it's only a little bit. Usually, they should have two or three variations of each route to utilize.

On a pass, I'm still reading the defense after the snap, still running down my keys. Your first receiver is your first target. And if he's not open, you don't take your time going to the next one or the one after that. You can't stop and think about what any of the other receivers are doing. As soon as you know the first guy's covered, you automatically move on, because you know, just by looking at the coverage, what the other receivers are supposed to do. It's like clockwork. Now, if I complete that first pass, I'll take a quick look to the side for the down and distance. Whatever they are, I know the available plays for that situation. And so on.

In this offense, the quarterback has to know what everybody's doing within five seconds. You have to know which way the offensive line is protecting. You have to read blitz pickup. If a blitz is coming, you have to read the receiver's sight adjustment, which turns it into a different pattern from the one he was originally supposed to run. If a blitzing linebacker isn't picked up in a certain protection, you've got to be able to hit the "hot" pattern out in the flat or over the middle—before you get knocked on your ass.

And you have to know what every single receiver is doing at all times. If it's a press, he's doing one thing. If it's zone, he's doing another. If it's man-to-man coverage, he's doing something else altogether. You also have to know how to pace your receivers. For instance, if I know a guy has just run his third streak route in a row, I'll tell him, "I'm not coming to you this time; take a break."

Once I'm on the field, I hardly ever look to the sidelines. But Ted would always be there, just in case I needed a play. Sometimes, after using a lot of the same material over and over, I'd glance at Ted or Frank to see if they had anything different in mind. More often than not, Ted would shake his head and say, "You have a good grasp of it. Just go with what you're doing." There were other times when they'd purposely avoid eye contact with me because they didn't think it was necessary to interfere.

The only time the play calling is taken out of my hands is in short-yardage and goal-line situations. Coach Levy prefers to handle that himself. He'll either signal me the play or tell it to me on the sidelines during a time-out. In those situations, he feels he can do a better job of seeing to it that we make all the right personnel changes, with small, fast guys coming out in favor of the big, powerful studs. And Coach Levy does a good job with it.

One big misconception about the no-huddle is that it diminishes the importance of coaching for the quarterback. Nothing could be more false. Although Ted didn't call the plays, he spent the week making certain I was thoroughly prepared to do so by kickoff. He advised me on what to look for on film, he explained things clearly on the chalkboard, he pointed out everything I should be seeing in practice, he showed me what plays to run on certain downs and distances, he told me what coverages to expect the opponent to use in certain situations. Ted's biggest contribution was putting me in the right frame of mind. And I always felt I was there—that is, unless someone delivered one of those hits that made me see double.

Ted also was an excellent teacher. To me, teaching is a major part of coaching, because a player never goes through a day during the season when his quality stays the same. He either gets better or gets worse; there's no in-between. In order to get better, he has to learn something, no matter how small, that allows his game to move forward. Otherwise, it takes a step back. And Ted would always manage to show me that one thing in practice—like the day I was keeping the ball too low as I set up to pass—that I needed to work on.

Thanks to him, I usually walked away from practice saying, "I had a good day today. I learned something."

Because of the added responsibility of calling plays, I started watching more film in the '90 season than I ever watched in my life. But it wasn't just the amount that mattered; it was the type. I had to make sure I looked at a lot of reels that showed how teams defensed the two-minute drill, which had been less of a concern when we were running our conventional offense. I had to see, when that hurry-up heat was on, how certain cornerbacks adjusted—whether they liked to give the receiver a lot of cushion or liked to press a little bit more. Just different things I might notice to help determine what play to go to or what individual to throw against.

My in-season work with Ted began each day at eight-thirty in the morning. First, we would watch film, along with Frank and Gale, for about an hour. Then we'd go to the general team meeting where Coach Levy addressed the entire squad. Then Ted, Frank, Gale and I would watch more film with the receivers. Then the three quarterbacks would get together to watch more film. Then we would break for lunch, come back and—you guessed it—watch more film. Finally, we practiced.

After each workout, I take home three to four reels of film (actually, we use videotapes nowadays) and watch them for an hour and a half or so in my film room downstairs. I grab about five pillows, plop down on the bed and work the play and rewind buttons until they're ready to fall off. I usually just make mental notes, but against teams I don't face regularly, I jot a few things down, because there might be some ideas I want to take back to the stadium. Ted would always joke that he should put in the game plan a day or two late, because each week Frank, Gale and I usually managed to persuade him to change about five or six plays or add a couple.

In fact, anytime he'd see Frank and me talking to each other at the chalkboard, Ted would get nervous and say, "Oh no! What do they want to change *now?*"

But he was really good about it. He'd listen to us, and I'd say about 80 percent of the time he'd install plays that we suggested. And if he didn't agree, he'd tell us that, too.

Ted's the type of coach every quarterback would love to have. He'll be greatly missed.

In Week Fourteen of the 1990 season, we took on the Giants at New Jersey in what was being hyped as the best of the AFC versus the best of the NFC. All we heard that week was how tough NFC teams were—and how superior they were to AFC clubs. We didn't buy that theory for a minute, of course. Nor did we like hearing Bill Parcells, the Giants' coach at the time, and some of his players refuse to acknowledge our effectiveness with the no-huddle.

So we were really looking forward to the chance to prove that we could hold our own against any NFC "bully," especially with the game being played on a Saturday before a national TV audience.

"K-Gun" was with us from the start, and, once again, we were rolling with it. After the Giants drove for a touchdown on the game's opening possession, we zapped them right back on our first drive, beginning with a 48-yard screen pass to Thurman that moved us all the way to the New York 26. Four plays later, I found Andre for a six-yard TD toss on a shallow crossing pattern to tie the score at 7–7. It was the fifth straight time and the seventh in the last/eight games that we put the ball in the end zone on our first offensive series.

We got the ball back at our 22, and with the help of my 36-yard pass to Andre, we were knocking on the door again at the Giants' 24. Some tough running by Don Smith and Thomas got us to the 2, from where Thurm ran a sweep for a touchdown to give us the lead less than a minute into the second quarter.

On both drives, it was obvious the Giants' defense was confused. Especially their linebackers, who didn't seem to know exactly where to line up and looked awkward in their movement at the snap. After all the scoffing they had done about the no-huddle, I think we caught them off guard with it. It seemed like we were one step ahead of them in everything we did.

The Giants were able to cut the margin to four on Matt Bahr's 23-yard field goal with 5:56 left in the first half. But we were on the march again 26 seconds later when, on second down from our 21, I threw a pass over the middle to Andre. After I released the ball, I got up on my toes to look downfield to see how the rest of the eight-yard play would develop. Then, all of a sudden, a hard pop in my left knee brought me down in a heap. I wouldn't find out until later that Will Wolford, our 295-pound left tackle, had lurched back into my left leg after his right knee was struck by Giants linebacker Carl Banks, who had been thrown aside by our left guard, Jimmy Ritcher. It was just one of those freak domino effects—*boom! boom! boom!*

The next thing I knew, I was on the ground holding my knee and feeling the worst pain I had ever felt in my life. First I was on my side moving my right leg and spinning in a circle. Then I sat up and just bobbed back and forth, grimacing with the thought that my season might have just ended.

But after a few minutes, the pain that had shot through my whole body was gone. I was able to get back on my feet, and although I was careful in putting weight on my left leg, I managed to walk slowly to the sidelines without anyone's help. As Frank came out to take my place, I told Kent that I'd be back in the game in a short while. He nodded his head, although I'm not sure he truly believed me. Having seen the kind of pain I was in on the field, I probably wouldn't have believed me either. But after overcoming the initial fear that I had torn my knee to shreds, I really thought it was the kind of injury that, like so many others, I'd just be able to shake off.

Once I got to the sidelines, I started doing deep knee bends to see how it felt. And it wasn't hurting all that bad.

"God, this is great," I said to the trainers. "I mean, if I can get hit the way I just did and move the way I'm moving now, this is pretty good."

Unfortunately, I had spoken too soon. I kept walking back

and forth in front of the bench to see how the knee would hold up, and it kept feeling better and better. Then I walked up to the edge of the field to watch the action. Forgetting myself in all the excitement of the game, I raised up on my toes to get a better view of the Giants' return of Rick Tuten's punt. And as I came down, my left knee buckled, just gave out completely. House happened to be standing right next to me, and caught me before I hit the ground.

Hopping over to the bench, I knew this time there would be no shaking it off. I didn't know how bad the damage was; you never know that until you get an X ray. But I had injured my right knee in 1985, during my second USFL season, and it felt similar to that. I avoided surgery then, wound up missing four games and returned for the playoffs.

Just before I climbed aboard the back of a utility cart that would take me to the dressing room where I would be more closely examined, I told Frank to encourage the coaches to keep using the no-huddle just in case they had any ideas of getting away from it because I was gone. They stuck with it, and as usual, Frank more than held his own as we would go on to win our third straight, 17–13.

When I reached the dressing room, Will was also in there, having his right knee checked. At first, neither one of us knew exactly what had happened. I didn't find out that it was Will who had fallen into me until one of the trainers told me several minutes later. And Will didn't find out until he spoke with me in the dressing room. In fact, as soon as he saw me he said, "Jim, what happened to you?"

"Well, I guess when you got hurt, you fell down and landed on my leg," I said. "At least, that's what they're telling me."

"You've got to be kidding me!"

"I find it kind of hard to believe myself."

"What were they having here today? A two-for-one special on knee injuries?"

My injury wasn't Will's fault, of course, just as his injury wasn't Banks's fault or Jimmy's fault. They just happened. When 200- and 300-pound bodies are flying around on every play, even a bizarre chain of events like that is a lot more possible than it might appear at first glance.

Dr. Weiss's initial diagnosis was that I had suffered a sprained medial collateral ligament. He estimated I would be out anywhere from two to six weeks, although he would have a better idea once I underwent a magnetic resonance imaging (MRI) examination on Monday. The first thought that came to mind was missing the following week's game at home against Miami, with our third consecutive AFC East championship and home-field advantage through the playoffs on the line. The second thought was the possibility of missing all of the postseason and what had been looking like a great shot for us to finally reach the Super Bowl.

I started wondering if being the top-rated passer in the NFL —as I was then—or the AFC, was some sort of jinx. A year earlier, at Indianapolis, I had been the conference's top-rated passer when I suffered a shoulder separation.

The MRI of my knee pretty much confirmed Weiss's diagnosis, indicating I would be out a minimum of three games and a maximum of six. With such a wide time range, we agreed the best thing to tell the media during a news conference a few days after the game was that I was expected to be sidelined for four weeks. No one knew for certain if that was a hundred percent accurate; you can never be positive about something like that. You really have to see the kind of progress you make day to day and week to week.

But if it was correct and if we beat the Dolphins, thus clinching the division and receiving a first-round playoff bye, I had a chance to return to the lineup in time for our divisional-round match on the weekend of January 12–13. Of course, if we lost to Miami, we'd have to play a wild-card game in three weeks. That left open the possibility of the season being over before I'd ever get to play again.

As always, Frank had my full support, although I don't think he needed it nearly as much as the previous season. Now, after that 3–0 stretch in 1989, the guy had a proven record of success as an NFL starter. No one saw him as a babe in the woods anymore. It wasn't a case where I thought Frank could get the job done; I *knew* he could.

Still, the idea of missing that Miami game was killing me. It was a game that every player and coach on the Bills and the whole western New York community were looking forward to. Everything was on the line, including the chance for us to redeem ourselves for that 23-point ass kicking they had given us back in September. This was the match-up we had all been dreaming about. This was the kind of game every football player lives for.

And I'd be spending it on the sidelines.

"What have I done wrong?" I asked a roomful of reporters the Tuesday before the Miami game. "I go to church every Sunday. I pray. God, I just don't know . . ."

The next day, I found myself in a familiar position—watching practice. Once again, I was standing around doing nothing while everyone else prepared for what, at the time, was the biggest sporting event to be staged in Buffalo since the 1966 AFL Championship Game against Kansas City. Once again, I hated it.

But just as they had so many times before, my family was there to provide the encouragement I needed to get through yet another injury.

"You're going to have to do what you did before," Pat told me during one of our many phone conversations. "Stay plugged in because Frank is going to need your help. I've said this before, and I'll say it again: Injuries are a part of football, you have to learn to accept them and you have to forget about them. The most important thing for you now is to do what it takes to get back into that lineup. This is nothing new for you, Jim. You've been through it before. You know how it's done."

I also knew that the trainers, Abe and Bud, would push me to the hilt so I could get back in there as soon as was humanly possible. Or shall I say, inhumanly possible.

For the time being, everything that all of us had worked so hard to achieve was riding on Frank's shoulders. It was a mammoth load, to say the least. But everybody on the team had faith in his ability to carry it, which isn't always the case when it comes to backup quarterbacks. Some just don't inspire a lot of confidence in their teammates, because either they've never had the chance to start in a regular-season game or when the opportunity came they didn't take advantage of it. Backups have a tendency to get a little lackadaisical in practice during the week because, for one thing, they don't get that many snaps, and for another, they usually don't anticipate seeing any action in the game.

But with those three starts in '89 Frank demonstrated to everybody on the team just how well prepared he was for each game. And a lot of that came from following an approach that Ted constantly pounded into his head.

"Remember, you're always just one play away from being a starting quarterback," Ted would say. "So you have to prepare yourself as a starter. You have to stay focused in order to be ready when you're called upon."

Frank had stayed focused. Frank was ready.

My knee was heavily taped and braced for a long day of standing on and watching from the sidelines. I didn't feel a lot of pain, but I was very leery about the way I moved. The last thing in the world I wanted was to have it pop out again and set back my recovery. I just had to be careful—a hell of a lot more careful than I was along the sidelines at Giants Stadium the previous weekend.

The best thing I could do for Frank that day was make myself available to answer any questions he might have during the course of the game. Occasionally, I might point out something I'd seen in the Dolphins' secondary and suggest one or two plays to exploit it with. But what I didn't want to do was bother him with all kinds of advice he didn't ask for. Frank had enough on his mind. He didn't need me to increase the burden.

Our playing styles are as different as our personalities. I'm a risk taker. Frank's conservative. He works with everything the defense gives him and usually won't challenge a defender to try to take something that isn't there. As a result, he keeps his mistakes to a minimum and comes out of almost every game having done more things right than wrong. But sometimes Frank will surprise you by taking a gamble, by going for broke. I guess all those years of watching me try to make the big play so often rubbed off on him a little bit. Like every other quarterback, Frank has a greedy side that will come out at a certain point in a game. You see the opportunity to take a chance for a huge play, and sometimes you just can't resist.

We stuck with the no-huddle; Ted saw no reason why he should give Frank less to work with than he would have given me. Which made perfect sense. "K-Gun" had been succeeding for us. The linemen, receivers and backs were used to it. Why change now? Besides, a game plan is supposed to be designed to attack the weaknesses of the other team. Although his pace might have been a hair slower, Frank was every bit as capable of operating the no-huddle as I was. One thing you knew for sure: He would usually have us in the right play.

And after a sluggish first quarter, he had us moving in the right direction in the second with a seven-yard scoring throw to James that gave us a 7–0 halftime lead. Frank also connected with Andre in the third quarter to put us in front 14–0.

The Dolphins finally got on the board in the third quarter with a 30-yard touchdown pass from Dan Marino to Mark Duper. But Frank guided us to a 21-yard Norwood field goal midway through the third and a 13-yard scoring run by Thurm, to cap off his 154-yard day, to give us a 24–7 lead early in the fourth. Feeling comfortable that the game was ours, I walked over to Frank on the sidelines to give him a big hug for a job well done.

Miami managed seven more points in the final minute, but that was all. We had our third straight division championship and the right to stay home for two playoff games. Now, all I had to do was get my knee healthy in time for the first one.

Helping along those lines that day was my bodyguard, Ed Perkins. Actually, Ed's a close friend and one of my hunting partners. But he happens to stand 6-5 and weigh 450 pounds, and he isn't the type of guy most people would want to mess with. Ed, whom I met in 1988 when he was riding a bulldozer to clear the land for my house, stood on the sidelines with me the entire game because, with the anticipation of the crowd storming the field and my inability to move out of the way fast enough, the team felt I should have some protection. Ed also does a little part-time work for JKE in that capacity, making sure things stay cool when I make a personal appearance and there are a lot of people around. He also helps me get through the crush of autograph seekers after games from the locker room to my family's tailgate party in the parking lot, and keeps an eye on things there as well.

Bill Polian had told me beforehand to be sure I headed straight for the tunnel a little bit early in case there were any problems with the fans. But I was enjoying the game too much and wanted to stay out there right until the last second. Besides, with big Ed by my side, how could I worry about anything bad happening to me?

But Polian was worried, and he and the Bills' security people kept coming up to me in the last couple of minutes yelling, "Go! Go! Get up in the tunnel, Jim!" I finally took off with 59 seconds showing.

And sure enough, there was a wild postgame scene, with fans tearing down the goalposts, despite the fact that we had at least one more game to play at Rich, and pulling out knives to take souvenir swatches of the artificial turf. Clashes between fans and the police/security force led to a bunch of people being treated for injuries. I've always said the violent stuff should be left to the players. At least we get paid to take the punishment.

The season ended with a meaningless 29–14 loss at Washington. You always hate to lose, but considering the fact that Coach Levy had substituted a lot of players and abandoned the no-huddle so potential playoff opponents would have a little less information on how to defense it, that one wasn't too tough to swallow. Our 13–3 record was still the best in franchise history.

Now we were looking to go 3–0 in a brand-new season.

I didn't practice during the week before our playoff bye. I spent the time going through a vigorous exercise program, which included running on a Stairmaster and a ton of leg lifts. But where the media was concerned, I went through that week in silence, deciding it was best for me to concentrate fully on getting my knee right. I planned to answer all their questions the following week, when I actually began to practice.

For my workouts, I wore a custom-fitted brace designed to give me greater stability when I twisted the leg while following through on my passes. It would take some getting used to. As I moved around on the field, I felt a certain amount of pain in the knee. Nothing I couldn't tolerate, but enough to stop me from wanting to do too much cutting on it as I ran. I couldn't help but think that at any time it might pop loose and I'd again be watching from the sidelines.

I wasn't prepared to go through that again.

As long as the knee was stable—and the doctor told me it was —I was going to play. It definitely wouldn't be a hundred percent ready for action by game day. It wouldn't even be eighty percent. But I had made up my mind I was going to play. My only concern was getting through the week, and then the game, without someone falling on my knee again or just hitting it the wrong way. Any sort of accident like that and I could be in serious trouble.

One thing that did feel a hundred percent ready was my throwing arm. All the rest it had received over the previous three weeks had done wonders. Normally, by the time you've practiced and played through a sixteen-week schedule (not to mention a four-week preseason and training camp), your arm is wearing down. After my first practice, I was showing much better zip than I had in quite a while. All my timing and all my throws were right on. Even in seven-on-seven drills, where you're working against the most concentrated pass coverage you can get in practice, I didn't throw a single incompletion.

Our divisional-round opponent ended up being the Dolphins, who were facing us because of their 17–16 wild-card victory over Kansas City and Cincinnati's 41–14 wild-card win over Houston. Had the Oilers won, they would have been packing for Buffalo.

Waiting to greet Miami was a semi-solid dose of "Bills weather." As had been forecast right along, the thermometer was down by the freezing point and a drizzle that began in the morning turned into snow by kickoff. It wasn't anything heavy, yet the Dolphins had packed about three thousand extra pounds of equipment. Most of it consisted of parkas, turtlenecks, gloves and hats. Maybe they were expecting a blizzard.

But they weren't the only ones taking precautions that day. Our trainers wrapped so much tape around my knee, I could have sworn I was wearing a cast.

Still, we all felt very confident going into that game. I wouldn't say we were overconfident. But we knew, on that day, we could handle them. After beating them twice already that season, we knew that our offensive line was better than their defensive line, and that our defensive line was better than their offensive line. We just knew, on that day, we were going to beat them.

And I honestly think, deep down, they knew it too.

We opened in "K-Gun," of course and, much to my surprise, I felt like I hadn't missed a beat from my last series in the Giants game. Despite being out all that time, I didn't feel the least bit rusty. I felt fully prepared for a big day. And I knew, once I completed that first pass, I'd have all the confidence I needed to complete some more.

One snap into the game, I put a 20-yarder into Thurman's hands. Four snaps in, I hooked up with Andre 30 yards downfield, and he ran the rest of the way for a touchdown. Bang! We were ahead, 7–0. Miami answered with a field goal. But before you could blink, we were lining up for a 24-yard field goal by Scotty, which he followed with a 22-yarder to give us a 13–3 lead at the end of the first quarter. We continued to make it look easy in the second, when I found Andre, who was being guarded by Louis Oliver (a true mismatch), for a 43-yard gain that helped set up a short touchdown run by Thurman to put us up 20–3.

Against a lot of teams, that would be a safe lead. But not against Marino. He came right back with a 64-yard touchdown bomb to Duper and, before long, I had yet another shoot-out going with one of the best golfing quarterbacks I know. (With that beautiful weather he has year-round in South Florida, his golf game should be great; I still haven't figured out how to blast out of a snowdrift.)

Actually, it's never really a case of Dan and me trying to out-perform each other individually on the field. That's something the media likes to fuss over. Our jobs are to help our teams come out on top. Yet it almost always seems to happen that, in the same game, we both put up a lot of passing yards and a lot of points. It was obvious this one wasn't going to be an exception.

I found James on a 13-yard TD pass to restore our 17-point advantage in the second quarter. As good a time as Reed was having against Oliver, James was having just as much fun going one on one with Tim McKyer. But a Marino bootleg made it 27–17 just before halftime, and Pete Stoyanovich kicked a 22-yard field goal early in the third quarter to make it a seven-point game again. Scotty booted a 28-yarder late in the third, but on a tackle-eligible play that faked out everybody in the stadium, Marino hit 284-pound Roy Foster for a two-yard touchdown to pull Miami within three at the start of the fourth.

For the first time, it felt like we were losing a little momen-

One of the early games of my "rookie" season in the NFL. (Robert L. Smith)

Helping me hunt for "big game" at the shooting of a poster we did for charity are, from the left, back row: Joe Devlin, Shane Conlan and Bruce Smith; front row: Thurman Thomas, Roger Trevino, my brother Dan, and Andre Reed. (Myers Studio)

Watching from the sidelines, out
of pads . . .

. . . and in pain. (Robert L. Smith)

With Bill Cosby; Sophia Bowen, Miss Georgia; and boxer Mark Breland. (Author's collection)

Showing them the ropes at my football camp. (Author's collection)

Making a point with the campers. (Author's collection)

Poised over center.
(Robert L. Smith)

Talking things over with Ted Marchibroda, my former offensive coordinator, and Frank Reich, a great backup and an even better friend. (Mike Groll)

When things get tough, I can always call on my boys to protect me. Clockwise from the left are Jim Ritcher, John Davis, Will Wolford, House Ballard and Kent Hull. (Cellular One/Buffalo Telephone Company)

The Kelly clan. From the left, back row: Pat and his wife, Tricia; Kevin and his wife, Charlene; my sister-in-law Pam and Ray; my sister-in-law Cynthia and Ed; middle row: Dan, Mom and Dad; the grandchildren: Brian, Allison, Matthew, Christian and Sean. (Jim Bush)

A triumphant moment! (Jim Bush)

That's my brother Pat, in a hopeless attempt to make contact after I was knocked silly in Super Bowl XXVI.

Nupe it! (Marty Heitner)

My corporate look.
(Jim Bush)

My "coaching staff" at Jim Kelly Enterprises. From the left: Roger Trevino, my brother Dan, and Dan Trevino. (Jamie Germano/Rochester *Democrat and Chronicle*)

tum. Then *bang! bang!* we had two more touchdowns—on a five-yard run by Thomas and my 26-yard throw to Reed—and a 44–27 lead with less than 10 minutes to play. Leave it to Marino to get in one more TD pass before the end of the day, but it wouldn't matter.

Final score: Bills 44, Dolphins 34.

I finished with my best playoff numbers to date, connecting on 19 of 29 passes for 339 yards and three touchdowns while throwing only one interception. Even with that "cast" around my left leg, I also ran three times for 37 yards. And I went out for a pass on what we call a "Skillet Left" play. That's where I hand off to Thurman, who runs to my right while I run a pattern to the left, and he throws me the ball. But that time, he hung on to it because some alert Dolphin came over to cover me. Why "Skillet," you ask? Because my *tremendous* ability as a receiver earned me the nickname Skillet Hands from my teammates. Get it?

Some people thought I was crazy for doing all that running around on a knee that was still in need of healing. Even a few Dolphin defenders looked pretty stunned as they saw me leave the pocket the first couple of times and come rumbling toward them. But when you're playing, you're not thinking about pain or whether all your joints are going to hold up. You're thinking about the things you have to do to win. The other stuff is just too distracting. If it reaches a point where you're thinking more about your aches than what you're doing on the field, that's the time to get to the sidelines for treatment.

Of course, the guys who truly were impressive with their legs were James (seven catches for 149 yards and a touchdown), Andre (four catches for 122 yards and two TDs) and Thurman (117 yards and two scores rushing; three catches for 38 yards). Besides their great talent, I think a lot of the success they had that day was due to the snow that completely covered the field by the second quarter. Miami's defense was hindered by the slick surface, which, in turn, made it a big advantage for us. Number one, our guys were used to it. Number two, our guys knew where they were going. A lot of times, when the Dolphin defensive backs tried changing direction on the fly, they wound up flat on their face masks.

At that point, we were feeling very good about our chances of reaching Super Bowl XXV. We were confident that we had the right material, offensively and defensively, to get there. Most important of all, we felt we were peaking exactly when we had to.

Everything just clicked for us. Not only the offense but the defense—which had the 1990 NFL Defensive MVP in Bruce Smith—and special teams, too. In all three areas, we were consistently coming up with big plays when we really had to have them. Anytime we were pinned against a wall, somebody would make the play that set us free. And that's the main ingredient of a championship team.

We definitely thought our time had come to go to the Big Dance. But we still had one more task to complete before receiving our invitation.

If the NFL had handed me a catalogue and said, "Pick an opponent for the AFC Championship Game," I couldn't have made a better choice than the Raiders, who were headed our way after winning their divisional-round game against Cincinnati, 20–10.

One obvious reason was, at 12–4, they had shared with Miami the second-best record in the AFC after us. What better way to settle the conference title than with a game between the two best teams in the conference? Another obvious reason was that they viewed our victory over them during the regular season, when we scored 24 points in the fourth quarter, as nothing but a fluke.

But for me, personally, there was yet another obvious reason: They were *the Raiders*. They were one of only two teams in professional sports that I was in awe of as a kid. When I wasn't daydreaming about throwing passes to Lynn Swann and John Stallworth at Three Rivers Stadium, I was fantasizing about completing long bombs to Fred Biletnikoff and Cliff Branch at Oakland–Alameda County Coliseum.

And even though I realized the players I loved watching as a youngster wouldn't be with them anymore, they were still *the Raiders*. There's a special satisfaction you get from beating a team that, in your heart, you once believed was unbeatable.

Yet I refused to buy all the talk about "Raider Mystique." Reporter after reporter would come up to me and ask, "What do you think about the Raider Mystique?" Or "How are you going to handle the Raider Mystique?" To me, the Raiders have always been a great organization with a long history of success. But to so many others in and around the NFL, they're the CIA in helmets and shoulder pads. Everyone gets so caught up with Al Davis and his reputation for having spies planted throughout the league who call him in Los Angeles with every opponent's secrets. When I hear that, I always picture a guy whispering into his shoe, like Maxwell Smart. It's crazy. I just don't think it's nearly as big a deal as some people make it out to be.

Still, as soon as we began preparing for the Raiders that week, we were all encouraged to take special precautions to make sure our game plans and any other vital information we had didn't slip into "enemy" hands. As always, I just laughed about it and took a business-as-usual approach. I had never come close to revealing our strategy to anyone outside the team, regardless of who we were playing, and I wasn't about to start then.

I've always had a lot of respect for Al Davis. He loves to win, period. That's why he's in the Hall of Fame—the Pro Football Hall of Fame, not the Spy Hall of Fame. I think, deep down, Al wants people to believe certain things about him just so he can get more pub.

I was a lot more worried about the players on the Raiders' defense than I was about whether the cleaning lady at Rich Stadium was on Al's payroll. We had a lot of respect for their defense. We knew exactly what they were capable of doing, which was a lot of damage to our offense if we weren't careful.

From what they showed us during the regular season and what we had seen on film, we knew the main thing they had going for them was a great pass rush. They were very quick off the ball, especially Howie Long. And having that ability to get good pressure up front made their overall defense, which might not have been loaded with great players, look that much better. A strong pass rush will always make a secondary seem a lot better than it really is, just as a weak pass rush will turn a secondary filled with great talent into Swiss cheese.

The expectation of a tough game kept us all pretty fired up during the week. To a man, we felt it would take the best game each of us could possibly play to beat those guys. I mean, we were as focused as ever. And I was among several players on the team who stayed late after every practice that week, putting in the extra study time to make sure I knew everything I needed to know about the Raiders' defense.

The attitude throughout our locker room was, "Let's make sure we have it all down, every last detail." Usually, that's a sign of: (a) You aren't all that familiar with an opponent—and even though we had played the Raiders earlier in the season, we didn't know them nearly as well as a team like Miami that we play twice a year; (b) You fully understand the importance of the game—and that was the biggest game of our lives at that point; (c) You have the utmost respect for your opponent; you're worried about them.

The only time our minds were pulled away from the Raiders and the game was early in the evening of Wednesday, January 16. That was when we all heard that war had broken out in the Middle East. With the game four days away, it suddenly dawned on us that the battle our soldiers were waging in the sand was a hell of a lot more significant than our contest at Rich. Many of the fighting men and women would pay the ultimate price in combat—with their lives.

Some guys on the team had relatives in the military stationed in the Persian Gulf. One of our linebackers, Carlton Bailey, had his father over there. He was as concerned as you would expect him to be at a time like that. But, just by watching him in practice, you could see he was still very much plugged in to the preparation for the game. You had to respect him for that.

All of our hearts and a hundred percent of our support were going out to those involved in the war and their families. At the same time, we knew life was still going on everywhere else in Buffalo and throughout the country. Sure, there was a lot of talk about both conference championship games being postponed or canceled. There was even speculation that the Super Bowl would be called off.

As far as I was concerned, it was just that—talk. There wasn't a single change made in our practice routine, which would have been the first sign the game might not be staged as planned. Very little of what happens in the executive offices at One Bills Drive doesn't make its way down to the locker room or the practice field at some point, and we weren't hearing or seeing a single thing out of the ordinary. The rest of the week was as normal as could be, except for the extra-large media contingent from all over the country.

Besides, from everything I was hearing, the majority of people in America wanted the games to go on. I received a bunch of letters from individuals from Buffalo who had been stationed in the Gulf since the fall saying how sad they were that they hadn't been able to attend any of our games and would remain on active duty through the Super Bowl. They were longtime fans, some holding season tickets, who felt they were missing out on all the fun of our great season.

That was what made the timing of the conflict so sad. Here we were, on the verge of accomplishing something a lot of people in western New York had waited their whole lives to see, and it was forced (rightfully so) to take a back seat to a war. Without a doubt, a damper had been placed on the game. However, in some respects, maybe we were providing something that a lot of people everywhere needed at that point—a little entertainment.

I was pumped for the Raiders game, really excited. As I got to the bottom of the tunnel, I felt goose bumps going up and down my arms. The stadium was packed. There were American flags all over the place. And once the national anthem began, it seemed like the number of those flags doubled. People were pulling them out of their pockets left and right. After the music finished and the crowd started to roar, it actually took a few minutes before you could get your mind back on what you had to do in the game. It was an emotional moment for all of us.

Obviously, I wasn't alone in the way I felt, because we got after the Raiders from our first possession. We rattled off five consecutive "K-Gun" plays and motored deep into Los Angeles territory. Then the Raiders, desperately looking to regroup, called another of those basketball-type time-outs that we had become used to seeing from our opponents. They looked more confused and disoriented than any of the other teams that had previously faced our no-huddle. It was as if we had caught them totally off guard, as if they hadn't bothered to spend one second preparing for it. Which didn't make any sense, because everyone in the world knew we were going to run it.

A few plays after the clock started again, we had the ball at the Los Angeles 13. The snap was dropped, which could have killed a great scoring opportunity and maybe given the momentum to the Raiders. But I ran forward and, instead of just falling on the ball the way your instincts normally tell you to do, I was able to pick it up. Not only that, but I was able to circle out of the pocket to my right. Not only that, but while I was circling I was able to adjust my face mask, because in bending over to get the ball, the top of my helmet came down too far and was impairing my vision. Not only that, but I was able to throw a touchdown pass to Lofton, giving us our tenth score (and ninth TD) in our last twelve opening drives.

That one crazy play told me, and I think everyone else, including the Raiders, that it was going to be one of those days when everything went the Bills' way. Sometimes you find out right at the beginning of a game that you have it; sometimes you find out right at the beginning of a game that you don't. Getting seven points on what should have been a disaster was a definite sign that we had it.

Boy, did we ever!

The Raiders came back about a minute later with a 19-yard field goal by Jeff Jaeger. Then they would sit back and watch as we scored the next 44 points.

I'm pretty sure by halftime, when we were holding a 41–3 lead, the guys in the dressing room across the hall were already thinking about what they were going to do once they got back to Los Angeles to begin the off-season. As much as I pride myself on never giving up, I probably would have been doing the same in their cleats. Of course, knowing what Al Davis's mood would be like after watching his team suffer one of the NFL's all-time humiliating losses, 51–3, I doubt the flight home was relaxing enough for thoughts about golf and lying on the beach.

In our dressing room at halftime, guys were saying the standard line you always hear at halftime, "OK, it's zero-zero going into the second half." Then they'd start laughing. You couldn't help it.

Of course, you also had to fight yourself as hard as possible to avoid losing your concentration altogether. You had to remember that the Raiders were still going to be out there when we went back on the field. And they weren't going to be happy.

I don't think there was a person on the face of the earth who could have predicted that score. Unless they were joking, drunk or both. It just wasn't possible for someone to guess we would beat a team that good by 48 points in any game, let alone with the AFC championship on the line. But everything we did, offensively and defensively, fell our way.

For most of the season, my pass protection was fantastic. That day, it was the best ever. The great pass rush we had been expecting from Long and Greg Townsend never came close to materializing. My guys didn't allow anyone to get near me, and as a result, I connected on 17 of 23 passes for 300 yards and two touchdowns. My completion percentage of 73.9 was an AFC Championship Game record, breaking the 70.8 of Jim Plunkett when he was with the Raiders in 1983. It was also my third consecutive postseason game in which I threw for at least 300 yards.

The defense that did all the terrorizing was ours. We ended up with six interceptions, including two by Darryl Talley. He returned the first one 27 yards for a TD.

I remember standing on the sidelines and feeling very satisfied with what we had done as a team and with what I had done individually. All the way around, it was an incredible performance—something that we could be proud of for years to come.

Our postgame celebration actually began at the start of the fourth quarter. By the third quarter, even the smallest doubts that might have remained about our victory were long gone. So in that final period, you had the whole defense dancing on the benches. You had players throwing all kinds of things into the stands—towels, sweatbands, footballs, whatever they could get their hands on. The fans kept yelling for souvenirs, and their orders kept being filled. Free of charge—for the fans that is. The NFL fined all of us for throwing the balls into the stands. But on that day it was well worth it.

I was also part of a plot that resulted in Coach Levy getting an unexpected Gatorade shower in the last couple minutes of the game. At first, I saw Darryl and Bruce Smith sneaking behind the bench to pick up the Gatorade bucket with five or six minutes left, and I said, "Hold on! Hold on! Don't make it look so obvious, guys. Let's wait a little while longer. I'll get his attention first, and he'll never see it coming. That way, we can douse him good."

They nodded. And a few minutes later, they got their cue as I walked around in front of Coach Levy, who was standing on the sidelines still concentrating on what was happening on the field. "Hey, coach, congratulations. We're finally going to the big one." With a smile, Coach Levy looked right at me. As he did, Darryl and Bruce emptied the icy bucket all over his head.

The smile quickly disappeared. In fact, Coach Levy was a little pissed off. He always believed in taking a businesslike approach to the game, and he thought it was kind of childish on our part to carry on the sideline tradition the Giants began with Bill Parcells in 1986.

"Couldn't you guys think of something more original?" he said.

Then, as he thought about it more, he finally said, "Oh, what the hell."

From that point on, I think Coach Levy loosened up a lot. I think that was a turning point. And the more time he spent around us, the better he understood the type of personalities he was dealing with. He realized that, every now and then, it was OK to be a little on the loose side.

By the time we got to the locker room, we were all pretty much partied out. Everybody was still happy. Everybody was jumping around, hugging and screaming at each other. But most of us were kind of drained at that point, and I think the fans were, too. Because if the game had been in doubt until the final seconds, like our division-clinching win over the Jets in 1988, I know that stadium wouldn't have been standing afterward.

I felt my thoughts and emotions being pulled in different directions. On the one hand, I still couldn't get over that incredible score or the incredible offensive and defensive statistics we had piled up. On the other hand, I couldn't believe I was actually going to the Super Bowl. That was the weirdest feeling of all. It was a good feeling, but it was weird because I could only think of being a kid in East Brady, the freckle-faced dreamer who had always envisioned himself celebrating—just as I was that day, except in a Steelers uniform—the fact that I would be playing in the game of games.

You never *really* expect to achieve a goal like that. You talk about it, you work toward it, you talk about it some more. But so do millions of other kids coast to coast. How many ever make it? How many ever really do get to go from a tiny place like East Brady to the top of the world?

I actually think I enjoyed it more for my family and friends in East Brady. My happiest feelings of all were for Mom and Dad. Dad could have spent his spare time doing any number of different things when I was a kid, but he gave it to me. He devoted himself to my achieving this, so it was as much his as mine. Without him, I know I'd have been watching that moment on television rather than living it.

And, of course, there was my mother, St. Alice. And all my brothers. And Uncle Ed.

I could imagine some of my old high school teammates and their parents, as well as others I knew, watching TV that day and saying, "Hey, that's one of our own right there . . . he's going to the Super Bowl." I could picture the same reaction from the guys I had played softball with in the summer, beginning in college and through my two seasons in the USFL (I had to stop playing after I joined the Bills because they were worried about the possibility of injury)—the Simpson boys (Pat and Pep) from the team sponsored by the Tootsie Roll Inn. The same ones who nicknamed me Spider-Man because I'd always wear a University of Richmond Spiders hat that my older brothers, who went there, had given to me.

It made me feel so proud to represent my little town in the biggest of sporting events. It made me feel that my football career, in which I had experienced so many great things from midget league on up, was finally complete.

Well, almost complete. There was still a matter of playing the game, which would be against the Giants. On the same day that we took apart the Raiders, they had stunned San Francisco in the final seconds, 15–13, for the NFC crown.

Unlike other Super Bowls, there would be no extra week between the conference championships and Super Bowl XXV. No chance for players from either team to pause, reflect, round up game tickets and hotels for family and friends . . . or just catch our breath.

Barely twenty-four hours after our point-fest against Los Angeles, we were on a chartered flight heading for Tampa. Most of us were still pretty well hung over from all the celebrating we had done at my house during the previous twenty-four hours. We broke out two cases of Dom Pérignon, as well as another bottle of champagne tall enough to look big even next to House Ballard.

Before we knew what hit us, it was Tuesday morning, our heads were spinning and our eyes were just too tender for all that Florida sunshine as we met members of the national media. Time to pull out the sunglasses, boys.

But even with the shades, it was impossible for anybody on the team to act cool about being in the Super Bowl. I felt a little in awe over the whole thing. And I think, coming as quickly as it did after the AFC Championship Game, the fact that I was actually there, actually a part of it, hadn't fully sunk in yet. It was hard for anyone in the organization to comprehend what was happening to us, including the owner, Ralph Wilson. His face was one big smile the entire week.

We approached the game with a lot of confidence, though. Just like the playoff contest against Miami, I wouldn't say we were overconfident. But we were confident enough, especially when you consider it was our first Super Bowl and we'd be facing a strong opponent that had been there once before.

The media circus was just that—a circus. On that Tuesday morning, the NFL made sure all the players were scattered throughout Tampa Stadium so we each could hold our own little news conference. There were almost enough reporters to fill every seat in the stadium. It was like watching a herd of cattle when they all walked into the place. And it was like watching a World Wrestling Federation match as they battled for position around each of us. I was standing in the bleachers, and guys were pushing and shoving all around me. It was wild.

The idea is to allow the national media to get to know the participating teams a little better, which is why you're asked a lot of basic questions about yourself, the team and the city you play in. I got a lot of questions about Buffalo, mainly because of all the negative things I had said about it before I signed with the Bills. And I was being totally honest when I said, "It's not anywhere near as bad as everybody in other cities says it is. In the summer, it's beautiful. In the winter, it's cold, sure. But it's also cold in places like New York City, Pittsburgh, and Cincinnati. We just get a little more snow in Buffalo. But I'll tell you,

I'd rather take that snow for a game than some of the windy days we've had in other stadiums."

I also got some silly questions like, "What's your favorite color?" What that had to do with the Super Bowl, I don't know. (For the record, the answer's yellow.)

Another reporter asked, "If you were a linebacker, rather than a quarterback, would you be approaching this game any differently?" All I could think was, "Are you serious?" But I tried to answer it as best I could, saying, "I'd be just as excited about the game, no matter what position I was playing. But of course, a quarterback has a lot of things to worry about that are different from what a linebacker has to worry about."

The wildest part of that day was when Downtown Julie Brown, the outrageous VJ from MTV, showed up to do interviews. She was dressed completely in black—her derby, her halter top, her super-skintight skirt that came down around the middle of her thigh, her fishnet stockings and her cowboy boots. Surrounded by all those frumpy-looking male reporters with cigar breath, she was a very nice change of pace.

Her questions were also kind of different, to say the least. She asked Kent Hull for his pants because, I guess, the temperature had dropped into the forties and she was cold. She asked Leonard Burton if she could bite his chest, and did so, gently. She even rubbed a few guys on the butt.

I guess some of the male reporters complained to the NFL for allowing Downtown Julie to attend the photo/interview day. But I liked having her there. A reporter's a reporter. She was trying to do her job just like they were. And she sure was a hell of a lot better to look at.

The only person who didn't get in on all this fun was Coach Levy. He never showed up. From what I heard, he decided to remain at our hotel after the buses carrying us to the stadium left because he wanted to work on the game plan a little longer. Then he was going to make the short ride—you could see the stadium from our hotel—in a separate car soon after the session began. The only problem was, the driver was from Buffalo and didn't know his way around Tampa. So he made a bunch of wrong turns, they got lost, Coach Levy got frustrated and finally told the guy to turn back.

That night, I saw Lawrence Taylor of the Giants at a Tampa

nightclub. It just so happened the place was holding a topless beauty contest, and L.T. and I were asked to serve as impromptu judges. We didn't talk a lot of football, but we did have a lot of discussion about the "talent" on the stage.

But I had every intention of staying focused on the game. This wasn't a pleasure trip. It was a business trip. Because the object was to win the Super Bowl, not just show up. A lot of teams had just shown up before. The last thing any of us wanted to hear twenty years down the road was, "Oh yeah, Buffalo was in the Super Bowl. But . . ."

There was one more river for us to cross.

After we went three and out on the game's opening possession—quite a change from our previous two playoff games when we promptly marched for touchdowns the first time we touched the ball—the Giants, with Jeff Hostetler replacing injured Phil Simms at quarterback, took over at their 31. From there, they immediately showed that they had a great game plan for us, which was to run the ball, control the clock and keep our no-huddle offense on the sidelines. On the way to Matt Bahr's 28-yard field goal to put them in front, 3–0, the Giants chewed up 6:15 in 11 plays.

I just chewed my fingernails on the sidelines.

Once we got on the field again, I managed to find James for a 61-yard completion to the New York 8. Unfortunately, we couldn't put it in the end zone and had to settle for a 29-yard Norwood field goal.

Then, in the second quarter, it looked like we were finally going to grab this game by the neck. We drove from our 20 for a one-yard touchdown run by Don Smith. Four minutes later, Bruce Smith scored a rare Super Bowl safety by chasing down Hostetler in the end zone to give us a 12–3 lead.

But we were unable to do anything with the momentum we had and the Giants proceeded to yank it away from us. With 3:49 left in the first half, they took their sweet time moving from their 13 all the way to our 14, from where Hostetler threw a touchdown pass to Stephen Baker to cut our advantage to 12–10, which was how it stood at halftime.

In the locker room, there was a sense that, instead of being up by two points, we were down by 10. Different guys, including me, felt like they had to stand up and say things like, "Come on! Let's get fired up! We can win this game! We've just got to take it up a notch! Come on!"

It wasn't really a sense of panic; it was more like a confused feeling. There we were, in the middle of the Super Bowl, and guys were actually trying to pump each other up. No one should need to have someone else pump him up in the middle of the Super Bowl.

Yet, the way we were playing, it was almost like we were a little flat. The Giants had moved the ball on us extremely well in the first half, and had just completely worn down our defense. And we hadn't done much on offense. We had scored some points, but we really hadn't put anything together that resembled one of our typical drives.

Whatever we did in those final thirty minutes, we knew we had to stem the tide—because it definitely wasn't going our way.

But when we came out for the second half, it felt like the first had never ended. The Giants were on the march again. We were watching from the sidelines again. And by the time Ottis Anderson scored on a one-yard run to give them a 17–12 lead, they had devoured another 9:29. Counting what they used on the scoring drive just before intermission, I had spent a grand total of 12:58 watching from the sidelines—and a hell of a lot longer doing nothing when you factored in the extra time for Disney's big halftime show.

It was torture. I mean, I had to start throwing passes on the sidelines just to keep my arm from getting stiff.

As the game progressed, the Giants' strategy kept looking more and more effective. Their best offense was also their best defense; they just stuck to the idea of running the ball down our throats all night and they never gave us a chance to score. When we finally did set foot on the field, it was with too much of a sense of urgency and we didn't execute as well as we were capable of. Moving fast in the no-huddle is one thing, but when you become as reckless as we were starting to become, you're not going anywhere. I was so caught up in trying to get us a fast score, I forgot to work the right combination of pass and run plays that kept defenses off balance and had gotten us to Tampa in the first place.

I just kept looking for the home-run ball, and that's usually when a quarterback begins hurting his performance.

From the start, the Giants sat in a very passive, very simple prevent defense. They were dropping everyone off into coverage. I mean, everyone. For instance Lawrence Taylor, a linebacker, was playing defensive end in front of our left tackle, Will Wolford. The only true linemen they had out there were a nose tackle (Erik Howard) and another end (Leonard Marshall). The rest were linebackers and DBs.

And those guys were just waiting for our receivers to come out so they could pound the hell out of them.

Their attitude was, "Fine, throw the ball. We're just going to kill your receivers." It's tough enough for any receiver to catch the ball over the middle. But having two linebackers waiting there to drill him is a hell of a lot tougher than dealing with two safeties.

If I had it to do over again, I'd probably call a few more running plays. But like I said, spending so much time on the sidelines while the Giants moved the ball up and down the field, I wasn't as patient as I should have been once I got on the field.

We did manage to move ahead, 19–17, when Thurman took an inside handoff from shotgun formation and broke 31 yards for a touchdown. But the Giants answered that with another marathon drive, holding the ball for 14 plays and 7:32 before Bahr kicked a 21-yard field goal to put them back in front, 20–19.

After an exchange of punts, we took over at our 10 with 2:16 remaining. I had one time-out and the two-minute warning to help me in stretching out the clock. I felt we were going to pull out another victory—this time, the biggest of them all.

At first, I was thinking end zone all the way. Scoring a touchdown is always your first objective when you begin a drive with the kind of time we had left. I was hoping to pick up the pace a little bit, but on the first play, I couldn't find anyone to throw to, so I ran for eight yards before the clock stopped at the two-minute warning. On the next play, I still wasn't able to find anyone open, so I ran again, picking up only a yard.

Finally, on the third play, Thomas shook free on a 22-yard carry to our 41. After that, I hit Andre with a four-yard pass. Then, for the third damn time in the drive, I had to scramble. And when I'm running rather than throwing, you know we're in trouble. I managed to pick up nine yards and a first down at the New York 46, but more precious seconds were wasted. We used our last time-out to stop the clock at 48 seconds. I was still thinking touchdown. But when play resumed, the best I could do was a low, six-yard pass to McKeller.

Now, having reached the final thirty seconds, the objective was to just get Scotty close enough for three points. The definition of "close enough" will vary depending on wind conditions and how he kicked during warm-ups. On that night, the winds were calm and I had watched him consistently hitting from 50 yards during warm-ups. So, in that case, "close enough" meant getting the ball at least inside the 30, which would set up a 45- to 50-yarder. Had there been strong wind in his face, we would have needed to get at least inside the 20.

After McKeller's catch, Thurman had an 11-yard run to the 29. "Perfect," I thought. "Just perfect: a nice 47-yard try." So I hurried everybody to the line and spiked the ball to stop the clock with eight seconds left.

You have to make the decision of where you want him to be, and once he's there, it's up to Scott to kick it. That's one time where you have to be extremely careful not to be too greedy. If you make one more attempt to move closer, you run the risk of being sacked or drawing a major penalty that takes you out of field-goal range, or of throwing an interception. With the kicker trying within his distance, you at least have a 50-50 chance at success.

As Scotty took the field, all of us stood on the sidelines and held hands. I'm not really sure why we did that, but if one person on the line thought it would help, then it was worth a shot. I didn't say a word. I just stood and watched.

I knew, as soon as the ball began its climb, it was going wide right. But I kept hoping and praying it would start to turn inside.

My only thought was: "NOOOOOO!" It never turned.

Minutes later we were in the dressing room. It was quiet. Very quiet. For those first few minutes after we walked off the field, we all were in kind of a state of shock. We were thinking that we had lost to a team that we knew we were better than— that we had blown a great opportunity to become world champions. There were hardly any words spoken because we were just so disgusted with the way we had played.

Then Coach Levy walked into the center of the room for his postgame speech. At first he just stood there, looking around at all of us as we sat in front of our lockers. You could tell he was having a hard time trying to find the right words. And who could blame him? What could he say about a game like that?

Finally, he cleared his throat and spoke.

"There's not a loser in this locker room," Coach Levy said. "So, guys . . . just hang in there."

That was his whole speech.

As much fun as there is in reaching the Super Bowl, there's even more pain in losing it. What made that game hurt so much was knowing that you had it right in your grasp, that you did everything possible to win it, that you used every ounce of energy you had—and it still wasn't enough.

Sure, there's satisfaction in knowing that twenty-six other teams wished they could have been in our situation. Being second best in a competitive league with so many great athletes isn't exactly a disgrace. But the problem with losing a Super Bowl is that, after all the hard work you put into getting there, you suddenly find that you have to start all over to get there again. You have to go right back to the bottom of the mountain and put on your climbing shoes.

It still hurts when I think about that game. It'll always hurt to think about it.

But when I do think about Super Bowl XXV, I don't feel any anger toward Scott Norwood. I didn't feel any then either. I was disappointed the field goal didn't go through, just like the rest of the team and the coaches and the management and the fans. But even though his locker was right next to mine inside Tampa Stadium, I wasn't pointing a finger at him. He didn't deserve to bear the brunt of any blame. To a certain degree, we were all guilty of maybe having been a little too pleased with ourselves after winning that AFC Championship Game. Maybe we spent a little too much time thinking about how easy that victory over the Raiders had been and we took the field against the Giants expecting the same thing to happen two weeks in a row.

Scotty tried to help us win, just as he had so many other times in his career. The way I looked at it, then and now, it just wasn't meant to be. But we had a damn good team and a lot to be proud of. All forty-seven of us.

• • • •

About ten days after Super Bowl XXV, I received the following letter from my brother Pat. I think it's a perfect example of what I mean when I talk about the tremendous support we constantly give each other in the Kelly family:

Dear Jim:

Just wanted to drop you a line and let you know how proud I am of you and how exciting you've made this past season for me.

I know winning the Super Bowl would have been the ultimate experience, but there's no doubt in my mind that you'll be back there again and come out victorious.

The most noticeable element I saw this year was how much more you seem to enjoy the game. I know winning helps a lot, but you seemed to have a lot more peace of mind than you've had over the past couple of years. I guess age has something to do with maturing. But putting all the distractions aside and totally concentrating on each week's game has made you a more complete player. Now, the hard part is being able to keep that same focus throughout your career.

I know looking back on myself, I'll always wonder what would have happened if I had done things a little differently. Where would I be today? What could I have achieved?

Don't let that happen to you. And don't let anyone or anything sidetrack you from your goals and dreams. See you soon!

Love, Pat

10

"Please Send Up Two Milk Shakes... and a Championship"

I'M VERY SUPERSTITIOUS. I know that probably sounds silly to some people. I know some people will probably smirk or laugh when they hear the steps I take to try to keep bad luck as far away as possible.

I don't care.

To me, the things I do for the sake of superstition are almost as serious as any other phase of preparing for a game. I believe that staying consistent, trying to do exactly the same things week in and week out, goes a long way toward my ability to help us win and keeping my body in one piece.

I have all kinds of little rituals. For instance, every Friday before a game, Frank Reich and I spend our half hour for lunch at the Orchard Park Cafe, near Rich Stadium. Just the two of us. We always sit at the same table, which Diane, who usually is our waitress, makes sure is ready the moment we walk in the door.

We always order cheeseburgers. Frank orders the soup; I just have the burger.

The conversation doesn't change much either. We talk a little football; sometimes Frank, with those X's and O's constantly swirling around in his brain, will even draw up a new play on his napkin. And I always ask him about his daughter, Lia. She's Daddy's Little Girl, and Frank is never short of new stories about something she said or did.

We have the option, as we do every day, of eating the catered lunch served to the team at the stadium. But Fridays at the Orchard Park Cafe have fast become a tradition. And neither of us has lost sight of the fact that the first year we started it, the Bills went to their first Super Bowl.

Another ritual involving Frank is that we room together the night before every home game. I always take the bed closest to the window. Frank calls the front desk to order extra pillows for both of us. And, the best part of all, he calls room service to order our milk shakes—chocolate for me, vanilla for Frank.

Always.

The morning of a game, all the players have their ankles and knees taped by the trainers. A lot of guys just come in, hop on the table, get taped and get out, never giving it so much as a second thought. But, again for the sake of superstition, I'm very particular about who tapes what. For my ankles, I go to Abe; for my knees, I go to Bud. Every once in a while, if I happen to be running a little late, I'll let Deano, one of the trainers' helpers, tape my ankles. But absolutely no one touches my knees except Bud.

Don't ask me why. I don't really have a reason. I'm sure Abe is capable of taping my knees as well as Bud does. It's just that I've done it with Bud ever since I joined the Bills and, in my mind, that's the way I have to keep doing it.

After I'm finished being taped, I put on my wristbands. With the ones that I wore through the 1991 season, I made sure the arrows on the Bills logo always pointed out, not in. (I'll be wearing different wristbands in 1992, which I'm sure will result in a new ritual.)

From '86 to '88, when I wore a flak jacket to protect my ribs, I always laced it with a black string that I kept in my locker. And it had to be laced just before the game. And I was the only one who could lace it, always starting with the holes on the bottom and working up. There were times, in putting on the jacket just before I walked out on the field, that I just about tore my locker apart trying to find that black string. Yes, it was *that* important to me. (Now the rib protector and shoulder pads are one piece.)

When we take the field for pregame warm-ups, I always walk with Steve Tasker. When we get in a circle and hold hands for our pregame prayer, I always grab Kent Hull's hand. And when we walk down the tunnel for pregame introductions, I always walk with Howard Ballard—the House is my bodyguard before, as well as during, each game.

These rituals will remain in place for as long as all of us play and work together. Otherwise, I just wouldn't feel right when I got out there to take that first snap.

And, believe me, feeling right before a game makes all the difference in the world.

I've had games where I didn't follow one of my little procedures—where I walked out of the locker room and noticed that I had forgotten to put on my wristbands. It upsets me no end, because even if I go back inside to get them, the mere fact that I didn't put them on in the first place is tempting fate. After something like that happens, I hope it's not going to be one of those days.

Most of the time, though, everything is where and how it is supposed to be. Most of the time, I walk onto the field feeling right, feeling ready to have a great day.

I felt as right as ever before our 1991 home opener against the Dolphins. And it wasn't just because I had had an especially tasty chocolate milk shake the night before.

After Super Bowl XXV, we knew we could hold our own with anybody in the league. It was a heartbreaking loss, but it was also a confidence builder. We had played well enough to win the biggest games of our lives, to be in a position to pull out what would have been one of the all-time great victories in sports history. It didn't happen. So instead of spending the off-season feeling sorry for ourselves, we spent it thinking about how much we all wanted to get back to the Super Bowl—to taste sweet redemption on January 26, 1992, in Minneapolis.

You could just see it during our first full-scale practice before the Miami game. Everyone was sharp. Everything was crisp. It had gone so well, in fact, that as we walked off the field, Ted Marchibroda said, "Guys, that was a championship practice today."

We were hungry. We were ready to eat up everything in the way of our ultimate goal.

I wasn't even bothered by the fact that I had missed quite a bit of preseason action because of the pulled right hamstring I had suffered on the first day of training camp and the left ankle I had sprained in our next-to-last exhibition game, against Green Bay. That second injury was scary because as I was rolling to my right to throw to Andre Reed along the sidelines, linebacker Tony Bennett hit me just after I released the ball and fell on the back of my legs, below the knees. The ankle rolled under my left leg and I heard a pop, which at first made me think it was broken. But it was only a sprain and, after sitting out the preseason finale at Chicago, I felt ready to play.

Everyone was saying we were the team to beat in the AFC. Many thought we were the team to beat in the NFL. But leave it to Coach Levy to come up with a statistic that, in the face of all those great things being said and written about us, would keep our cleats firmly on the ground: Only four teams that lost in the Super Bowl managed to return the following year.

The team I worried about the most in our quest to repeat as AFC champions was Miami. Overall, I thought the Dolphins were going to be even tougher than they were in 1990, when they fought us right down to the wire for the division title and home-field advantage in the playoffs. It looked like they had beefed themselves up in key areas on offense and defense. And any time you have Marino and Shula on the other side of the field, you run the risk of getting your ass kicked.

There were other factors that made the Dolphins a big concern for our opener. One, they were really looking forward to playing us for the first time since we knocked them out of the playoffs seven months earlier, 44–34. When you score 44 points on a team, you have to expect them to change something defensively the second time around. We expected every team on our 1991 schedule that had either played us in 1990 or watched us on film to look for different ways to slow down, or stop, our no-huddle attack, which had helped us rank first in the NFL in scoring with 428 points and score 95 in two playoff games.

Number two, we wouldn't have Bruce Smith, who would miss most of the season while recovering from arthroscopic surgery on his left knee. Number three, we wouldn't have Jamie Mueller, a great special-teams player as well as a powerful fullback, who would be lost for the year with a nerve disorder.

Sure enough, it started out as a typical Bills-Dolphins shoot-out and stayed that way for the better part of three quarters. But in the end, our "K-Gun," firing even straighter and truer than it had the year before, came out on top. We generated a single-game club record for total net yards with 583 on the way to a 35–31 victory.

I would also be in a hell of a lot of pain after aggravating my injured left ankle in the third quarter. The trainers kept telling me that I wouldn't be able to go back into the game. In fact, up in the press box they were announcing that I definitely wouldn't be back. But it was going to take a hell of a lot more than a bummed ankle to keep me out. I never want to give anyone the opening to call me a big puss, and that injury just wasn't severe enough in my book to keep me on the sidelines. I knew that if I kept trying, I'd be able to walk it off.

Meanwhile, Frank came in and did his usual great job. He finished the drive with a 13-yard touchdown pass to James Lofton. That's why we call him Chill Factor 14, because he's so cool in those clutch situations and, of course, 14 is his number.

But I know what my offensive linemen and other players on the team expect of me—if I'm not carried off that field, they know I'll usually be back. And I was. And I took us on touchdown marches of 80, 70 and 55 yards while finishing off a career-high day for passing yards with 381. But a lot of credit had to go to the defense, which set up the last drive after Ray Bentley used his helmet to knock the ball loose from running back Mark Higgs and Mark Kelso recovered at our 45.

Thurman Thomas was incredible, becoming the only player in Bills history to have 100 yards rushing and receiving in the same game. As we expected, the Dolphins tried to mix up their coverages to cause confusion. But I stuck with plays that, with proper execution, would work against any type of defense they were in. And I audibled a lot from passes to runs. Either way, Thurman was going to have his hands all over that football.

It was a costly win, though. Jeff Wright, our standout nose tackle, suffered a dislocated left kneecap in the third quarter that would land him on the injured-reserve list for the next seven weeks. That left us with only one healthy starting defensive lineman, left end Leon Seals. And he was still gimpy from off-season arthroscopic surgery on both knees.

But I'm a firm believer that one segment of the team must always be prepared to take up the slack for another, because you never know when injuries are going to hit, where they're going to hit and how hard they're going to hit. At that time, our defense was being clobbered by injuries, so our offense had to come to the rescue. I can remember times when it was the other way around. And I wasn't ruling out the possibility that they'd be bailing us out at some point down the road.

My ankle was fine for our next game, at home against Pittsburgh. But when the final gun sounded on that one, I was as mentally drained as I've ever been in my career. We pulled out everything we had offensively and threw it at the Steelers. By the time we were finished, we scored 52 points to their 34. And I had a team-record six touchdown passes.

I used so much of the playbook that, by the fourth quarter, I was fresh out of material. Honest to God, I walked into the huddle and said, "Kent, what play can we run now?"

"I don't know, man," he said. "We've used so many variations, I just don't think there's anything you can call that we haven't already used more than once."

He might have suggested another pass to Don Beebe. After all, by that time, Don had made four touchdown catches, to equal the single-game club record Jerry Butler set against the Jets in 1979. The funny thing was, after the first two I went up to him and said, "OK, Beebes, now you owe me two more." I was just kidding, of course. But he took me seriously and got open for his third and fourth TDs.

Actually, it wasn't that big of a surprise when you consider Don's great speed and the fact that the Steelers decided to cover him one on one all day. They were doubling Andre and James and leaving Don all by his lonesome. As a result, during the course of the game I called a bunch of plays specifically for him.

It was almost like sandlot football, because I'd be taking him aside and giving him different patterns to run. Before one of his scoring catches, I just said, "Take him up deep, bro'. You've got him beat." Then I'd say, "Run a post this time." Or "Give me a streak route."

I normally just call a play and look for the open man, spreading things out the whole time. But if the Steelers were going to insist on leaving someone as fast as Don singled up, I'd have been stupid not to take advantage of it any way possible. It just became a question of "How can we beat the guy who's covering Don now?"

Going into this game, I studied film like I'd never studied before, because, for one thing, the Steelers had the top-rated defense in the NFL in 1990 and some great cover guys in their secondary, like cornerback Rod Woodson. They also gave us a lot of different looks. At times, their defense tried to play games with me, and I loved it because you can mess with them right back with real audibles and dummy audibles.

But they did get me good in the third quarter when linebacker Bryan Hinkle, whom I never saw, intercepted me and returned the ball 57 yards for a touchdown. I guess if you throw the ball enough—and I threw it 43 times in that game—you're going to have one picked off. When somebody asks me how many touchdown passes I had that day, I say, "Seven. Six to us . . . and one to them."

It was hard to believe that, after only two games, our offense had generated 1,119 yards, 87 points and 64 first downs. It was even harder to believe that I had thrown six scoring passes against the Steelers. You just never expect things like that to happen. I know the Steelers didn't. After the game, Neil O'Donnell, their backup quarterback, told me they honestly thought they were going to shut our offense down. And I'm sure they still don't know how we scored 52 points on them.

To a certain extent, they struggled to keep up with the pace of the no-huddle. You saw a lot of their guys leaning over, hands on their knees, physically exhausted. In fact, Woodson, who is one of the best athletes in the NFL, took himself out of secondary and kick-return duty for a while just to rest.

But whether you're running "K-Gun" or anything else, the biggest factor of all is execution. If you execute the way we have and you stay focused on what you're doing and nobody has a letdown, you're going to succeed most of the time. In our offense, every receiver must run his pattern to the fullest because he never knows where I'm going to throw the ball. It doesn't matter if the play's designed to go to James's or Andre's side; if they roll up a different coverage and I see something else, I'm going to come back and throw it to Don, Thurman or Keith McKeller. Ted's favorite saying to the receivers was, "Always be running, always be alert. Because you never know if the ball's coming your way."

I had a lot of fun through those first two weeks. I was enjoying every minute of it. And I'm sure I had plenty of company. Nowadays, I don't think people want to see the pitch right and the pitch left, the dive right and the dive left. They want to see exciting football, and our no-huddle offense is exciting.

But it's never a one-man show. The people around me were just as responsible for all those eye-popping numbers as I was. So when the NFL named me AFC Offensive Player of the Week for my performance against the Steelers, I regarded it as a nice honor but I thought Don Beebe deserved it as much as I did. The coaches also give out weekly team awards, and I received Player of the Game. The prize was a 14-karat-gold Buffalo Bills ring, which a local jewelry store sells for $550. I gave it to Don, telling him, "I don't know if any receiver will ever have a game like you did. You earned this. It's yours."

I had said all week that our third game, against the Jets at the Meadowlands, was going to be extremely tough. But I could see in the eyes of the reporters and everyone else I was talking to that they didn't believe me. They gave me a look like "Yeah, right, Jim."

Believe me, I never wish for a tough game. I'd love to win them all 51–0. But I'm also realistic. And the Jets had the talent, especially on defense, and the overall desire to give us a hard time. Hard enough so that we barely escaped with our eighth straight victory over them, 23–20. In fact, the win wasn't safe until the last 16 seconds, when Pat Leahy's 51-yard field-goal attempt fell just short of the crossbar.

As we went out for the kneel-down to kill off the rest of the clock, I saw the expressions on the faces of the defensive linemen. They were really depressed. But they had nothing to be ashamed of. They played one hell of a game, they fought us right to the end.

A lot of people were stunned that, after two weeks of dominating the NFL, our offense produced "only" 304 yards. Everybody always asks, "Do you think you're unstoppable?" And I always answer, "No," because this is a game of physical talent and the Jets matched up pretty well against us with the physical talent they had on defense. They covered our receivers well, they made me throw the ball a little quicker than I wanted to and I had a couple of throws where I hurried a little bit more than I should have.

In a sixteen-game schedule, you're going to have to pull out a few like that one. You're going to have to come up with the big plays when you need them. And we did. Such as when, with five minutes left and the Jets leading 20–16, we had a fourth-and-six at the New York 30. I dropped back to pass and everybody was covered. With a pass rusher closing in on me, I looked over to James's side, and although he was covered, I had to take a chance and throw it to him; I couldn't get sacked. Just before my release, I saw James starting to move to the outside, so I threw the ball there. Somehow, he caught it for a 10-yard gain and a first down. Two plays later came the biggest play of all, when I hooked up with Thurman on a 15-yard pass over the middle for the winning touchdown. I had told him to split the seam right up the gut. He had two linebackers to beat, and I figured he wouldn't have any problem getting open. The only problem on the play was that the ball slipped out of my hand as I threw it, and fortunately it managed to get to him just fast enough for the score.

When we play the Jets, there's always a little more hostility among the players of both teams than you usually see. We're always ready for a tight, bruising, beat-up type of game. And that was exactly what we got this time.

Kent was telling me afterward that during pregame warmups, Chris Burkett, the Jets' receiver who used to play for the Bills and is one of Kent's good friends, wouldn't talk to him. Wouldn't even look at him. Most of the time, players from both teams make small talk before a game, especially the ones who are friends with each other. But things are different when we're sharing the field with the Jets.

And after we won the game, Chris wouldn't say a word then, either.

"I got a feeling the guy's not going to speak to me until sometime this summer," Kent said with a smile.

It was a huge win. With a 3–0 record and losses on the same day by Miami, Indianapolis and New England, we took a commanding two-game lead in the AFC East.

Next we had to travel to Tampa Stadium to face the 0–3 Buccaneers. Ordinarily, I love playing in Florida; I had a lot of fun there during my college career. But the thought of going to Tampa Stadium made us all feel a little uneasy. We couldn't help thinking about what happened the last time we were there —for Super Bowl XXV. We also couldn't help thinking about the fact that the Bills hadn't won a game in the place since 1976, my junior year of high school. A lot of that was due to a lack of mental preparation going into the game. Through the years, Tampa Bay's win-loss record hasn't been that great, and sometimes you tend to take teams like that lightly. Which is always a big mistake.

Sure enough, we struggled again in 1991. But at least we had something to show for it with a 17–10 win.

The deciding points came when I beat a blitz to throw a 29-yard touchdown pass to Keith McKeller with 5:21 left in the fourth quarter. On that play, I put the free safety right where I wanted him by having Andre run a pattern that I knew would pull the guy over to that side and allow Keith to get open. I saw the blitz coming and I stayed in there until the last second before I let go of the ball. That cost me a whack in the head from one of their pass rushers, although I thought that he still had time to avoid nailing me and that the officials should have called a penalty.

The Bucs' defense seemed ungrateful for the favor I did for Keith McCants early in the second quarter when I was sacked by Reuben Davis. On the same play, McCants somehow got one of his fingers caught in the earhole of my helmet. It was the strangest thing I had ever been involved in during a game. Fearing I would lift my head and rip his finger off, he started yelling, "Please, don't move!"

I couldn't believe it. A defensive guy was actually begging *me* not to hurt *him*. And the funny part was, because I stayed so still on the ground while McCants worked his finger out, people kept coming up and asking if I was all right.

The Bucs had a chance to force overtime in the final two seconds. But on second and goal from our 8, Chris Chandler bounced a pass on the ground in front of Mark Carrier, who was standing in the middle of the end zone. During that last drive, I did so much pacing back and forth on the sidelines, I just about wore out the bottom of my cleats. My feet were killing me.

To me, teams like Tampa Bay are the scariest of all. Because in the back of their mind, they know that you're probably the better team, that they're playing the role of the underdog and have absolutely nothing to lose. And the closer a game like that stays and the longer it lasts, the more excited they become. All of a sudden, they're able to raise themselves to a little higher level, which was exactly what the Bucs did.

Offensively, we played as poor a game as we had all year that day. Watching film the next day, we could see that we had opportunities really to hurt their defense and we didn't take advantage of them. For example, they blitzed us a lot more than they had done previously. And we didn't hit enough big plays when they were blitzing and leaving some of our receivers single-covered.

As poorly as we played, we just had to consider ourselves lucky to come away with the win. Three or four years earlier, the way things were going, Chandler's pass probably would have hit Carrier right in the numbers. And we'd have gone home with a loss.

After we all finally got into the locker room, I stood up and made my best call of the day: "Let's pack our bags and let's get the hell out of here!"

We couldn't wait for what came next on our schedule—a home meeting with the Chicago Bears. We were 4–0 and they were 4–0. We were the early-season powerhouse in the AFC and they were the early-season powerhouse of the NFC. This was a game that interested a lot of people throughout the country, and we were geared up to make a statement.

It was just so much easier to get mentally ready for a game

like that than it had been to prepare for the Tampa Bay game. All you had to do was look at the name "Bears" and you automatically thought about a team with a long history for having big, physical, strong people.

We figured the only way we were going to have a chance to come out on top against them was to be just as physical and powerful as they were. But what we were doing was playing right into their hands. The Bears love to get into that kind of game because they're a team that wins on defense. They're going to keep the score low. They're going to keep pounding on you and pounding on you. Then, in the fourth quarter, they're going to pull out a win.

When we went into the dressing room at halftime holding a 7–6 lead, we realized we had been lured right into their trap. So we made an adjustment in our running game by using a bend-back play that had been in our offense for a while but we had hardly used up to that point. It's just a simple case of having Thurman Thomas take a couple of steps in one direction, then bend back and run behind the guard or tackle on the opposite side. When Thurman does that, overly aggressive defenders like they have on the Bears will overpursue to the side where he begins the run and take themselves right out of the play. In the first half, there were several times when Thurman would run to his left, take one or two steps, and find himself heading straight for the waiting arms of Mike Singletary, the Bears' great inside linebacker, who would already be standing outside of left tackle Will Wolford.

Once we ran the bend-back successfully about two or three times in the second half, the whole game opened up for us. Now Singletary was saying to himself, "I can't be overaggressive anymore and just run to the point of attack; I've got to wait on this guy to see which way he's going to go."

When that started to happen, Thurman would end up getting two extra steps on Singletary in any direction he went. You give Thurman two extra steps, he's going to blow right past you. And once our running game started clicking, things loosened up enough so we could use everything else in our game plan.

As a result, we scored four more touchdowns in the second

half, including three in a span of 10:26, and piled up 422 total net yards on the way to a 35–20 victory.

The spark that the offense had been waiting for came in the final 12 seconds of the first half, when I connected on a 33-yard scoring pass to Al Edwards to give us a 7–6 halftime lead. I went on to throw for two more TDs (including a 77-yard strike to Lofton that was my longest of the season) and 303 yards while completing 19 of 29 passes.

The pass to Al was a perfect example of a play that Frank and I had put together late in the week and presented to Coach Marchibroda. He decided to insert it in the game plan. As we'd planned it, the pass was supposed to have gone to Beebe, but he was knocked out of the game early after taking a shot to the face mask from Singletary. We had practiced the play all week with Don and it worked every time, so there was no reason to think it wouldn't work with Al. What we did was have Andre run a crossing pattern to bring the free safety up, and that left Al, who has pretty good speed, all by himself in the deep zone; I got so excited when he broke free, I almost overthrew him.

Another thing that helped make our passing game so effective that day was the fact that the Bears' cornerbacks were very quarterback-conscious and took most of their reads from watching my eyes. Just by studying film, you could see that that was their only key. If I looked right, they moved right; if I looked left, they moved left. Their corners also do what we call press-bail, meaning that they line up like they're going to press the receiver and try to slow him up at the line, then bail out just before the snap, but always while keeping an eye on the quarterback. So as they were bailing, I could give them false reads to pull them away from the man I wanted to throw to.

One thing you always have to be mindful of when running the no-huddle is the pace. We want it moving as fast as possible, getting everybody on the ball in a 1-2-3 rhythm. Yet in the first half of that Chicago game we were taking too much time between plays for some reason. As a result, the Bears had a chance to dig their cleats in for the pass rush and sack me three times, and were able to make more personnel substitutions than most teams do against us, which hurt our running game.

So besides using the bend-back play, the other change we made in the second half was to make a more conscious effort to move the no-huddle quicker. As a result, we caught the Bears with the wrong people on the field to defend a pass play and a couple of runs. We also caught them with too many men on the field once, and they were penalized. But our goal wasn't to purposely draw a penalty; that was Cincinnati's trick. We just wanted to get them in the incorrect defense for the kinds of plays we were running.

The game also marked the return of Bruce Smith, who is the catalyst of our defense. When we need a big play, a sack or something behind the line of scrimmage, Bruce usually comes up with it. And he's done it year in and year out. Although we all knew he was still hurting with that knee problem, he managed to be a factor through the first half and early in the second, drawing five penalties—three false starts and a hands-to-the-head call on rookie offensive tackle Stan Thomas, and another false start on veteran Ron Mattes, who replaced Thomas. Unfortunately, Bruce spent the final two quarters on the sidelines. Afterward, he developed fluid in his left knee and returned to the injured-reserve list for the next seven weeks.

During my postgame news conference, somebody mentioned to me that on a radio interview in Chicago a few days earlier, Bears defensive end Tim Ryan said he thought their defense would be able to rattle me. I wasn't sure where he got that idea. Maybe when I'm retired from football and sitting in some nursing home somewhere they'd be able to shake me up pretty good. I don't want to sound cocky, but it's going to take a lot to get me rattled during a game. Even after those three first-half sacks, I wasn't the least bit concerned about hanging in the pocket as long as I usually do. Heck, if I was going to get rattled, that would have happened when, as a kid, my older brothers would often mistake me for a punching bag.

With all the media hype about how a larger, more physical NFC team like the Bears would have no problem pushing around a supposedly smaller, more finesse-oriented club like ours, we were proud of the way we handled ourselves against the so-called big boys. Over the years, the Bears have always had one of the best defenses in the league and we wanted to prove to ourselves that our offense could move the ball against them.

At 5–0, we had our best start since 1980 and only the third

such record in franchise history. With Miami and New England losing on the same weekend, we opened a three-game lead in the AFC East—after only five weeks.

A lot of people saw our sixth game, against the Chiefs at Kansas City on *Monday Night Football,* as a preview of the 1991 AFC Championship Game. Whether or not that was true, we considered it very important to our goal of winning home-field advantage through the playoffs—provided we first won our division. If we beat the 3–2 Chiefs, we'd go three games up on them in the home-field race; if we lost, we'd only be one up in terms of win-loss records, but they'd be one up as far as the head-to-head tiebreaker was concerned.

The Chiefs do a lot of things like Chicago. Offensively, they want to pound you with their running attack; they're not going to throw long that often. Defensively, they have a bend-but-don't-break philosophy. They play loose enough to get you into a throwing mode, then their pass-rushers—led by outside linebacker Derrick Thomas—just pin their ears back and come after you.

We knew all those things beforehand. So, we thought, if we could establish a running game early, wear down their defense and keep those pass-rushers honest, we'd be fine. Little did we know our appearance at Arrowhead that night was going to resemble the Alamo. And we would play the part of Custer.

The Chiefs were hosting their first Monday-night game since 1983, and a crowd of 76,000 had the place rocking. There was a rare (at least in the NFL) pregame fireworks display, and for the rest of the night all we heard was a continuous roar and all we saw was a sea of tomahawk chops.

We got chopped, too, 33–6, for our first loss of the season.

Instead of us wearing their defense out, they used their big running backs—Christian Okoye and Harvey Williams—to tire our defense early in the game. And that was a huge problem, because our defense was already missing Bruce Smith and Jeff Wright, who were still out with knee injuries. Before we knew what hit us, we were behind 10–0. Trying to play catch-up against a team that can rush the passer as well as the Chiefs is almost always going to be a losing proposition. I got sacked six times, four by Thomas. On three of those sacks, I fumbled to set up scores. In all, we lost the ball five times, with three leading to touchdowns and one to a field goal.

Right before the game, Coach Levy told us, "Whoever wins the turnover battle is going to win the football game." As usual, his analysis was right on the money. We gave them so many gifts, they should have been happy until Christmas 1995.

The Chiefs had a great pass rush, and that was part of the reason for the sacks, but most of it was because I hung on to the ball too long trying to find open receivers. I also blame myself for the fumbles; you just can't drop the ball three times no matter how much you're hit back there.

I tried doing a couple of things to minimize their rush. I tried speeding up the pace of "K-Gun," as I did in the second half of the Chicago game the week before. I tried to throw while rolling to my right; I tried to throw while rolling to my left. We managed to pick up a few big gains from those rollout plays. But they weren't enough.

With Thomas being as quick as he is around the corner, I wanted to mix up the snap count to keep him guessing so he wouldn't be able to come off on the snap of the ball all the time. But with the fans as loud as they were, that was tough to do. So when a great athlete like Thomas doesn't have to guess, he's going to have time to get around a player and put pressure on a quarterback.

It was also a night of living hell for our defense, which gave up 239 rushing yards (including 100 each by Okoye and Williams). That was 28 more than our whole offensive output for the game! The last time we played this bad was in our 23-point loss to the Dolphins in the second week of the 1990 season.

A reporter asked me afterward if I felt particularly upset because the loss came on Monday night and was seen by millions of television viewers throughout the country. I told him I didn't care if it happened on Monday night or Wednesday afternoon. I don't like to get beat. Period. Thank God there were still ten more weeks left in the regular season.

I did know this: The Kansas City Chiefs were not 27 points better than we were. It was just one of those games where everything they did went right for them, and everything we did seemed to backfire. I hoped it was only a short-term virus that we had to get out of our system.

Just as we had done after the previous season's disaster in Miami, we set out on a mission to get the winning feeling back. We had to get another streak of victories going. We had to get back to where we were in the first five weeks of the season. Because how you rebound from a game like that shows what you're made of. More than anything else you do, it determines the kind of character you truly have as a team.

I could sense, from our first day back on the practice field, the desire throughout the squad to show that that performance at Arrowhead had nothing to do with the *real* Bills. And I just knew it wasn't going to allow us to have any sort of letdown against the 0–6 Colts, the first of three straight visitors to Rich in our longest home stretch of the season.

Judging by the final score—Buffalo 42, Indianapolis 6—I'd say I was right.

"There was no question in my mind we played our best football game today . . . offensively and defensively," Shane Conlan said. "We knew it wasn't going to be another Kansas City Chiefs game."

I had to take Shane's word for it. With 1:36 remaining in the second quarter, I left the field for the rest of the day with a mild concussion after Jon Hand blasted me in the head with a forearm—yes, the same Jon Hand whose hit caused me to suffer a shoulder separation in 1989. We were leading 21–6 at the time. Once again, Frank was brilliant in relief, leading us to 21 more points, which gave us our largest margin of victory ever against the Colts. From what I understood, the offensive linemen were even calling plays for Frank in the second half, including a 78-yard touchdown run on a first-down play that Kent suggested.

I needed all the play-calling help I could get on the four snaps I somehow managed to take following Hand's hit, including a fumble on the first that I recovered. I guess the first sign that I was out of it came when I asked Will Wolford if we were still in the no-huddle. We were, of course. A bunch of the other players just rolled their eyes. When Ted signaled from the sidelines a basic off-tackle running play we call, say, a "19," which we had been using steadily from the start of the game, I asked someone on the field, "Do we have '19' in our offense?" After Thurman, on his way to a 117-yard rushing day along with the 108 of Kenneth Davis, ran for a yard, I trotted over to the sidelines to talk things over with the coaches. They all thought I looked OK.

But while walking back on the field, Kent and Thurman noticed right away that my eyes didn't look right. Thurman then put his finger by his earhole and made the "coo-coo" sign to the bench. The next thing I knew, I was turning around and heading back to the sidelines and Frank was coming in.

From what I was told, after the game I walked over with Ed Perkins to our family's tailgate party. As I approached the motor home, my brother Kevin noticed I was signing footballs for some fans in the parking lot. He started laughing and shouted, "Hey, you'd better check to see whose name he's signing."

When I saw Dad by himself, the first thing I asked was "Where's Mom?"

He reminded me what I had already known—that Mom had stayed back in East Brady for this trip.

During the party at my house that night, most of the players came up to me to put their two cents in about how strange I was acting in the huddle after the hit. And as each story began sounding more bizarre than the other, I said, "OK, OK. I think you guys are spicing it up just a little bit." Of course, they had me at a disadvantage—I really didn't remember much of anything.

The next morning, I was still pretty groggy as I did my weekly call-in radio show with Marc Stout and Pete Weber on WGR AM/FM. People kept asking questions and I kept answering, "I wish I could answer you, but I can't because I can't remember."

For a while, I was also forgetting things like telephone numbers that I call regularly. I'm talking about important numbers, like the ones belonging to certain female friends of mine. Now, that's when you know you're a little fuzzy upstairs.

Talk about perfect timing, the next day I was scheduled to travel to Giants Stadium to shoot a TV commercial—for Nuprin. Although I was still shaking out cobwebs, I couldn't have been in too bad shape. Because what I was told would probably be a twelve-hour shooting lasted only about seven and a half hours. And it wouldn't have taken that long if we didn't have to stop every five minutes while planes taking off from nearby Newark International Airport roared overhead.

If there was a personal turning point for me in 1991, it came on October 21. That was when we faced the 0–6 Bengals in our second Monday-night appearance in three weeks.

Soon after the opening kickoff, I began having what I'm sure the 80,000 fans at Rich and millions of viewers throughout the country thought was going be the all-time worst game of my life. Before the first quarter ended, I had thrown three interceptions. The first one set up a field goal. Luckily, the defense, playing its best game to date, held Cincinnati scoreless after the other two.

I hadn't been picked off in 85 attempts before that night. The last time I had three interceptions in a game was against San Francisco in 1989. And I never had three in a half, let alone a quarter.

But I can say, with all honesty, I didn't feel my whole world was crashing down around me. I felt embarrassed, for sure, especially with the entire nation tuned in. But I firmly believed things would change. I never doubted, not for an instant, I would get myself turned around.

After the third interception, I walked over to my offensive linemen, all of whom were sitting on the bench, and said, "Just hang with me, guys, and I promise we'll be all right." Some people might think I said that just because it sounded good at the time. Others might think I was trying to convince myself, more than my linemen, that things were going to get better. But that was the way I *really* felt. Because it was one of those games where I knew I was ever so close to making big plays. It was just a matter of an inch here, an inch there and the disaster I had in progress would become a night to remember for all the right reasons.

And it was. The rest of my completions were to Bills players, including five for touchdowns, as we rolled to a 35–16 triumph. I finished the night 18 for 27 for 392 yards, which topped my performance in the opener for a new single-game career high and a club-record fifth 300-yard game for the season.

My linemen hung in there with me. So did the receivers. Everybody kept working. When you have that many guys in a football game operating on the same page, pulling together, things are going to take a turn for the better, without fail.

I also felt a big responsibility to hang in there. As the quarterback, the leader of the team, my reaction to adversity can make or break our chances for a comeback. If everyone else sees me falling apart and feeling sorry for myself, they're bound to pack it in. You always have to stay strong and show that you have your emotions completely under control. I can't count the number of times I've gone up to teammates at all levels of football after they made a bad play or a bad series of plays, and said, "Forget about it! The play's over. It's how you come back from it that matters."

And the best thing I could have done after those interceptions was go right back out and throw the ball, which was exactly what we did. There was no reason for us to shy away from the pass. Because we knew all along that Cincinnati's defense could be exploited through the air. We knew that if we were going to win the game, we were going to have to throw the ball.

One of the biggest reasons was that James Lofton, our best deep threat, was being covered by Richard Fain, a rookie who was filling in for injured veteran Lewis Billups. A veteran quarterback's eyes will always light up when he sees a rookie cornerback lined up across from any wide receiver—let alone one as smart, experienced and fast as James. It wasn't that I was spending the whole night looking to burn Fain and no one else, but I thought we had a good chance of getting something big to that side. And sure enough, on the first play of the second quarter, I hit Lofton 40 yards downfield along the sidelines. Fain, who had been badly beaten, lunged, got a handful of dark blue jersey, then fell on his face as James ran for the rest of the 74-yard touchdown play.

I would throw four more scoring passes, including a 51-yarder to our veteran tight end, Pete Metzelaars, who normally doesn't get to catch a lot of balls with McKeller in the lineup. It came on a third-and-one play, a play-action pass off tackle. Since I joined the team, we had run that play three or four times. And that was my first completion with it. Because it is a designed short-yardage play, Coach Levy sends it in, and when he did so that night, I was actually nervous.

"Please, God!" I said. "Help me complete this one."

It's something we run all the time, but unlike most teams, the Bengals sucked up well on the run play fake and I just threw it right behind them. I was thinking back to when we played Seattle a couple of years earlier on *Monday Night Football* and I had Butch Rolle wide open for a touchdown—and I overthrew him. Now, I was saying to myself, "Don't overthrow Pete."

It was nice to get the monkey off my back. Not to mention a touchdown.

With a 7–1 record and a three-game lead over the Jets in the AFC East, we could kick back and relax through our bye weekend. The timing of the break was just perfect, coming right at the middle of the season. My elbow was feeling a little sore, we all had our share of bumps and bruises, not to mention the more serious injuries to Bruce Smith and Jeff Wright. It was a much-needed time to rest and heal.

We returned from the bye to face the Patriots, who were 3–5 and looking revitalized under new head coach Dick MacPherson, for our last game at Rich for three weeks.

No matter who coaches the Pats, they always manage to give us a difficult game. And this time, there was an another opponent—wind. It was whipping all day, bringing with it a first taste of winter in cold temperatures and light snow.

As a result, we struggled with our passing game, we had a couple of muffed punts that led to a pair of second-half Patriot touchdowns, New England made a 93-yard punt that blew all the way to our 1-yard line—and we still managed to win, 22–17.

In weather like that, you can't throw your 20-yard outs, it's hard to throw your deep posts, it's hard to throw streak routes. It's just tough to get in there and do what you do best. So that had something to do with the fact we scored 17 fewer points than we had been averaging at home during the '91 season. But what counts is that we won another division game. When the clock read all zeroes, we had our sixteenth straight win at home as well as a one-game edge over Houston in the battle for home-field advantage through the playoffs.

Besides the scoreboard, another great sight was that of Jeff at nose tackle after he missed the first half of the season. At least we had one of our two mainstays back on the defensive line. And that was especially important as we worked our way down to crunch time.

Fred Smerlas, the man he replaced, was playing nose tackle for the Patriots that day, his first appearance at Rich since leaving the Bills. And one of the things we were determined to do was get him to jump offsides, which was his trademark during eleven seasons in a Buffalo uniform. I figured Fred would remember some of the audibles we used in 1989, his last season with us. So I called one as a dummy audible. He bit and jumped offside, although the official never called his number.

I went over to the sidelines to Bud Carpenter, our assistant trainer, and said, "I told you I'd get Fred today."

"Yeah, but they didn't announce his number over the PA system," Carp said. "And I'll bet, if you pull him off and get them to announce, 'Offsides, number 76, defense,' the crowd will go nuts."

Sure enough, I managed to get him a second time. And when the announcement was made, the crowd went crazy. I looked over at Carpenter on the sidelines, and he was laughing so hard that he was doubled over.

"That one was for you, Bud," I yelled.

I like Fred a lot. Everybody likes Fred. He's a down-to-earth, good person.

And he's a real comedian. He always came up with one-liners when he was with the Bills, and it was no different after he joined the Patriots. A few days before the game, he told reporters, "I want to knock off the two hairs left on Kelly's head."

I wasn't worried. Of all the guys on the New England defense, Fred was the one I knew I could outrun. Besides, he has enough hair on his chest to cover my entire body.

The only thing I have to say about Fred is that his locker has been a hell of a lot cleaner since I took it over. Before I moved in, I got our equipment guys, Dave Hojnowski and Woody Ribbeck, to hire a maid. We had that locker sterilized and fumigated. So there are no more mice, rats and whatever else there was crawling around inside.

We got off to another slow start offensively the following week when we played the Green Bay Packers at Milwaukee County Stadium. But considering our history, that wasn't a surprise. Two things we hadn't done well on the road was score (in six games at Rich to date we had averaged 37 points; in three on the road, we had averaged 15.3) and win (we had won 31 of our last 33 games at Rich; since 1988, our road record was 14–16).

And let's not forget our problems on grass (a 5–10 record since the middle of the 1986), which was the surface at Milwaukee.

We did manage to buck those trends, however, with a 34–24 victory over the Packers, although I paid the price with my ribs. Early in the third quarter, while throwing a pass that would draw a big interference penalty for us, I was speared by free safety Chuck Cecil. I wore padding over my ribs but the bottom part lifted as I threw and he managed to jam his helmet right into the exposed part of my back. At first, I couldn't breathe; I had the wind knocked completely out of me for several seconds.

Cecil is the type of player who frequently hits with his head. He's gotten a couple of penalties for spearing, but not that time. It seems like he goes in with his eyes closed and whatever happens, happens. Sooner or later, it's not going to be what happens to somebody else that will be his problem; it's what's going to happen to him. He has to worry about his own neck.

Anyhow, I missed our next two series while being examined in the dressing room, where it was determined I had bruised ribs on the left side of my lower back. I was still in a lot of pain when I came back out to the field. I tried to keep loose on the sidelines by throwing, although every time I twisted, it hurt. But it wasn't the kind of pain that would cause me to miss the rest of the game. We had a 21–10 lead, and I didn't feel secure about it.

So after going back in, I guided us to 13 more points, including a one-yard touchdown run by yours truly. Before the play, I told Thurman, "Be ready for a pitch, because I don't want to run the football." But after the snap, someone came up to cover Thomas, and . . . oh, well . . . I took it over myself. As I crossed the goal line, my back got twisted on the left—the same side as my tender ribs.

"Thanks," I told everybody who came up to congratulate me. "But please don't touch my back."

Combined with the Jets' loss to Indianapolis that day, our 9–1 record now gave us a four-game lead in the division with six games to go. Only a collapse that nobody wanted even to think about would prevent us from winning our fourth straight AFC East crown.

The following week, in what probably was our best road performance of the season, we cashed in on four turnovers for 24 points and rolled to a 41–27 *Monday Night Football* win over Miami at Joe Robbie Stadium. Our two-game seasonal sweep of the 5–6 Dolphins mathematically eliminated them from the AFC East race, which we still led by four games.

The first eight games of the season, we were pretty pitiful in the turnover department. But in the last two, it looked like we were finally showing an awareness that we had to start taking the ball away and stop giving it up so much. We protected the ball very well against the Dolphins, which, in the smothering South Florida heat, wasn't easy for our running backs. Thurman still had his third straight 100-yard game, but had to be spelled frequently by Kenneth Davis, who chipped in 98 yards. Despite my aching ribs, which forced me to throw everything short and to the right (because I couldn't twist my body to the left), I managed to keep the ball out of Miami hands while completing 20 of 28 passes for 185 yards and three touchdowns.

And the defense made big plays when we needed them, such as Cornelius Bennett's superhuman exhibition that broke the game wide open from a 10–10 tie midway through the second quarter. He blew past offensive tackle Mark Dennis, stripped Dan Marino of the ball, grabbed it on the ground, got up and ran for a six-yard touchdown that put us in front for good. On one play, he had a forced fumble, a recovery and a touchdown. I guess that's what he means by a "C.B. Triple" in those TV commercials he does for McDonald's.

Even with all those turnovers, though, I never believe you can steal a game from Marino. You always earn it, because just by breathing he poses that constant threat of getting his team back in a game in a hurry. When we were up 21 points with six minutes left on the clock, I honestly didn't feel comfortable. I was so uncomfortable that I was up out of my seat on the bench watching the defense and screaming at the top of my lungs, "Come on, guys! Come on, defense!" I know exactly what Marino's capable of doing.

As Coach Levy says, never look for an opponent to lose. Always think of yourselves as winners; go out and take care of your own business.

For some reason, however, we totally forgot about that six days later when we traveled to rain-soaked Foxboro, Massachusetts, for another go-around with the Patriots. The result was a bitter 16–13 loss.

With our offense executing as poorly as it had all season, we wound up blowing a 10–0 lead on the way to seeing our five-game winning streak come to an abrupt end. All because of five turnovers, including my NFL career-high of four interceptions. To give you an idea of the kind of day we were having offensively, my longest pass covered 14 yards and Thurman's longest run covered eight.

There were no excuses. Reporters kept asking me about my ribs after the game, but they weren't the problem. I just wasn't following through on my passes, and when I don't follow through, I'm not going to put the ball where it's supposed to be. I made mistakes I normally don't make; the entire offense had breakdowns that we normally don't have.

A perfect example was our final drive, when we found ourselves in the familiar position of being able to pull out a last-second victory. On third and three from the Patriots' 35, I took a six-yard coverage sack. I couldn't find anyone to go to, but I should have thrown the ball away and I didn't. That was a mistake on my part. Then, on fourth down, there was a miscommunication between James and me and I wound up under-throwing him with 43 seconds left to kill our last hope for victory.

The defense played well. So did our special teams, blocking two field goals and a punt. But our offense stunk up the entire Northeast. We just weren't making the plays when we had to, which was so different from the way things had been going up to that point. I mean, how, in a matter of six days, do we go from dominating the Dolphins to looking like we don't even belong in the NFL? Something's definitely wrong with that.

And it didn't have anything to do with the Patriots' defensive schemes; it was simply a lack of execution on our part. The Patriots did a good job defensively. You have to give them credit for the big plays they made. But it wasn't a case of them taking the ball from us; we gave it away. Anytime you block three kicks, you should win. No two ways about it.

At halftime, those of us on offense got quite an earful from Ted Marchibroda. A lot of people saw Ted as an easygoing, soft-spoken, mild-mannered kind of guy. Most of the time, he is.

What pisses Ted off is when people look like they just don't give a damn, which was exactly what he thought he saw through those first two quarters.

And when Ted gets pissed, he gets *pissed!*

"You guys are stinking it up," he yelled. "You aren't playing the way you're capable of playing. Now get your head out of your asses. Because the way you're playing, you're going to get those asses beat today. Wake the hell up!"

After the game, Coach Levy took his turn to express his dissatisfaction to the whole team. He's another one who isn't seen as much of a yeller, and he isn't. And he didn't say a lot that day, but what he did say and the tone of his voice were enough to grab everyone's attention—and keep it.

"We embarrassed ourselves out there today," he said. "You should all feel embarrassment for that performance, every single one of you. That was just awful . . . awful!"

If I didn't know better, I'd have sworn I saw snot bubbles coming from Coach Levy's nose.

Besides the 10–0 lead, we blew a chance to increase our one-game edge in the home-field advantage race with Houston, which had lost to Pittsburgh. At 10–2, we also saw our four-game division gap over the Jets shrink to three, although we could wrap up the AFC East crown by beating them the following week at home.

On top of that, we lost starting right guard John Davis to a knee injury that was expected to sideline him well into 1992. John was a catalyst in our offense. He was playing exceptionally well. Glenn Parker would be expected to step in and take up the slack, but we were going to miss John.

When I first joined the Bills, reaching the Super Bowl wasn't among the goals we set as a team at the start of the season. Goals are supposed to be realistic. And with us still in the early stages of rebuilding, we knew we had no business thinking in terms of the Super Bowl or even the AFC Championship Game.

Back then, our main concern was just to become competitive in the AFC East. We geared all of our thoughts toward establishing ourselves as the best team in the division. Once we accomplished that, in 1988, we started to focus on the conference crown. And, finally, the Super Bowl.

But even after we experienced what it was like to stand at the top of the AFC mountain and get to the Big Dance in 1990, it was important for us to maintain proper perspective in 1991. We had to remember that we wouldn't be going anywhere unless we first captured the AFC East, which, for the third time in four years, would be the prize for beating the Jets in a late-season game.

We prepared for a typical Bills-Jets slugfest—a tight, low-scoring, back-and-forth kind of game. And when you get into a game like that, you have to be extra careful to avoid killer mistakes like turnovers and penalties. The team that usually wins a slugfest is the one that has been the most fundamentally sound the whole way. It's the one that still has its head in the game in the fourth quarter when there's a temptation to start thinking about how tired and sore you are rather than what you're supposed to be doing on the field.

"Whatever we do, let's not beat ourselves," I reminded more than one person in practice that week. "Remember the last time we played them. We aren't going to be that lucky twice."

As the week progressed, I felt a lot more comfortable seeing the great attention to detail that everybody was showing. The linemen were taking all the right steps and picking up all the right people in pass-protection. The receivers were running perfect patterns and concentrating on each catch. The running backs were making sure they held the ball just a little bit tighter and were hitting all the right holes. Even our equipment guys, Hojo and Woody, had a flawless week. They didn't give me the wrong laundry bag once.

It was obvious our team, from top to bottom, was ready.

Of course we figured that even with better execution than we showed against New England, we were in for as tough a time as we had had at Giants Stadium in September. But we ended up turning the ball over four times, and found ourselves trying to protect our 17–13 lead with 7:36 left in the fourth quarter.

Darryl Talley then made the day's biggest play by forcing Jets wide receiver Rob Moore to fumble after his 13-yard catch to our 10-yard line. Mark Kelso recovered at the 7. And I proceeded to march us 93 yards, hitting Lofton on a 54-yard pass and then a 27-yard touchdown to ice our 24–13 victory.

Both times, we ran the exact same play, a quick post pattern.

On the touchdown, on which my line did a great job picking up the blitz, James gave cornerback Tony Stargell an unbelievably great fake to the outside (we call it a "stick move"), Stargell took it, then James came back inside and was wide open. It was the kind of play that a Hall of Fame-bound receiver is going to make.

The availability of those passes is something that you recognize through experience and developing a feel for what certain teams like to do and don't like to do. For instance, in both cases, we expected the Jets to be in man-to-man coverage, and they were. Now, if you went by all of their tendencies, you'd be expecting them to play zone. But knowing the mentality of their coaches and players, we just had a feeling that they were going to try to come after us at that point with a blitz. And they did.

Earlier in the game, I took some pretty good punishment from the Jets' defensive linemen. On one play, I waited too long for a receiver to get open and end Jeff Lageman drilled me from behind, causing me to take a hard fall on my right knee-cap. Although I didn't miss any plays, that caused a bursa sac to explode and my knee wouldn't be right until the off-season.

Then defensive tackle Scott Mersereau was twice given roughing-the-passer penalties for hitting me late. The first time, I thought his momentum took over and I didn't take it as a blatant cheap shot. But the second one was clearly a case where he wanted to hit me late. Not only that, but he came in low after my knees. So I got in his face right away to let my feelings be known.

"You sonofabitch! What are you trying to do?" I yelled. "I'm out here playing football just like you are. So I don't need any cheap shots to try to take me out of the game."

I don't make a habit of trying to piss off defensive linemen for no good reason. They have enough incentive on their own to come after you, so there's no need to add to it. But you can't let anyone on that field think he can get away with a cheap shot that might end your career. I'm only a 225-pound person going against a 285-pounder. But you have to let them know how you feel.

The interesting thing is, Mersereau came up to me about three or four series later and apologized for the low hit. Three or four series after the fact!

"I didn't mean to try to injure you or anything," he said.

"Yeah, right," I said, making it clear that I didn't believe he was being sincere.

And that was the end of the conversation.

After the game, there was an almost somber atmosphere in the stadium. I'm not saying we weren't thrilled with the win. I'm not saying the fans weren't excited, either. The electricity was as high as ever through that entire game. We needed every ounce of support we could get from the crowd because, with the game being so close, any edge for us would make a major difference.

And it did.

But afterward, it seemed like everybody, the fans as well as the players, knew we had much bigger fish to fry. After a 13–3 record and one Super Bowl appearance, our expectations had grown a lot taller than they were before the 1990 season—and I think they had finally outgrown the satisfaction that goes with being crowned king of the AFC East. The message on the front of the red baseball caps we were all handed as we entered the locker room said it best: "Four for four and looking for more." We had our fourth straight division title, but it was only the first of four steps we needed to take to reach Super Bowl XXVI at Minneapolis. Next was securing home-field advantage through the playoffs (our lead over Houston would grow to two games after the Oilers' loss to Philadelphia that night). Then we had to win our divisional-round playoff game. Then we had to repeat as AFC champions.

But we never thought about losing to the Jets. We had a healthy respect for their defense, and between their pass rush and some great coverage work by their secondary, we had our problems throwing the ball. Still, we approached the game with a lot of confidence, helped by Bruce Smith's return to the lineup after missing seven games.

We saw ourselves as having an excellent opportunity to get back to the Super Bowl—while taking one step at a time.

The one thing we knew about our meeting with the Raiders in Week Fourteen at the Los Angeles Coliseum was that it would have nothing in common with the last time we played against them—for the 1990 AFC championship. We expected it to be a lot tougher, a lot tighter than the landslide victory we scored at Rich.

And it was.

It also was a lot crazier.

After missing four kicks earlier in the game (three field goals and an extra point), Scotty finally found success on a 42-yard field goal to give us a 30–27 overtime win.

As important as the victory was, assuring us of a first-round bye in the playoffs, the way in which we achieved it was even more important. Through the previous two games, our offense had stagnated. We were in dire need of a lift—something that would get us back to the aggressive personality we were showing earlier in the season.

I took it upon myself to find it in the second half. That was after going through most of the second quarter with the no-huddle plodding along with off tackle left, off tackle right, a little dump pass here, a little dump pass there.

"The heck with this," I said to myself. "I'm going to go with my own type of football, with a Jim Kelly offense. I'm going out there and winging it. I'm going to let it all hang out. And whatever happens, happens."

Then everybody on offense started clicking. We upped the pace of "K-Gun," which definitely fits us better than the slower approach we had taken in the second quarter. I wound up hitting 33 of 52 passes for 347 yards and two touchdowns.

But the two biggest passes I threw that day weren't for scores. The first, on fourth and one from the Raiders' 29, went to Andre for 20 yards and set up my nine-yard touchdown throw to James to tie the game in regulation. The second came in overtime, on first down from our 36, when I found Andre again for a 31-yard gain to set up the winning field goal.

In between, Scotty would be wide left on a 36-yard field-goal try with 11 seconds left in regulation. After we went into OT, I walked up to him and said, "Scotty, we're going to get you another chance." We hung in there with him, got him the opportunity and I had all the confidence in the world he would finally do it—even after Raiders strong safety Ronnie Lott made what looked to me to be an obvious attempt to break Scotty's concentration. Just after the field-goal unit broke its huddle, Lott walked ten yards across the line and right in front of

Scotty, then walked back to the other side. So I ran onto the field to let Ronnie know that I didn't appreciate his little psych-out tactic.

"That's not very professional," I said. "That's not cool to do something like that, Ronnie. It's bullshit!"

He said it was something he always did before an opponent's field-goal try, just for the sake of superstition. I'm as superstitious as anyone, but to me it still looked like a cheap way of giving the kicker something to think about.

Then the crowd of 85,000 got into the act by chanting "Super Bowl! Super Bowl!" trying to remind Scotty of his miss in Tampa. But he had enough support from his teammates to offset all those distractions. As his holder since the beginning of the 1990 season, the one thing Frank knew about Scotty was that when he was having trouble, it was because he either wasn't keeping his head down or he wasn't following through.

"Just visualize the kick going through the uprights," Frank kept telling him.

In pro football, as well as other sports, the key to everything is keeping your poise. Ultimately, we did so that day.

With a 12–2 record, a win by us or a Houston loss in the final two games of the regular season would settle the home-field battle once and for all.

We took matters into our hands the following week by traveling to Indianapolis for a Sunday-night game and pounding the Colts, 35–7. That tied the franchise record of 13 victories which we had set in 1990.

After throwing three first-half touchdown passes, I was pulled out, along with several other starters, for the rest of the night. We made the game so boring that fans began cheering when the Colts forced us to punt—that is, the few who remained beyond halftime. ESPN ran a split screen with the game on one side and the world's longest live TV interview with Walter Payton on the other.

Thurman's pursuit of the NFL rushing title ended on our first series when he suffered a sprained ankle. Later in the game, James twisted his foot. But neither injury was considered serious. Thurman got a great consolation prize for missing the rushing crown when he was named the league's Most Valuable Player by the Associated Press.

Having satisfied both of our regular-season goals, we basically just went through the motions in our regular-season finale at home against Detroit. I didn't play, nor did Thurman or James. Andre and Bruce played sparingly. And for those potential playoff opponents who were scouting us, Frank was given a very limited offensive package and did quite a bit of huddling.

Some people wanted to make a big issue about Marv's decision to rest several of his starters for the playoffs. I wanted to play as much as anyone else, but I had no qualms with the approach he was taking. It is up to the head coach—not the players, fans or media—to determine who plays and who doesn't. Period.

We did, however, leave most of our starting defense intact for the whole game. And those guys played their hearts out, pushing the Lions—who were seeking their first NFC Central title since 1983—to the limit. We lost in OT, 17–14.

Our Rich Stadium winning streak was stopped at 17. We had taken a lot of pride in keeping it going. But we also knew it was much more important that we start a new winning streak there in January.

Besides, it had been a great season. It was far and away the best and most satisfying year I had had since joining the team because of all the great things we accomplished offensively.

After the 1990 season, practically everyone I spoke to—relatives, friends, fans and reporters—asked the same question about our fantastic offensive output: "How can you top this? How can you possibly get better?"

Well, we did. We scored an NFL-leading 458 points, breaking the club record of 428 set in 1990. We also shattered team marks for total yards (6,252 yards), net passing yards (3,871), completions (332), first downs (360), passing first downs (208), touchdowns (58) and touchdown passes (39).

I broke my own team records for passing yards (3,844), touchdown passes (33), attempts (474), completion percentage (64.13), and 300-yard games (six). I also finished as the top-rated passer in the AFC with 97.6 points and led the NFL in scoring throws.

In our backfield was the NFL's Most Valuable Player, Thurman, who led the league in combined yardage for the third straight year and became only the 11th player in NFL history to gain 2,000 combined yards in a single season (he had 2,038). We had two of the NFL's top receivers in Andre (81 catches for 1,113 yards) and James (57 for 1,072). (At 35, James also became the oldest player in league history to gain 1,000 yards receiving.) We also had one of the greatest offensive lines around.

And the best part was we still won 13 games, just as we did in '90. It was more than every team in the NFL except Washington, which won 14.

I couldn't have been happier . . . But I was hoping, in about five weeks, to be in Minneapolis.

We had hoped our divisional-round opponent would be the Chiefs. Getting another crack at them in the playoffs was the only chance we would have to redeem ourselves for that humiliating Monday-night loss at Arrowhead Stadium in October. We wanted to prove to the nation's viewers that we weren't nearly as bad as we looked when the Chiefs and their noisy fans gave us a tomahawk chop between the eyes.

Our prayers were answered when the combination of Kansas City's wild-card victory over the Raiders and the Jets' wild-card loss to Houston sent the Chiefs packing for Buffalo.

Now we would get them in our backyard. Now their offense would get to experience what it's like to try to call plays and audibles over the nonstop roar of 80,000 strong.

There was no way that what happened to us three months earlier was going to happen twice. And it didn't. With our defense performing better than at any time during the regular season, and my three touchdown passes, it was our turn to do the humiliating, 37–14.

Led by Cornelius's great imitation of Superman, our D allowed only 77 yards on the ground—quite a change from the 239 it gave up in October. And after being forced into a passing mode, the Chiefs, with Mark Vlasic replacing injured Steve DeBerg at quarterback, threw four interceptions.

"The last time we played the Kansas City Chiefs, we learned one thing: If you don't play physical against them and hit up in the holes as linebackers and linemen, they're just going to run the ball right down your throat," Darryl Talley told a reporter afterward.

We were also pretty physical on offense as well, rushing for 180 yards, which, combined with my net of 268, gave us an impressive 448 for the day to the Chiefs' 213.

We had a sense of confidence in our minds that the game was going to go the way it did. We knew we were going to have to face a tough team with a very good defense. But they weren't going to have the benefit of the noise that made things so easy for their pass rushers and so difficult for us in pass protection the first time around.

They blitzed a lot, but we just called the right plays at the right time and I didn't have to wait too long for receivers to get open. Plus, our offensive line did a great job picking up some of the blitzes.

To me, having the crowd on our side always gives us a big advantage no matter who we're playing. But as I've said, there's an equally big edge to just staying in familiar surroundings while you prepare for a game and not going through the hassles of traveling. That's the main reason most teams usually play a hell of a lot better at home than they do on the road.

Now only the Broncos were the final obstacle between us and our second consecutive Super Bowl appearance.

Watching film, it wasn't hard to develop a healthy respect for Denver's defense. They had two of the better safeties I've seen in Steve Atwater and Dennis Smith—guys who not only can cover people but also can knock the shit out of them. Overall, the Broncos were very sound in everything they did defensively. We fully expected to have problems scoring on them, because they defense us as well as anybody.

It was going to be a matter of staying patient and waiting for the big play to occur, if not on offense then on defense and special teams. In other words, it was going to take a lot more work than it had in the 1990 AFC title game.

What we didn't expect, though, was to find ourselves in a 0–0 tie at halftime. And you could tell how frustrated we all were on offense during those twelve minutes in the locker room. Normally at halftime, the quarterbacks go one way, the line goes another way, the receivers go another, the backs go another. Then, after a few minutes, we all come together and talk. But the thing I'll never forget about that game was that nobody could say anything at halftime because everybody was talking.

Everybody was chattering about his own version of why things weren't going our way, so nobody was really listening to each other.

The main reason for that frustration was that the Broncos' defense did something a little different from all the other teams we had faced up to that point in the 1991 season. Usually, when we go with three wide receivers in our no-huddle offense, as we did that day, teams counter by taking out one of their linebackers and replacing him with a defensive back. But the Broncos stayed with their regular 3-4 personnel—three down linemen, four linebackers, two corners and two safeties—and put all of their linemen and linebackers on the line of scrimmage. Because we only had six blockers going against a front seven that, without the extra DB, is larger than we normally see, the Broncos were able to shut down our running game right away.

Then, when we threw the ball, sending five guys out for passes and leaving only five in to block, Denver just blitzed the hell out of us with all seven guys. The three defensive linemen occupied Kent and the two tackles. The two inside linebackers took up both guards. And the two outside linebackers—Simon Fletcher and rookie Mike Croel—were usually able to get free shots at me.

When a defense is going with an all-out blitz, receivers have to cut their patterns off because the quarterback is going to be throwing the ball a lot quicker. That means most of the passes you're going to be able to complete are short. And the Broncos had really done their homework well, because they had a pretty good grasp of how our receivers were going to cut off their patterns and how I was going to react. Their attitude was, "Sure, you might make a big play here and there. But you aren't going to beat us with a bunch of short passes. And we're going to be hitting the quarterback all day long."

Believe me, I felt their attitude.

The last team to try that all-out blitzing strategy against us was the Eagles, and we managed to score 24 points before they knew what hit them. So at halftime, we all knew what the Broncos were doing. We just figured, if we hit them with a big one, then we would be able to force a readjustment.

But even though we were playing in the AFC Championship Game, there wasn't a great sense of urgency at halftime for us to get into gear offensively, because we weren't feeling any pressure. The Broncos' offense couldn't get anything going against our inspired defense, either.

"I'm almost hoping that Denver will go ahead and get a touchdown," Will Wolford said to one of our other linemen as they sat together in the locker room. "Maybe that'll wake us up."

The Broncos would finally get a TD, but not until the fourth quarter. By that time they were down 10–0. No, our offense never did wake up and hit them with a big one. We continued to look flat, we continued to just go through the motions, we continued to allow the Broncos to frustrate us.

But we still won the game, 10–7.

All I can say is thank God for our defense. In fact, our only touchdown was scored by a linebacker, Carlton Bailey, on an 11-yard return of a tipped John Elway screen pass by Jeff Wright. And the deciding points came on a 44-yard Norwood field goal. Thank God, too, that David Treadwell missed three field goals, bouncing two off the right upright.

Basically, those of us on offense were just along for the ride. Sometimes, we were stopped by the Broncos and sometimes we stopped ourselves with poor execution. Nothing major; just some missed assignments that we aren't in the habit of missing. All things that could be corrected.

I completed 13 of 25 passes for only 117 yards, and was intercepted twice. Thurman averaged only 2.8 yards on 26 carries and saw a postseason streak of four 100-yard rushing games come to an end. Sure, we were surprised. We expected a tough time, but not a shutout. We thought we were going to be able to score at least a couple of touchdowns.

But were we complaining? Hardly. Whatever we did or didn't do that day, the most important thing was that we were going back to the Super Bowl. Nothing else mattered.

Ever since Super Bowl XXV, we couldn't wait to get back into it and start all over again. Losing a Super Bowl isn't like losing a regular game, because there isn't another game to prepare for the following week—and take your mind off the loss. Our one-point defeat to the Giants lingered in our minds for four, five, six months. I didn't like that.

Now, we had the chance to go back.

There are not many teams that get a second opportunity, but we were going to have ours. It was a matter of going out and capitalizing on it.

Like almost everyone else around the country, I figured the Redskins would be a lot tougher to beat in Super Bowl XXVI than the Giants had been in Super Bowl XXV.

The Redskins had a great defense, a powerful offense with all kinds of different weapons and outstanding special teams. The Giants were good in all three phases, but they weren't, in 1990, at the level the Redskins were in 1991. Not even close.

That isn't to say I expected us to lose. I never expect us to lose a game. In fact, I had very good feelings on our way to the Metrodome in Minneapolis because we had had probably the best week of practice in all the time I had been with the Bills. I was certain that we were prepared to play our very best game— the kind of game it would take if we were going to stand a chance of winning.

But even before the officials made Brad Daluiso kick off twice for us for some silly reason, things had gotten off on the wrong foot for me that day. There I was, down on the field, trying to prepare for the biggest game of my life and the next thing I know CBS sticks a camera in my face and wants to interview me. Now, I've always considered myself a pretty cooperative guy where the media's concerned. And I rarely, if ever, miss any of the countless appointments that are made for me with network interviewers who come out to Rich Stadium or my home or even our hotel on the road.

But there is a time and place for everything, and less than an hour before the Super Bowl down on the field is neither the time nor the place to interview a player. At least, not this player.

I mean, I'm getting ready to play in the *Super Bowl,* I'm on the field warming up and thinking about everything I have to do in the game, and a CBS announcer (he knows who he is) wants to have a full-scale discussion with me. I realize he has a job to do, too, and I respect him for what he does. But sometimes people go overboard and expect you to drop everything you're doing to fit what they're doing. They don't stop and consider what it might be like to be in your shoes and show some understanding about what you might be going through and say, "Maybe I should leave him alone because I know he's getting himself ready for the game and needs to concentrate."

Unfortunately, some of the people in the TV business feel that, since they know you and you're friendly with them, you're obligated to mold yourself to their schedule. I like the gentleman from CBS, I respect him. But when he did that, it kind of pissed me off. I cooperated with everything that his and other networks wanted me to do before the game, but at that time, right before kickoff, I didn't want to be bothered. I didn't want to have a camera in my face while I was warming up. And it put me in an awkward position, because I'm trying to get away from him and his camera is on me live to millions throughout the world.

Was I feeling a lot of pressure on my shoulders? Hell, no. I don't really get nervous before any game (after I throw up, that is). I used to get very nervous before high school games. I used to be scared to the point where I'd shake under center.

But not anymore. In fact, I was probably more nervous taping my appearance on *General Hospital*. Before a game I get excited, I get pumped up. And I transfer those feelings into my performance.

Besides the incident that I had with the announcer just before the game, which was still nagging at me, there were other indications that things might be headed in the wrong direction for us.

For instance, Thurman Thomas somehow lost his helmet on the sidelines and wound up missing the first two plays of the game. I'm still not exactly sure what happened; I don't think anyone is, including Thurman. My best guess is that he left it sitting somewhere and another guy on the team mistook it for his helmet, picked it up and moved it to a spot where he'd be able to find it later. When Thurman went back to get it, it was gone and he wound up scrambling to find it.

Not the kind of distraction you want to have right before a game of that magnitude.

Meanwhile, Kenny Davis had to start in Thurman's place at halfback. On the first play, he ran for a yard. On the second, I audibled from a running play to the left side to a running play to the right side. But Kenny didn't hear me. So while everyone else went right, Kenny went left. I had no one to hand the ball to, and ended up carrying it myself for four yards.

Things like that are going to happen. You wish they didn't happen in the Super Bowl, but what are you going to do? The sad thing is that the line had opened such a great hole on that play. If Kenny had heard the audible, he might still be running.

On third down, I was sacked for a 10-yard loss and we had to punt.

Shortly after that, we lost Shane Conlan to a knee injury. We were already weakened by the loss of Leonard Smith to a freaky knee infection that came after the AFC Championship game. Losing Conlan made us weaker.

After falling behind 17–0, I thought we were going to get some points in the final minute of the first half. We drove to the Redskins' 28 where on third-and-18, I threw to Andre Reed. It looked like he had been interfered with by free safety Brad Edwards, but there was no call. Andre got so mad that he took off his helmet and slammed it to the turf. That drew a 15-yard penalty for unsportsmanlike conduct and knocked us out of field-goal range.

We were having a total loss of poise. You could sense that things were getting out of hand. And we were glad when half-time arrived so we could regroup.

I heard some guys yelling here and there in the locker room, but there wasn't any single memorable speech that got everyone fired up for the second half. The only thing I concentrated on was what Ted told me during our usual one-to-one halftime meeting.

"Continue to do what we're doing," he said. "You just need time to throw."

By that point, I had already been sacked three times and hurried on several other occasions. We couldn't figure out what was happening. The Redskins didn't surprise us with their all-out blitz; we expected them to attack us the same way the Broncos had. And all week during practice, we were getting great blitz pickup by everybody. As I said, it was a fantastic week of practice.

For some reason we didn't carry it over into the game. As a result, we ended up on the wrong end of a 37–14 shellacking.

We, as an offensive team, didn't make the plays we usually

make. Sometimes I had guys open and didn't hit them. Sometimes balls were there that we didn't catch. Sometimes blocks slipped away. Overall, though, I just have to give credit where credit's due. The Redskins were very well-prepared. They were the better team that day.

Maybe the best thing that happened to me was getting knocked into a state of semi-consciousness in the fourth quarter and, as a result, not being able to remember very many details. I haven't watched a videotape of the game yet, and I don't think I ever will. What's there to analyze? We were outplayed. Period.

The parts of Super Bowl XXVI I do remember, I'm trying to forget about. When I even start thinking about the game, I automatically put my mind on something else.

It hurts that much.

11

Picking Up the Pieces

AFTER ABOUT AN HOUR of being with my family and friends at the "Irish wake" following Super Bowl XXVI, the heaviest emotional pain I felt began to subside a little.

It helped hearing everyone, especially my brothers Pat and Ray, come up to me and say things like: "Jim, you made it this far and you have nothing to be ashamed of. There are twenty-six other quarterbacks who would love to trade places with you, who would love to be able to say they were a starting quarter-back in the Super Bowl.

"So what? You lost. There is always another time to think about. Remember how much it hurt last year? Remember how down you were? And you were able to make it all the way back. You'll make it all the way back again!

"Now it's time forget about it, brother."

And to that we each downed a shot and a beer.

Looking at my brothers' faces, I saw the same kind of support and encouragement I had come to expect from them through the years. But I also saw some pain. My brothers feel for me just as I feel for them. They are living it with me. When they watch me in a game, I'm not just another player out there wearing number 12; I'm their flesh and blood.

When I hurt, they hurt.

The combination of losing, feeling groggy and not finding my way over to my family's hotel right after the game like I was supposed to was almost too much to handle at one time. I had to have people around who loved me, people I could talk to. And, thank God, they were all there for me to turn to when I needed it most.

I realized I wasn't ever going to get over the loss completely. I don't think any player ever gets over a loss of that magnitude. Even if I go on to win a Super Bowl or Super Bowls, I'll always carry the memory of losing my first two in a row. I'll always think about the things I could have done better in both games to change the outcome.

That's just human nature. That's also the nature of someone as competitive as I am. A competitor can never live down a loss; it sits in the middle of his gut forever.

But being with my family and friends that night was comforting. I wasn't just with them, I was part of them.

"You have to remember one thing," Ray said. "No matter what happens on the football field, you'll never be a loser in our book. It's just another football team that beat your football team. Nobody defeated you as a man."

I also realized a quarterback can be down, but never out for very long. I still had a football team counting on me to help lead it back into another season. We lost the Super Bowl, but we hadn't lost the pride of winning all the games it took to get there. We still were recognized as one of the better teams in the National Football League.

I had been voted as the starting quarterback for the American Football Conference squad in the Pro Bowl, which was scheduled for the following Sunday, February 2, in Hawaii. In fact, eight of us from the Bills were due to fly from Minneapolis to Honolulu the next morning so we could be there in time for the first practice session on Tuesday.

But my first thought that night was to skip the trip. My head was still hurting big-time. Both my knees ached, and the right one, which I had injured in the second Jets' game, was swollen almost to the size of a grapefruit. I had received a pretty good pounding in the Super Bowl—on top of the poundings from the preseason, the regular season and two playoff games—and I was sore from top to bottom.

The last thing I felt like doing at that point was playing in one more football game.

But then I thought about four very close friends of mine, Jeff Peck from Miami, George and Debbie Schichtel from Orchard Park, and Boomer Connell from Buffalo, and the gifts I had given them for Christmas—all-expenses-paid trips to Honolulu so they could watch me play in the Pro Bowl. We had planned to spend the week together there. It was something we were all looking forward to.

And if I made the trip, I'd have to play. I couldn't just go there and vacation when the NFL was counting on me to appear not only in the game but at other functions it arranges each year for players to attend.

I realized, even though I could have been medically excused from the Pro Bowl by our team physician, that I had to go. I had an obligation to my friends.

So early the next morning, my brother Danny and I took our seats on the plane. I stretched out as best I could and slept most of the way to Hawaii, hoping my body would do some fast healing during the flight.

I didn't practice in pads that whole week, although, because I was supposed to start, I still did some drills and spent time away from the field getting a quick lesson in the plays our AFC coach, Dan Reeves of the Broncos, wanted us to use.

He left the play calling up to all three AFC quarterbacks—Warren Moon of Houston and Ken O'Brien of the Jets were the others. But because we'd be using formations and terminology different from those of our own teams, we each had all the information printed for us on wristbands.

Of course, it wasn't a very intense week of football. It never is. And it was relaxing to a certain extent to kick back on the beach.

With each day I was there, the thought of losing the Super Bowl drifted a little further from my mind. I have to admit, however, the sight of Redskins quarterback Mark Rypien throwing a pair of touchdown passes to help the National Football Conference score a 21–15 victory did bring back a few unpleasant memories.

On the other hand, there are plenty of good thoughts to cheer me up. For instance, later that month I became one of eight inductees into the University of Miami Sports Hall of Fame. Other former Hurricane football players in the group were Don James, head coach of the University of Washington team that shared the 1991 national championship with Miami, and Rubin Carter, one of the NFL's all-time great nose tackles, who starred with the Broncos. I'm proud to be recognized as one of the first contributors to UM's reputation as Quarterback U."

Looking back on my career, there are a lot of reasons for me to feel proud and, at the same time, very fortunate. There's so much to be said about faith. Faith in God, faith in yourself, faith in your family. I've kept the faith. I've received a lot of love and support and a few lucky breaks along the way, and now I'm doing exactly what I wanted to do all my life.

I can't predict the future, but I believe the best is yet to come.

Jim Kelly grew up in East Brady, Pennsylvania, played college football at the University of Miami, played for the Houston Gamblers in the USFL and has been the Buffalo Bills' quarterback since 1986. He now lives in Orchard Park, New York.

Vic Carucci is an award-winning sportswriter for the *Buffalo News* and a special correspondent for *Sports Illustrated*. He is the author of three previous books, including the autobiographies of Fred Smerlas *(By a Nose)* and Conrad Dobler *(They Call Me Dirty)*. Carucci lives in East Amherst, New York.